Vivian Vance

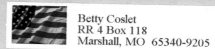

From Saundra
Dec. 23, 2001
My 70th Birthday

The Other Side of Ethel Mertz

The Life Story of Vivian Vance

Frank Castelluccio and
Alvin Walker

BERKLEY BOULEVARD BOOKS, NEW YORK

Permission to use images of Lucille Ball and Desi Arnaz kindly given by Desilu too. Photographs from the *I Love Lucy* episode entitled "Ethel's Hometown" and from *The Lucy Show* episode entitled "Steamboat Bessie" courtesy of Photofest and Desilu too. All other photographs from *I Love Lucy* and *The Desi-Lucy Comedy Hour* are from the authors' collection.

THE OTHER SIDE OF ETHEL MERTZ:
THE LIFE STORY OF VIVIAN VANCE

A Berkley Boulevard Book / published by arrangement with Knowledge, Ideas & Trends, Inc.

PRINTING HISTORY
Knowledge, Ideas & Trends, Inc., hardcover edition published in 1998
Berkley Boulevard mass market edition / August 2000

The Penguin Putnam Inc. World Wide Web site address is http://www.penguinputnam.com

ISBN: 0-425-17609-6

BERKLEY BOULEVARD
Berkley Boulevard Books are published by The Berkley Publishing Group, a division of Penguin Putnam Inc., 375 Hudson Street, New York, New York 10014.
BERKLEY BOULEVARD and its logo are trademarks belonging to Penguin Putnam Inc.

PRINTED IN THE UNITED STATES OF AMERICA

10 9 8 7 6 5 4 3 2 1

Per Anna,
Grazie per i sogni
Franco

with love to my sisters and family, Marina, Mina, Patricia,
Marianna, Vincent,
Julianna, Arianna, Joseph, Anthony,
Meagan, Brittany, Vinnie, Gino & Nino

Jorge Soto Vega, un dia

My respect and love always to
Bonnie & Oscar Walker

In memory of my brother,
Curtis Walker

Robert Morrissey, this was the purpose
To my dear friend Ted Van Why

Contents

Foreword

There are times I realize we all would have done ourselves a favor if we'd followed the lead of Garson Kanin, the playwright, director, raconteur, and friend to the rich and fabled. By Kanin's own admission, immediately following a conversation with one of his famous friends, he'd make copious notes. In Kanin's book about novelist W. Somerset Maugham, *Remembering Mr. Maugham,* he says the minute after he'd have a chatty visit with Maugham, usually at the Dorchester Hotel in London, he wouldn't even wait until he got home but would head immediately to the hotel's writing room and put pen to paper, writing down everything that had been said—conversations, impressions, opinions, minute details. All of which came in very handy when, years later, Kanin would want to recall times past.

I wasn't so smart (or industrious). Nor did I realize when I was spending time around people like Lucille Ball and Vivian Vance in the late 1950s that I was privy to anything worth remembering. They were, after all, actresses doing a TV series. Famous, sure, and interesting people to be around—not always fun but certainly interesting—but I had no inkling that at the time I was enjoying some adventure with Lucy and Viv that they were making history. To me, history was something that only happened in Washington, D.C., on Wall Street, or in Buckingham Palace. I now wish I'd been much more of a sponge.

My reason for being in their presence in the first place needs an explanation. In the late 1950s, at the time Lucy, Viv, Desi Arnaz, and William Frawley—the triumphant four—had finished doing their weekly half-hour *I Love Lucy* shows and were filming a monthly one-hour version called *The Lucille Ball–Desi Arnaz Westinghouse Show*, Lucy hit upon an extracurricular idea—to create a contract stable of young actors to be trained for leads in future Desilu shows. Once upon a time, she'd been a contract player on the very studio grounds she now co-owned with Desi, when it was known as RKO. At her Desilu Studios, she wanted to give new actors some of the opportunities (and weekly paychecks) which had once been such a help to her.

I was one of those chosen, and a lifelong friendship began between Lucy and myself, for reasons that belong in a book about Lucille Desiree Ball, not Vivian Roberta Jones. But it was through the times spent in Lucy's circle, primarily when I'd watch those TV shows being filmed, or hang around the set, or be invited for a dressing room lunch, that I first got to know Vivian V. Later, when my path turned to writing, Viv's husband John Dodds became my literary agent so our connection both widened and deepened.

But there were certain invisible roadblocks. For one

thing, I was basically "Lucy's friend," which put me slightly off limits as far as Viv was concerned, negating any kind of deeper-level friendship. Those two ladies loved each other but both were also very territorial. And of the two of them, Lucy was the official star, something Vivian respected although it didn't always make for harmony between them.

It's time all that was investigated further and put down on paper, one reason I couldn't be more pleased, on behalf of all the Ethel Mertz and Vivian Vance fans of the world, that Frank Castelluccio and Alvin Walker have written this book. There have been dozens written about Lucy but this marks the first ever written about her marvelous cohort, and it's time we all knew more about Vivian. And about that complicated, sturdy-but-fragile relationship with Lucy both at work and away from it.

From my p.o.v., they seemed to be great but cautious friends. Bonded together but leery of each other, like two great ballerinas (or prizefighters) with enormous mutual respect but fiercely competitive until the final grande jetè or gong. After their work together was finished, Lucy adored Vivian wholeheartedly, and I don't think she ever quite recovered from Viv's death. But while they were still performing on camera, I think their competitiveness was stronger than their devotion to each other.

Another reason the Vivian Vance story needs to be told is because of the many dramatic turns in her personal life, things one would never suspect had happened to "Ethel Mertz." Also to spread the word about the extensive theatrical career she had before her *I Love Lucy* days. Also because she was such an interesting paradox. Vivian Vance was the world's greatest second banana, male or female (some may argue that but millions of us would argue that argument), but she was never comfortable in that guise. As far as I could see, Vivian fancied herself a

glamour girl, not someone who should ever play a neighborhood housewife married to an old duffer like Bill Frawley. I think she resented the fact the world saw her as E.
Mertz when she saw herself as Constance Bennett. She
loathed wearing sackish dresses and aprons while Lucy got
to, at least occasionally, be the more chic of the two.

In real life, she got to do it her way. I'll never forget one
summer when our paths crossed, long after the Desilu
days. I was doing summer stock in Sullivan, Illinois, in a
show which was to follow one in which Vivian was the
star (playing, by her choice, a very Constance Bennett–ish
part). Vivian suggested we have dinner together on her one
free night. The only problem, she said, was that there was
only one restaurant in town, but she knew it well and recommended the food. So far, so good.

I got the surprise of my life when I went to pick her up.
You would have thought we were headed for the Copa, or
21, or Maxim's rather than a roadside diner (plastic table-
cloths) which also doubled as a saloon (pool table in the
corner). Vivian had on a strapless gown. Fur coat. Hair
coiffed and upswept. Long earrings. High heels. Let me
tell you, her entrance at that pub caused more than a few
gasps, mine included. More than one farmer put down his
beer and stared. At the pool table, no one moved. But
Vivian was completely comfortable. If people were staring, well, in her opinion, that's what people did when
checking out someone glamorous, vibrant, of the theater. I
couldn't recall seeing her happier.

I hope you'll enjoy this journey into Vivian's life via
Frank and Alvin. She deserves the attention and our deep
affection.

—*Robert Osborne, columnist and critic for the* Hollywood Reporter *and host and anchor for the Turner
Classic Movies Cable Network*

Preface

In late July, 1994, we were watching the *I Love Lucy* episode entitled "Ethel's Hometown" in which the famous foursome of Lucy, Ricky, Ethel, and Fred, en route to Hollywood for Ricky's screen debut, makes a stopover in Albuquerque, New Mexico. Misled by letters from Ethel, her father informs the whole town that Hollywood has summoned his daughter for movie stardom. The townspeople welcome their hometown girl with a banner proclaiming "Ethel Mae Potter We Never Forgot Her" in hopes that she will entertain them on the stage of Albuquerque's Little Theatre. The next evening, her ego now well inflated, Ethel "the star" gives an evening of "songs and readings." Lucy, Ricky, and Fred, their noses bent out of joint, decide to take the spotlight away from Ethel by upstaging her with vaudeville routines while she sings

"My Hero" from *The Chocolate Soldier*, and, as Ethel says, "One of my favorites and yours, 'Shortnin' Bread.'"

As Ethel sang "Shortnin' Bread," we both agreed that Vivian Vance was genuinely funny and seemed very at ease. As she prepared to start her second number, we laughed out loud at the way she waved her kerchief and nodded to the orchestra to begin.

Once the episode ended, we shared our favorite moments from *I Love Lucy* and the knowledge we had of the players. To our amazement, we knew very little about the actress we both consider our favorite on the show. The next day, I decided to go to the library hoping to find a book on Vivian Vance's life. Much to my surprise and disappointment, I discovered that no one had written a biography on television's most recognizable and popular second lead. Apparently the only available information was bits and pieces included in books about Lucille Ball and the history of *I Love Lucy*.

The next morning, I awoke and my first thought of the day struck me like a thunderbolt—Alvin and I are going to write Vivian Vance's biography. When I telephoned him and asked if he wanted to take on this project, he simply answered "Yes." I am convinced that whoever or whatever put the thought in my head that morning had also convinced him. As we drove to the library, we questioned whether we were making a mistake undertaking a project of this magnitude. But if any doubts did exist, they vanished completely the moment we read in *Who's Who in Television* that that very day, July 26th, would have been Vivian's 85th birthday. Neither of us realized that our decision would put our lives on hold for the next three years while all our thoughts focused on the life of someone we knew only as a character on a 1950s television show. When we told friends of our plans, they always asked, "How did it come about?" and we have often wondered if any of them believe our explanation. The circumstances surrounding our decision, though completely true, at times sound fabricated even to us.

This book evolved out of curiosity and a desire to know more about a woman who graced our lives with her presence. The force behind this project comes from elsewhere. Whether that elsewhere is coincidence or intervention from beyond, someone else can figure out. We just knew we could not ignore this message and felt that something or someone had chosen us for the task.

Even though we had both worked in the arts for years, neither one of us had experience as a professional writer. But we did not allow this little obstacle to stop us, clearly, many problems lay ahead. Despite the many difficulties that arose on our foolhardy yet well-intended venture, we somehow always managed to move toward our goal. Often the obstacles of researching, interviewing, and writing overwhelmed us but we never thought of quitting. Instead, to put us back on track, we'd pop in a video cassette and watch an episode of *I Love Lucy*. The next day we'd start again.

Anne Denove Farleigh, Vivian's understudy in a 1939 show, once remarked, "If we were going into the unknown I would like to go with Vivian 'cause she would be able to bluff her way through." Vivian's constant bluffing during certain periods in her life and the fact that she reinvented herself several times made our journey of discovery even more difficult. But little by little we uncovered the truth by peeling back the many thinly veiled lies she scattered throughout her life so as not to hurt those she loved. Gradually the pieces of the puzzle we came to know as Vivian Vance's life began to fit and a very human being emerged.

A driven woman, Vivian lived a life filled with turmoil, excitement, and a thirst for inner peace which eluded her for many years. Through it all, she used humor to mask her pain. She had an obvious gift for acting yet her struggle to achieve stardom caused constant frustration and stress throughout most of her career. And when Vivian finally attained fame as Lucille Ball's sidekick, that fame associated her with a role she came to despise.

The words of those who knew Vivian helped us to erase from our minds the image of Ethel Mertz and allowed the real woman to come forth.

"I think Vivian Vance would have made a smashing director because she knew her craft extremely well."
—Bret Adams, talent agent

"The Vivian I knew was a working actor on a very successful show and was a very kind human being."
—Jay Sandrich, director

"Viv was down to earth and never made you feel like she was a celebrity. She was just one of us. You never knew she was a star."
—Helene Lobherr, neighbor and friend

"She was absolutely the funniest woman I ever met in my life, just a down-to-earth person with a lot of wisdom."
—Corinne Wiley, friend

"Vivian thought that [the] oddballs in life are really the most interesting; the odder you were, the more she loved you. She gave me my humor, she gave me the way to look at life through kind and gentle eyes and taught me how to live as a sane, thoughtful, and considerate person."
—Paige Matthews Peterson, neighbor and friend

"I felt I could tell her anything. One thing I learned from Viv was an essence . . . being extremely professional

and disciplined. I behave a certain way because of that angel . . . she was more apt to laugh at something than to denigrate it . . . she was a broad in the best sense of the word."

—Lucie Arnaz, actress

"*Vivian was the best second banana in the business.*"
—Mary Wickes, actress

"*She was a brilliant foil. For too long, Vivian has gone unsung.*"

—Herbert Kenwith, director

"*Vivian was a strong, brassy woman that no one pushed around. She was direct, honest, with no phoniness or artificiality.*"

—Marjorie Lord, actress

It is this essence that we wanted to capture in this book.

Vivian once wryly commented, "When I die, there will be people who send Ethel flowers. I'll get to heaven and someone will say 'Hi, Ethel! I see you are still in re-runs.' "

Undeniably, the public will always remember Vivian Vance for her work on *I Love Lucy,* but we hope that this book will enable those whose lives she touched to also understand and appreciate the other side of Ethel Mertz.

Actress . . . comedienne . . . humanitarian. This is the story of Vivian Vance.

Acknowledgments

First and foremost, we'd like to thank Ralph Bowyer who helped pave the way into the lives and hearts of Vivian's family. Thank you.

A very special thank you to Dorothy O'Neal without whose recollections and deep love for Vivian this book would never have been written.

Our heartfelt appreciation to Lou Ann Graham for her honesty and directness. She opened her heart to us during an extremely difficult period in her life and for that we will always be grateful.

To Robert Jones for helping us shape an honest picture of his parents through his memories.

To Lucie Arnaz for allowing us in and sharing so many of her memories. Her validation of this project opened many doors for us and for this we are forever grateful.

A special thanks to Elisabeth Edwards. No matter how inundated she was with work, she was always willing to help.

Through the tears and laughter of Paige Matthews Peterson we were able to see the other side of Vivian. Thank you.

To Coyne Steven Sanders, who never seemed to tire of answering "just one more question."

And we are very grateful to the following people for their time, their memories, and their help: Bret Adams, Johny Aitchison, Steve Allen, Bill Asher, Lauren Bailey of AFTRA, Kaye Ballard, Lorra-Lea Bartlett of CBS, Paul Blake, William Blake, Jay Bell, Stanley Bergerman, Kathleen Brady, Dorothy Brewster, Jim Brochu, Ken Brown, Ned Comstock of the University of Southern California, the late George Coleman, Oscar Collier, Carole Cook, Albert Cranor, Joan Crawford, Emily Daniels, Madelyn Pugh Davis, Terry Davis, Ann Driscoll, Nanette Fabray, Anne Denove Farleigh, Pat Farrell of the District Court of Albuquerque, Alice Featherngill, Charles Forsythe, Adele Longmire Franz, Kathleen Freeman, Robert Fyrolent, Martin Garcia of CBS, Helen Garrett, Tom Gilbert, Dody Goodman, Ross Graham, Frank Guerrasio, Carl Guilkey, Ruth Johnson, Herbert Kenwith, Hal King, Dorothy Konrad, Irma Kusely, Martin Leeds, Ralph Levy, Imogene Littel, Ed & Helene Lobherr, Bruce MacClain, Michael McClay, Brenda Madison, Tammy Maimon, Larry Maraviglia, Agnes Marchese, Trula & Gary Marcus, Hugh Martin, Irene Miller, Walter O'Neil, Gregg Oppenheimer, Robert Osborne, John Patrick, Pat Patrick, the late Pat Paulsen, Rex Reed, David Roman, Jay Sandrich, Bob Schiller, Michele Scutti of the Albuquerque Little Theatre, Jane Sebastian, Mark Sebastian, Doris Singleton, Henry Speer, Max Showalter, Ed Tabbitas, Rosalyn Targ, Robin C. Thompsen of Actors' Equity, Maury Thompson, Gary

Tomlin, Tom Toner, Michael Van Duzer, Marjorie Lord Volk, Tom Watson, Bob Weiskopf, Bernie Weitzman, the late Mary Wickes, Neil Wilburn, Corinne Wiley, Harry Wilkison, Vivian Wilkison, Janice Williams, Walter Williamson, Kevin Winkler of the New York Library for the Performing Arts, Dr. & Mrs. Ziegler.

A special thank you to Angela & Freddie Towler.

To our energetic and precise transcriber, Shaquita Jackson, a world of thanks.

Many thanks to the staffs of: the American Federation of Television & Radio Artists Association; CBS, Inc.; the Connecticut Mental Health Association; the National Mental Health Association; Cherryvale County Clerk; the Los Angeles Museum of Television and Radio; the Los Angeles and New York Actors' Equity Associations; Teresa Sanborn of Independence High School, Independence, Kansas; the New York Library for the Performing Arts; the Albuquerque Little Theatre; the Margaret Herrick Library of the Motion Picture Academy of Television Arts & Sciences; the New York Museum of Television & Radio; the University of California at Los Angeles Theatre Arts Library; the Screen Actors Guild; the Writers Guild.

In special memory of Vivian Wilkison and William P. Hall.

Thank you, Sandra Brown, for believing.

To our editor, Sonja Hakala, whose guidance and patience made the journey oh, so very pleasant.

Vivian Vance and Lucille Ball

Chapter One

A Quiet Visit

Belvedere, California, 1979. This quiet community, hidden across the bay from San Francisco, looks much like a summer setting in a Currier and Ives print. The New England–style houses lining Beach Road are still, except for the gentle splashing of the waves. Daily activities go on with just the occasional notice taken of a limousine standing by outside the fence numbered 84. A familiar woman emerges from the house. On the way to her car, she stops momentarily and looks back, pensively. When she finally lets go of the cheerful facade kept in place throughout that afternoon's visit, the strain on the woman's face is clearly visible. Still, she seems hesitant about leaving. Then, unable to cope with the overwhelming pain of the situation, Lucille Ball turns and hurries to enter the car, quickly closing the door behind her. Just as swiftly, the limousine drives away.

On the second floor of the house Lucy has just departed,

Vivian Vance faced the final days in her struggle against a disease which would soon claim her life. Actress Mary Wickes, who accompanied Lucy that day, remembered that no one said a word on the drive home. "We cried all the way back," Wickes said. "We knew we wouldn't see her again."

During their visit together, Vivian and Lucy told stories that flooded them with memories, both good and bad. "I remember that day very well," recalls friend and neighbor Paige Matthews Peterson, who, along with a few family members, kept a vigil for Vivian. "Viv and Lucy had liked their separation and rightly so. But Viv was thrilled that Lucy had come to see her and told me that they talked about everything."

According to Viv's sister Dorothy O'Neal, when Vivian initially received the news that Lucy and Mary planned to visit, she tried to keep the reunion from taking place. "At first she was very unhappy that Mary and Lucy came. It was very near the end at that point and she didn't want anybody to see her and she didn't want to see anybody."

"Vivian was always helpful to others whenever they were getting scared, but being comforted was not her style," lifelong friend Jane Sebastian explained.

Max Showalter, who shared a close bond with Vivian for over forty years, points to the intimate concerns which so often accompany a slow and lingering death. "Vivian had always been very proud of her looks," he said, and during her illness she took great care to guard her appearance, out of both vanity and a realization that the disease was winning. Nevertheless, those who were there that day agree that upon seeing Lucy and Mary Wickes, whatever fears Vivian may have had vanished.

During the afternoon, the twosome who made television history reminisced about their antics on and off the screen. During the final moments of their visit, while having a quiet conversation, they faced their own mortality together.

Once alone, Vivian's thoughts drifted to the past. Needing to tell her friend a few more things, she wrote "Lucy! My mind is full of thousands of memories—what to say? What to say? Wish I could repeat every nice thing and take back every bad? Thank you for *all* . . . you, the show, the *years* have brought? What a novel, part hilarious and part sad? Please know dear Lucy tho' I am giving into a glorious life there is a lump in my throat and a very large rock lodged in my heart today—something like *Our Town* at the last curtain."

The final page of this letter is now lost. The famous scene from Thornton Wilder's *Our Town* to which Vivian alludes questions one's ability to recognize the beauty of life while living it moment by moment. While Lucille Ball struggled to find a place in an ever changing world, Vivian Vance had reached an understanding of life. "Vivian liked herself . . . she had come to terms with herself and the fact that she was a very, very smart woman who had lived her life well," Paige Matthews Peterson said.

By recalling the scene from *Our Town*, Vivian tried to encourage Lucy to appreciate and enjoy life to the fullest. This note is an indication that Vivian's and Lucy's relationship was not all love or all hate, as some would like to think. Instead, their relationship embodied both these elements as well as jealousy, rivalry, dependency, and admiration.

The character traits which they shared—dominance, impatience, and directness—sometimes caused friction between the two women but it never diminished the natural chemistry that existed between them. Clearly, this chemistry kept both their temperaments and their relationship balanced. The best known female comedy team in the world shared almost twenty years perfecting a brand of comedy still imitated today. They shared personal strug-

Lucy! My mind is full of thousands of memories — what to say? What to say? Wish I could repeat every nice thing and take back every bad? Thank you for all you, the show, the years have brought?

Vivian's last note to Lucy

Write a novel part hilarious
and part sad?

Please know Dear Lucy
tho' I am going into a
glorious life there is
a lump in my throat
and a very large rock
lodged in my heart
today — Something
like "Our Town" at the
last curtain —

None of us ever

gles, watched each other like hawks, and ultimately learned to accept each other's shortcomings.

Near the end of her life, Vivian came to terms with her existence, finally concluding a journey filled with contradictions. After all the years spent trying to achieve stardom, Vivian finally recognized that acting could not provide her with the happiness she desperately needed. Born with an insatiable hunger to act, she later dismissed its importance by telling playwright John Patrick that performing "was like being a shopkeeper—at five o'clock you lock the door and go home."

According to writer Bob Schiller, Vivian Vance "was loved by all but known by none," and spent most of her life utilizing a well-oiled and finely tuned sense of humor to survive and shut out painful feelings. Some saw beyond her facade but most people mistakenly labeled her the jolliest woman who ever lived. Friends, family, and business associates repeatedly refer to her most prominent trait— her sense of humor—when defining her persona. After all, Vivian used her comedic talents on every occasion and in every manner possible—as a convenient way to influence people, as a shield to protect herself and manipulate others, and as a carefully planned career ploy.

Vivian always knew that with a little laughter, she'd get along all right. Consciously or not, her calculated banter developed out of a need to survive and fit into a society that constantly judged her unconventional personality. Ultimately, this humor served her well.

Chapter Two

Waking Up in Kansas

❧

*"Dorothy was so happy to wake up in Kansas. Not
I! I'd have looked for another cyclone and stood right
in its path!"*

—Vivian Vance

Vivian's parents, Euphemia Mae Ragan and Robert
Andrew Jones, came from large, hardworking families filled with steadfast characters whose ancestors emi-
grated from England, Ireland, and Scotland. Proud of their
heritage, the Joneses and the Ragans often boasted of their
families' accomplishments. Robert Jones's grandfather
often recounted adventurous tales of forebears who sailed
with Captain John Smith. Euphemia's father, who participated in Sherman's march to the sea, wore the Civil War
uniform of a decorated acting-captain with pride. And her
brother played professional baseball for fifteen years,
pitching for the Cincinnati Reds.

Euphemia was born on August 28, 1884, in Oswego,
Kansas. Known to her family as Famie Mae but referred to
by everyone else as Mae, she grew up with two sisters and

five brothers. Two other siblings died at birth. According to her youngest daughter, Lou Ann Graham, Mae ". . . was raised with five brothers who teased her a lot, and experienced a very hard childhood."

Thin, with long dark hair and delicate, pretty features, in photos Mae's eyes hold a reserved and guarded gaze, making her seem inaccessible to those around her. Growing up, Mae surrounded herself with as many positive influences as possible and made it a point to find the things at which she excelled and then perfect them. As a young girl with a passion for music and singing, she taught herself to play piano and harmonica.

"Mama wanted very much to [be] a performer," Lou Ann remarked. "Relatives said that as a girl she was the life of the party, singing and dancing until all hours."

At age sixteen, a singing teacher coached the young mezzo-soprano improperly and ruined Mae's voice. Later in life, she became partially deaf, a condition the Ragans were prone to, which forced her to rely on a hearing aid. Wanting to appear as much like everyone else as possible, Mae became so proficient at lip reading that eventually her impairment went almost unnoticed.

Even though Mae had an aching need for approval from her family, no one supported her aspirations to sing professionally and eventually she abandoned all such dreams. Once she realized that a career on the stage was not in her cards, Mae chose to belittle anything and everyone connected with show business. She dropped out of school in the eighth grade and, following the usual pattern of her day, began to search for a husband with whom she could settle and rear a family.

In other women, these early setbacks would have produced a timid and reserved individual but in Mae they created a strong and willful woman. In spite of this self-reliance, which she would someday pass along to her children, Mae needed comfort and turned to what seemed to be her only viable source—religion. As an adult, Mae used this religious fervor as a weapon to shield and control her family, as a substitute for her broken dreams, and as the way to make sense of her life. As her devotion deepened, she lashed out at anyone and anything that did not conform with those beliefs. Lou Ann believes that this self-imposed piety turned Mae into "a disapproving, frustrated, and aggravating woman." And, paradoxically, a devoted and caring wife and mother.

When Bob Jones was born on March 26, 1880, he arrived loaded with charm, a contagious love for life, and an adventurous spirit. His father took him out of school to work on the family farm when Bob was in the third grade. Although this was a normal way of life for many, it clearly did not suit Bob's purposes. He liked fishing and hunting but had no inclination for work in the fields. Instead, he dreamed of a more enterprising way of life.

Because of his small frame, Bob was allowed to run an elevator in the coal mines while in the third grade. The other workers nicknamed him Cager but by age nineteen, when Bob topped out at six feet two inches, they changed it to Tallie. Handsome, well built, and charming, he attracted the attention of many young local girls. He eventually married a woman named Daisy but she died soon after the wedding.

Known for his quick temper, Bob Jones never turned away from a good fight. The claustrophobic confines of the coal mines and the tedium of the work often combined to ignite tempers and fights among the workers. At first, Bob enjoyed being challenged. Enjoyed it, that is, until the day he lost his first fight. After that, according to his son Robert Max Jones, "he swore he would never lose another and he never did."

Later in life this philosophy changed and Bob came to

believe that fighting never settled anything. As he mellowed, so did his temper. Yet he retained the ability to raze anyone in his path when he did lose it.

Still, Bob Jones was better known for his caring and giving nature rather than his bouts of anger. And because he did not readily conform to popular opinion, his peers often judged him as an eccentric. His family tells the story of a time during the Depression when Bob gave a five-dollar bill to a beggar while on his way to buy an item at a hardware store. When he arrived at the store and asked the price of the tool he needed, the salesman quoted a price of less than a dollar. Bob, who had just given away five dollars, thought the tool too expensive and proceeded to another store on the far side of town just to save a few pennies.

It is often said that opposites attract and such was the case with Bob Jones and Famie Mae Ragan. Despite their great differences in temperament and philosophy, they fell in love, married, and spent the rest of their lives together. They met around the turn of the century in a rural farming community in Kansas. Their mutual appreciation for music brought them together at weekly socials in Cherokee, Oswego, and Cherryvale.

Mae gave Bob a sense of stability while he always felt a need to protect her. Once while attending a dance in a neighboring town, one of the locals got smart with Mae. In a flash, Bob came to her defense. Like a scene out of *West Side Story*, the boys from different towns divided up. But Bob's fighting reputation had preceded him. When some of the boys circled the couple in a show of strength, Bob calmly and very quietly locked stares with the biggest guy from the opposing mob and waited for the next move. But no one took Bob's silent dare. One by one, they backed down and allowed the couple to leave without a struggle. On their way home, Mae asked him what he had planned to do. His response was, "I would have turned around once and taken 'em all out."

Two years after their June 10, 1903 wedding, Bob and Famie Mae welcomed their firstborn, Venus Athiel. At the time, Bob made a promise to his wife to give up two of his favorite vices, drinking and smoking. According to family members, Bob stuck by his pledge until the day he died.

Under the close watch of her mother, Venus became a shy and obedient child, very much her mother's daughter. When Venus was still a baby, the family moved to 311 East 5th Street in Cherryvale and Bob put his entrepreneurial dreams into motion, opening a cafe at 218 West Main Street called The Bob Jones Cafe.

On July 26, 1909, Vivian Roberta Jones made her debut in Cherryvale, Kansas, not, as she later led so many people to believe, in Albuquerque, New Mexico. The confusion about her birthplace started during Vivian's early days in New York and quickly became gospel when columnists regularly referred to her as "Albuquerque's own" or "Albuquerque's favorite daughter." Vivian never set the record straight because she had indeed lived in Albuquerque for years and, more importantly, because she received financial backing from its townspeople early in her career.

This confusion persisted when Vivian played Ethel Mertz on *I Love Lucy*. The actors and writers on the show often made references to actual people and places from their own lives. So when the character Ethel went home in the episode "Ethel's Hometown," that town was Albuquerque. According to childhood friend Ruth Johnson, several years went by before "Vivian finally came down to earth and let everyone know she was originally from Cherryvale and not Albuquerque."

Growing up neither shy nor obedient, Vivian required a

Vivian's father, Robert Andrew Jones, her older sister, Venus, and her mother, Euphemia Mae Ragan Jones, circa 1909

Vivian and her older sister, Venus, 1913

firmer hand than her sister, Venus. Raised alongside the Jones girls, Alice Featherngill remembers that "Venus was a more retiring girl while Vivian was willing to always try something new." Though a natural mother-daughter love existed between Mae and Vivian, Mae had her hands full with this active and mischievous child right from the start.

Blond and blue-eyed, Vivian possessed an outgoing charm and, like her father, an adventurous spirit and love for life. Like her mother, she was headstrong, opinionated, and dedicated. While the similarities Vivian shared with her parents should have produced naturally harmonious relationships, they often brewed conflict.

When the family relocated to 322 West 2nd Street, four blocks away from Vivian's birthplace, Vivian and Venus befriended a local girl whose warm smile and expressive eyes exuded that special something. Later on, Louise Brooks's dark and exotic looks launched her career in the silent cinema of the late 1920s.

Brooks was the epitome of the flapper. She began her career as a dancer but soon graduated to starring roles in two classic films, *Pandora's Box* and *Diary of a Lost Girl*, both produced by G.W. Pabst. During the height of her fame, females of all ages copied Brooks's signature coif— a bob with sleek bangs. Today this distinctive look is often used by stylists on fashion models and remains synonymous with Louise Brooks.

Louise gave Vivian her first experience playing second fiddle to a leading lady. Years later, Venus recalled, "If Louise was born dancing, Vivian was born funny. Viv was comical when she was just two and three years old."

When his business at the cafe didn't do as well as he expected, Bob decided to sell it and take a job as a switch-man with the Frisco Railroad. It didn't last, so when Vivian turned six, Bob and his small clan moved to another town in Montgomery County, Independence.

For years, the economy of Independence had depended on farming but by the 1920s, oil had become the major source of wealth in town, turning some farmers into millionaires overnight. Oil companies leased their land, drilled wells, and if the wells produced, the farmers were paid royalties. Bob and his brother, Ralph, saw an opportunity to capitalize on the farmers' newfound financial power and opened the Jones Brothers Grocery at Sixteenth and Myrtle Streets.

As a little girl deeply in awe of her daddy, Vivian proudly announced to one and all the news of her father's move into retail. She believed, as he did, that riches loomed just around the corner. But as an adult she looked back and assessed the situation a bit more realistically. "Daddy went into a different kind of business with Uncle Ralph, running the Jones Brothers Grocery Store, and always with a twinkle in his eyes for the best-looking customers. If he hoped to find that the rainbow ended in Independence with a crock of gold, he must have been disappointed, but it didn't show. Mama found a new church and we remained what I came to recognize as chained Methodists."

The youngest daughter of the Jones clan, Lou Ann, revered her father just as her older siblings did. She tells this story, handed down to her by the family, about an unwelcome visitor to the Jones Brothers Grocery Store.

The Ku Klux Klan came into [Bob's] store to make him join up and he said, "Absolutely not!" Dad was not a man you argued with. He served anyone, he didn't care what color you were or what you were. Once, some of the surviving members of the Dalton Gang came in and he served them; he didn't care that they were crooks. He didn't like to be told that he *had* to do anything.

Vivian's closest lifelong friend turned out to be her sister Dorothy, born in 1915. Throughout their lives Viv and Dorothy, better known as Dot, confided their deepest secrets to each other while looking out for each other.

According to family friend Paige Matthews Peterson, "Vivian adored Dot and truly loved her. I spent a lot of time with them and saw how they worshipped each other."

The special bond between the two sisters appears to have shut out other family members who may have been hurt by their exclusion. But over the years, they accepted and came to understand the pair's inherent closeness. In fact, Lou Ann states that if "Viv asked Dot to lie on the floor so she could walk over her, Dot would do it."

Vivian did not enjoy anything about domestic life. While she did have assigned chores, she would try to find a way to pass them on to someone else if she could. Vivian preferred being outdoors playing with friends, inevitably finding something to do that her mother disapproved of. "When it snowed, we used to tie our sled behind Mr. Jones's delivery truck and ride around town," remembers family friend Alice Featherngill. "It was pretty dangerous, but Vivian loved it."

According to psychiatrists, every child has a preordained place in a family and every child seeks attention. In the Jones's household, Mae praised Venus while admonishing Vivian for everything she did. In addition, Mae told her second daughter that the couple, especially her father, had wanted a boy instead of a girl. This knowledge and Mae's constant criticism hurt, but Vivian masked her vulnerabilities by projecting the image of a conceited and rebellious child.

A tug-of-war between mother and daughter began early in Vivian's life. She bitterly resented her mother's claim on her father and challenged it by seeking constant approval from her daddy. Vivian recalled, "I still clung to

Vivian and her younger sister Lou Ann

the idea that Daddy wanted a son as his second child. I thought I ought to make up for his disappointment somehow. I grew up doing my best to be a boy so that he would give me the love that I felt I lacked from him. As I first remember him he was flagman on the old Katy railroad. He was a rugged and handsome man, in a uniform, with eyes the same piercing blue as Mama's. Daddy had roved around Kansas most of his life. Oh, what a man he was!"

Like his daughter, Mr. Jones's behavior was often rebellious and it usually took his wife to set things straight. Once while attending a car show, he fell in love with and decided to buy a Lexington Lark, a less costly version of the very expensive Duesenberg. When he proudly arrived at home, Mae brought him down to earth. According to Featherngill, "Mrs. Jones knew they could not possibly afford it and told him that he would have to take it back immediately. Mr. Jones always wanted to live higher than he could while Mrs. Jones took things more seriously."

While Mae worked and sacrificed in a world of self-imposed restrictions, Vivian struggled against her family's rigid norm to create a world of endless, fun-filled possibilities. In all, Mae had six children: Venus, Vivian, Dorothy, Maxine (Mickey), Robert Max, and Lou Ann. Neighbors remember Mae forever cooking, laundering, and cleaning the house, and as Featherngill says, "Always having a baby and working very hard. I kind of felt sorry for her."

With every new addition to the family came added stress and worry for Mae, which in turn caused more strain in her relationship with Vivian. Her precarious position in the family enhanced Vivian's feelings of rejection and she tried to make up for this by seeking the approval of her friends. She always did the opposite of her mother's wishes, turning Mae into an even stricter disciplinarian. Vivian later recalled, "It was Mama who used to make me go out and cut a switch from a bush in the garden so she

could whip me with it. She was the conscience, the pun-
isher, the voice of a vengeful God."

An indifferent student, Vivian attended school only
because she had to. "I don't think she applied herself.
Vivian was out for a good time," her childhood friend Ruth
Johnson said. Dorothy agrees that her older sister's true
interests did not lie in achieving scholarly kudos. Rather,
"Vivian was always in clubs in high school and always
rehearsing or doing something. She was very popular and
dated boys from other towns."

The blue-eyed spitfire got her first taste of fame performing impassioned readings for family and neighbors in
local recitals. Vivian enjoyed the attention and praise she
received during these home talent shows and these positive
assessments filled the void she felt at home. At this point,
Vivian decided she wanted to be an actress and dreamed of
stardom and fame. But the strict religious atmosphere surrounding her at home did not support her decision.

"I was entered in grade school and after awhile I was
pushed by the elocution teacher into my first part in a play,
something called *Miss Busby's Pink Tea*," Vivian said.
"Even then, if you acted in a school play and took elocution lessons and stood up and performed in the parlor as I
did, hellfire was already starting to singe you, in the judgment of most Bible Belt Ragans. Some of my aunts
wouldn't let my cousins play with me for fear they'd be
contaminated. Mama agreed to the elocution lessons in the
firm belief that they would prepare me to be a teacher. She
approved of my singing lessons too. She had wanted to be
a singer herself, but I can't tell you how many times she
told about the Sunday morning she stood up in church and
not a note would come out. That was one of her first crack-
ups. 'If you don't mend your ways, Vivian,' she'd say,
'you will have a nervous breakdown just as I did.' "

According to Vivian, Mae suffered several nervous

breakdowns in her life and with every one of them, she chose to burrow deeper into her religion instead of trying to find the root of the problem. Lou Ann remembers her mother telling her "that she had a breakdown at age fourteen because of the constant teasing from her brothers. It might just have been nervous fatigue. That term 'nervous breakdown' is used rather loosely, I think."

While Vivian's singing and elocution lessons added more financial burden for the Joneses, Mae obviously understood that her second-born had talent. She did not, however, encourage Vivian to pursue a career as an artist. Instead, in an effort to deter Vivian's dreams, Mae pushed her daughter to polish her talents for a career in teaching. Unaware of her jealousy, Mae justified her opposition to Vivian's plans by spouting quotes from the Bible.

In spite of her mother's objections, Viv still found ways to cultivate her talents. Those who attended Independence High School with Vivian Jones remember a willful girl whose goals and dreams of grandeur made some uncomfortable. This self-sufficient cockiness is often part of the personality of those with a natural gift. Vivian believed that "people who are innately talented should just trust themselves—just visualize it, and go do it."

Anna Ingleman, who taught Vivian speech and drama, noticed these abilities and decided to cultivate them. "Miss Ingleman," Vivian later wrote, "was a petite, exquisite little thing with curled white hair, always well groomed in pretty dresses with dainty shoes." Miss Ingleman gave young Viv the encouragement and vision she lacked at home. "She had me reciting Sail on, O' Ship of State! Sail on, O' Union, Strong and Great! to develop my voice. I was so eager to please that I could put any Fourth of July tub-thumper to shame. She drilled me in tongue-twisters so that I might handle any known combination of vowels and syllables, especially 'Theotholis Thistle'."

Years later, Vivian returned to Independence regularly to visit Miss Ingleman and she helped support the retired school teacher financially. There are also indications that Vivian assisted her first mentor in purchasing a home.

Miss Ingleman also had the distinction of tutoring famed playwright William Inge. In 1961, the Kansas Centennial Committee honored Vivian and Inge for their achievement in the arts. Vivian admired the playwright who based his works *Picnic*, *Come Back Little Sheba*, and *Bus Stop* on their town and Kansas. However, their classmate Ruth Johnson disagreed with the picture Inge drew of her hometown in his work. "Teenagers in Independence, Kansas, were innocent, naive and straitlaced. We tried to live by what was considered correct. We did not always live up to those expectations. One needs to be aware that Independence also created a Vivian Vance and a William Inge. The images he created bore no resemblance to the world as I knew it."

When she turned thirteen, Bob Jones urged Vivian to learn to drive. He did not like to see his girls dependent on others and pushed them to develop and use their own resources. Vivian, determined to please her father at any cost, accepted every one of his challenges without question, learning to change a flat tire, fish, and shoot a gun. At the same time, she learned about the benefits of using her smile, wit, and persuasive charm.

In a place where girls were expected to blossom into modest young ladies, Vivian found her free spirit stifled and unable to flourish in Independence. Still, she tried her best. In 1925, sporting a Dutch boy hairdo (bangs and a straight bob), Vivian took part in the Independence High School girls quartet and the girls glee club, soloed on the piano, acted in every school play, including *Whose Little Bride Are You?* and *East Is West*. Audiences who saw Vivian Jones on the stage of Independence High still vividly recall the high energy and off-beat quality she projected.

She also belonged to the cheerleading squad. William Inge was the only male member of the squad and friend Irene Miller recalls, "I looked up to her (Vivian) because she led the cheers. We were playing a game out in the fields and I said, 'Where is the scoreboard?' Viv looked me up and down and said in that snappy way she had, 'Honey, you're gonna have to keep count 'cause we don't have one!'"

Because she was involved in so many projects, Vivian often neglected to invest the time that certain tasks demanded. More than once while on stage, she befuddled her acting partners, including Ruth Johnson, by forgetting her lines. "You would have to think real fast when she forgot her lines because she would just start to ramble and improvise and you'd have to go right along with her," Ruth said.

As time went on, Vivian trained herself to learn not only her lines but those of the other actors. Upon graduating, she had mastered the art of memorizing a play from cover to cover. This gift stayed with her throughout her career. Carl Guilkey, who appeared in several high school productions with Vivian, said, "She was my memory in the plays. Having a tremendous memory and I a damn poor one, she'd help me memorize my lines and could prompt anyone. She became an excellent ad-libber."

Popular with everyone, Vivian associated with the "in" crowd. To appear well-off, she often swapped clothes with her girlfriends. "She wanted to impress people that she was something she wasn't," Ruth Johnson recalls. Vivian longed to attend social events at the local country club. "In a town our size," Johnson said, "the most prestigious club you could be a member of was the country club. In the twenties, it was more exclusive. The members were affluent, had time for golf now and then, planned dances and dinners and socialized. Some were millionaires." Vivian tried relentlessly to join this inner circle in hopes of dancing with the oil tycoons of Independence. While she would later sing in similar places, she never achieved her goal of mingling with the town's elite.

Vivian had a knack for getting friends to do what she wanted and often lassoed them into her schemes. Once, needing to pass a biology test in order to graduate, she convinced Ruth, the brain in the class, to cheat for her. For each question, Ruth raised two fingers for a true answer and one finger for a false answer. "I didn't want to do it and I don't know why, but we all did what she told us to do," Ruth said. Vivian once dragged her neighborhood friend, Dorothy Brewster, to see a movie playing in a church that neither of them belonged to. According to Dorothy, "[Vivian] convinced me to go along so she wouldn't be the only one to get into trouble if we were found out."

Banned from showing movies on Sundays, the downtown theater featured live concerts, and for two dollars music lovers could buy tickets for the entire season. Vivian often attended these events with friends and heard the likes of lyric soprano Rosa Ponselle, John Phillip Sousa and his band, and vocal soloist Madame Schumann-Heink performing at these weekly functions.

Like other teenagers in Independence, Vivian played tennis, went sledding and to football games, and piled into any available car along with as many as a dozen other people to chug along on day trips to nearby towns. The New York Candy Kitchen was the local hangout, specializing in homemade chocolates, ice cream sundaes, and adolescent gossip. The young ladies "were especially attracted to the soda jerk," admits Johnson, "including Vivian, who had made the rounds of the best catches."

Another friend, Albert Cranor, agrees that "Vivian went out with any boy who was ready." Of course, this caused even more problems at home. Vivian wrote years later, "I was called 'boy crazy' and it was true. Adolescence is a healthy time of life to be in love; it's good for your growth and your inner being. But in my family it was to be ashamed of and shunned."

When Mae once tried to stop her from seeing her latest beau, Viv called on Albert Cranor for assistance. "I put up a ladder at a window so she could go see the boys. Vivian was a rounder, in and out of trouble; nothing big, but she was very active."

Her actions produced enough fuel to generate gossip in the close-knit community. Vivian remembered that "Sometimes I fell for boys who didn't love me, and I suffered worse than Stella Dallas (the poor and tragic heroine of a 1923 book and 1937 movie of the same name, whose love affair with a wealthy man didn't have a happy ending). I had some marvelous, close girlfriends as well but nobody gossiped about that. I was a girl who was always in love, boy crazy and glad of it."

Carl Guilkey dated Vivian in high school. When he grew up, he became an insurance adjuster for the Independence Public School System and handled vandalism claims. Imagine his shock when the school superintendent accused Guilkey of vandalism. Not knowing what to expect, a worried Carl arrived at the scene. He recalls, "I pulled open a drawer of one of the old desks and inside, underneath, was my name carved in the wood." Smiling secretaries and assistants surrounded him, waiting for an explanation. Guilkey smugly replied, "Well, if you report me on charges, you'll have to report that person whose name is beside mine. Now, you may not remember her as Vivian Jones, but I'm sure you've heard of Vivian Vance!"

Outside of school, life in the Jones household could best

be described as a roller-coaster ride. Bob and Mae regularly opened their door to sick relatives and helped nurse them back to health. But the small house did not have enough space to accommodate everyone and the close quarters often caused tempers to flare and arguments to erupt. Privacy became a luxury.

But all was not gloom and doom. Dorothy remembers music, dancing, and lots and lots of laughter, and describes the Joneses as a witty and musical family. When not engulfed by feelings of morality, Mrs. Jones joined in the festivities, playing her harmonica and dancing along. Imogene Littel, Mae's niece, recalls of these rare times, "I loved Aunt Mae because she really was the actress in the family. She was very talented. I think that was where Vivian got her acting ability."

The fun ended abruptly whenever an argument broke out between Bob and Mae, as it usually did when the subject of paying bills came up. Lou Ann remembers, "Dad may have been very hard on Mother, unkind to her. He would never have struck her, but he had a very loud voice and they did have some fights. When he got really angry, boy he got angry. I only saw him that way once. My older sister Venus was there at the time and sent me to the movies because Dad was throwing things and she didn't want me to see it. She evidently had seen it before. I think it was both their faults but Mother could be very aggravating."

The finale of most of these arguments came when Bob packed his bags. Then the angry words would subside as he uttered renewed promises of devotion. These repeated arguments deeply affected Vivian and she naively vowed never to involve herself in a relationship with that kind of turmoil. "I watched my mother weeping so often around the house that I made it a point of honor that I was never going to be like that. 'No man was going to see me cry,' I promised myself. I would be strong like Dad, who in my eyes was either the bravest or the most foolhardy man alive."

In Bob's opinion, Mae's constant needling to become a good Christian and take life a bit more seriously caused their marital rifts. But for Mae, Bob's philandering topped the list. His outgoing personality and good looks gave him lots of opportunities to wander and he took advantage of them often.

But Bob Jones always provided for his family. A strict father, he rigidly enforced a 10:30 curfew. If one of his girls did not make it home from a date by 10:31, they found him fuming and wielding a shotgun on the front porch of the house.

The imbroglios in the Jones household gave Vivian even more reason to escape. She found refuge and comfort at Miss Ingleman's home, a "pretty, immaculate, and above all, peaceful place." During the many nights they spent together, pupil and teacher sketched blueprints for the future. By the age of seventeen, Vivian realized she'd taken advantage of most of the opportunities available in Independence. Voted Best Girl Bluffer in high school (someone "who can put up a big front"), and labeled in the yearbook as "always going out of town," she'd made her mark on the stage, in the quartet as a soloist, and in the Dee Dee Club, an all-girls social club. She even tried her luck at beauty pageants. She worked to buy herself a Jantzen swimsuit, convinced it would make her look glamorous and clinch her a title, and entered a beauty competition sponsored by the Kiwanis. Even though she didn't win, Vivian wasn't rattled.

Knowing full well that Vivian would never be a star in Independence, Vivian's grandmother Ragan encouraged her to leave. Vivian later recalled her grandmother saying, "You must leave, since you are just like me. You are the only one to carry on in my place."

A tough-as-nails survivor who never gave in to adversity, Louisa Mae Ragan "was the easiest member of my mother's family to get along with," according to Vivian. Certain that her granddaughter had inherited her sense of independence, Louisa Mae often advised Vivian to explore all options and not limit herself to her present circumstances. Then when Louisa confided in Vivian that the two were twin souls, Mae placed Vivian firmly in the enemy camp.

This grandmotherly support increased the tensions in Vivian's always delicate relationship with Mae. Louisa had not supported her own child's endeavors and had given her little protection from the ridicule of other family members. As Mae nursed the psychological wounds inflicted on her as a child, she found it difficult to watch Vivian getting the nurturing she had never received.

Mae rarely found any of Vivian's endeavors worthy of notice. There was one time, however, when Vivian won a medal for recitation in a contest sponsored by the Women's Christian Temperance Union. Mae called all her relatives and acquaintances to make sure everyone heard of her daughter's accomplishment. "Mama thought it was the greatest thing that ever happened," Vivian said.

Unbeknownst to Mae, the night Vivian arrived in Emporia for the event, a Presbyterian college boy took her on a drive. "He parked in the country somewhere, then brought out a flask of something and a bottle of near-beer. He poured out some of the beer in one bottle and topped it with the stuff in the flask, turned it upside down for a minute or two to produce what in those days was called shot beer," Vivian said when she told the story years later. After drinking several shots, she could not feel her legs, and worse, she could not see. Back in the hotel, friends nursed her through the night. The next day, after a wobbly presentation of O. Henry's "The Last Leaf," Vivian discovered that she barely missed being permanently paralyzed because the flask contained embalming fluid.

By the time she finished high school, Vivian had grown into a striking young woman. Her 5'7" frame, shoulder-length blond hair, and blue eyes caught the attention of a woman scouting new talent for *Ziegfeld's Follies*. Producer Florenz Ziegfeld's popular *Follies* showcased the loveliness of American women by parading dozens of near-naked beauties on stage to popular tunes of the day. A staple of the theater during the 1920s, these musical extravaganzas seemed to some risqué and sinful.

When the company came to Independence, it played to packed houses in a downtown theater. During the run, a scout went to pay Mae a visit to discuss the possibility of hiring Vivian. "She came to the house to ask my mother if she'd consent to my joining them," Vivian said. "Mama raised the roof so high you'd think a tornado had struck. She couldn't have been more disturbed if I'd been invited to Buenos Aires as a recruit for white slavery." After the tongue-lashing, Ziegfeld's representative didn't choose to press her offer any further. And any doubts that Vivian may have had about leaving Independence completely disappeared.

When she announced to her family that she would be leaving to seek work on the stage, Vivian ignored Mae's anticipated opposition and advice that she go on the Chautauqua circuit, a religious camp meeting with a few amusements added for good measure. Mae warned her daughter that "you are going to hell, you're going to burn, you want to be an actress, trying to lead men into sin."

Vivian cared for her family but saw herself as an outsider. As the secondborn, she had always vied for attention. But all the praise she received from friends and Anna Ingleman could not fill the void in her childhood. Because of this lack of attention, many, including Paige Matthews

Peterson, agree that Vivian "never gave much of herself to her family or spoke about them, though she adored them."

This sense of failure overshadowed all of Vivian's early accomplishments. "I couldn't remember ever having been first class at anything," she later wrote. "I had grown up so far thinking that I would never amount to much. I was the little girl who practiced a piano piece for a year, ready to play at a recital, then sat frozen on the platform, staring at the keyboard. Something inside was always pushing me to be ahead in any parade, yet I knew that if I got up front, I'd be panic-stricken. It took most of my life to understand the reasons why."

One night at a party at Miss Ingleman's, the subject of names came up. After examining the possibilities, a young playwright suggested Vivian take his surname. She liked the sound of it and decided from that moment on she would be known as Vivian Vance.

So in 1927, wearing a marcel hairdo (waves with curls at the sides) to add a few years to her look, Vivian left Independence for Tulsa, Oklahoma, where she managed to land her first professional gig singing at the Crystal City Amusement Park. Struggling with the layers of guilt and shame instilled by her mother, Vivian Roberta Jones began her journey as Vivian Vance.

Vivian in Cushman's Revue. This picture was taken at the stage door of the KIMO Theatre in Albuquerque between shows.

Chapter Three   .

Albuquerque, Here We Come!

❧

Vivian was always reluctant to disclose the details of this period of her life, so reconstructing the years from 1927–1930 is difficult. In articles written about her early career, no one mentions her trip to Tulsa, or any of the subsequent events. But this is what is known.

A year after Vivian left Independence, the rest of the Joneses decided to head west. The Jones Brothers Grocery store had run into financial difficulties because Bob and Ralph were too willing to give credit to too many customers. That meant their own creditors were knocking on their door.

Mae's health was often delicate and it took a turn for the worse not long after Vivian left home. Every time the seasons changed, Mae had severe asthma attacks and she found it increasingly difficult to recuperate from them. But the deciding factor behind this move was Bob's philandering. His latest conquest had developed into more than a mere fling and this time, Mae would not stand idly by. She gave Bob an ultimatum—either the woman or his family. His family won, so in 1928 Bob and Mae packed the car with their possessions and headed to Albuquerque with their five remaining children.

Albuquerque's charm, natural beauty, and perpetual sunshine enticed many new settlers to this southwestern town. Known as "cow country" because of its vast grazing land, many physicians advised consumptives and patients suffering with respiratory diseases to relocate to Albuquerque for its curative climate.

Years later, Vivian recounted her family's journey to Albuquerque in great detail. But according to siblings Dorothy and Robert, she did not make the trip with them. Her stories about this event are an example of how Vivian often chose to rewrite her past, glossing over particular details of her life when certain events made her uncomfortable or would put her in an unflattering light. In fact, her niece, Dot's daughter Vivian Wilkison, said that all the Joneses had a tendency to forget the bad times and recall only the good. "My mother (Vivian's sister Dot) dwells on the positive and doesn't like to talk about anything negative. She tends to put a rosy light on everything. But if my Mom is a Pollyanna, Vivian was even more so."

It is certain that before her family left Independence for Albuquerque, Vivian had already moved to Tulsa, Oklahoma. "Whenever my parents spoke of Vivian's leaving, the impression was that she went without their permission," her younger sister Lou Ann said.

While in Tulsa, Vivian appeared at the Crystal City Amusement Park. This was the heyday of parks like Crystal City, with their neatly trimmed lawns for strolling lovers, a pond or lake, picnic areas, and lots of games and rides for children. These pleasure gardens lured adult customers to dance halls featuring live entertainment. Usually set on one side of the park, these pavilions vibrated with the sounds of big-name orchestras. It was in one of these pavilions that Vivian sang her nightly serenades.

High school friend Alice Featherngill says Vivian lived alone in a small hotel room in Tulsa while performing at Crystal City. "She was very excited to have me see her perform. She did not talk about her family or anyone else. I was in college, and felt pretty independent, but I really did not understand how she could survive by herself." There are very few other details of her life in Tulsa. Even her confidante Dot can say only that "Vivian did not stay long at Crystal City."

While Vivian was performing in Tulsa, a touring company brought the show *Broadway* to the midwest. This colorful, Runyonesque musical, which was a hit when it opened in New York on September 17, 1926, follows characters in search of success on the Great White Way while getting mixed up with a little murder and revenge. Written and staged by George Abbott and Philip Dunning, and produced by Jud Harris, it contained numbers directed by John Boyle.

Joe Danneck worked as an advance man for *Broadway*. His duties included traveling to cities ahead of the cast to secure accommodations, book theaters, and publicize the show. He arrived in Tulsa just in time to catch Vivian's act at Crystal City. Attracted to the outgoing, charming eighteen-year old, Joe asked Vivian out for dinner once her show ended. Vivian instantly saw opportunity in the smooth-talking publicity agent and decided to leave Tulsa and move on to something bigger.

Joe used his influence to secure a position for Vivian in

the chorus of *Broadway* through his uncle, Jay Prothro, the touring show's producer. Once on the road, Vivian promptly graduated to playing the part of Pearl, "the gal who gets revenge on the guy what got her man." Theater critic Brooks Atkinson once described *Broadway* as a "garish, strident background of cabaret singers, hoofers, midnight parties, visiting gunmen from Chicago on a drunken spree, with a jazz band outside beating the appropriate tempo." This realistic view of the Great White Way opened Vivian's eyes to a side of show business foreign to her. In a way, the seedy world depicted in the play prepared her for the realities to come once she reached New York.

Before the Joneses left for Albuquerque, the producers scheduled a special benefit performance of *Broadway* in Independence. Vivian may have influenced the decision to have the show booked there but considering her position, it seems unlikely. Vivian's ego, nevertheless, did receive a boost. Except for Mae, Vivian's family proudly basked in the limelight while she proved to her detractors, who had judged her so harshly through the years, that she had the ability to be a professional.

The relationship between Joe and Vivian intensified. Prompted by her desire to prove her mother's prophecies wrong, Vivian chose to marry Joe rather than just sleep with him. So when the company reached Dubuque, Iowa, nineteen-year-old Vivian married the twenty-three-year-old Joseph Shearer Danneck, Jr. No one from either family attended the brief ceremony when the couple was married by Reverend H.D. Atchison on October 6, 1928.

Though Vivian never talked much about this marriage, it's clear she did not marry for love but for other reasons. Perhaps she fell victim to her mother's belief that marriage meant respectability. Perhaps she was trapped into thinking that having a man in her life would provide security even though she projected the image of a confident, self-made woman. Or marriage may have let Vivian set aside any guilty feelings arising from past indiscretions committed for the sake of her career. Whatever the reason, the marriage was difficult to sustain and Vivian experienced a great deal of distress. In fact, her search for true love proved difficult for many years to come. Her sister Lou Ann believes that Vivian spent most of her life expecting "the man on the white horse," someone just to love her and carry her away.

Joe kept traveling ahead of the show while Vivian appeared in *Broadway*. Regardless of the constraints placed on her by Mae, there are indications that Vivian missed her family and contemplated going home. However, when the company headed east, so did the newlyweds. New York hit Vivian with the sobering reality that she had a long way to go before calling herself a professional singer or actress. But Joe had a few contacts on the Great White Way, so before long his connections helped launch them on yet another tour of a successful Broadway hit.

Peggy Fears was a popular personality of the twenties who used her beauty and smarts to achieve success in show business. After a brief but notable stint with *Ziegfeld's Follies*, Fears married a millionaire and gained notoriety as a socialite. She divorced, went to Hollywood, and tried her hand in movies but had little success at the box office. So she returned to the stage, this time as a producer as well as an actress. Although this allowed her to choose her own parts and gain respect as a businesswoman, Fears had only one hit with *Music in the Air* in 1932.

But in 1929, Fears produced a touring company of the Richard Rodgers and Lorenz Hart musical comedy *Peggy Ann*. Vivian sang in the chorus and Joe resumed his work as advance man. During a run of the Gulf Coast cities, Vivian realized that her hasty decision to marry left her in a union void of any love. Joe and Vivian shared only one thing—the desire to make it in the theater. This reason, however, was not enough to hold the young couple together. In addition, Joe did not financially support his young wife and continued to lead the life of a bachelor, a sore point with Vivian who had grown up dreading the violent arguments that erupted whenever the topic of money came up.

Though her association with Joe had exposed her to a world she only dreamed about, it also taught her two difficult lessons about life and acting—it was not a good idea to try to succeed in professional theater without training or marry just to get ahead. If she wanted to use her manipulative abilities successfully, as she had as a teenager, Vivian needed to hone her skills and target bigger game.

When the *Peggy Ann* company ended its tour, prospects for the couple looked bleak. In the wake of the 1929 New York stock market crash, there were few opportunities for employment of any kind and New York did not tempt either Vivian or Joe. Instead, the couple headed to Albuquerque in 1930 and the safety of her family. They moved into an apartment near Bob's latest enterprise, the Jones Grocery located at Coal and Broadway.

Vivian's father's latest venture did not last long. The Depression and Bob's trusting nature made yet another business go under. Lou Ann was only five years old when Bob Jones lost this store. "I remember he brought me a sack of pennies from the cash register," she recalls. "He'd given out too much credit to monied people who could have paid him. If he had gone to court he could have made them pay." Among others, Bob owed money to his butcher, Butch, who worked in the store, and his wife, Eva, who made dresses for the Jones girls. "My mother felt so guilty that they couldn't be paid, that she sold butter, eggs, and homemade pies, and gradually paid them what was owed," Lou Ann said.

For her part, Vivian had no inclination to decorate a home and create a cozy atmosphere like most young brides. Little, if any, effort went into turning their apartment into a real home. Vivian and Joe both had other plans.

Joe began to promote wrestling matches while Vivian modeled clothes for a local dressmaker, and, while he was still in business, worked for her father in the grocery store. This was a sad period for Vivian, both personally and professionally. She found herself in the same familiar dead end she'd run into in Independence and all the plans she'd made with her teacher, Miss Ingleman, had not come to pass. In addition, she was living with a virtual stranger she was supposed to call husband.

Joe apparently agreed with Vivian's assessment of their relationship and not long after their move to Albuquerque, he disappeared. On April 8, 1930, Vivian filed a complaint against him for divorce, citing abandonment and lack of support. On further investigation, it seems Joe had no choice but to leave New Mexico because of a shady deal gone sour that ended in a shoot-out which left one man dead.

The last Vivian heard, Joe Danneck had moved to Detroit. This whole episode might have given other twenty-year-olds enough reason to live a simpler life but Vivian remained adamant and would not allow Joe's leaving to dishearten her. She kept up the appearance of a happy-go-lucky girl who demanded that no one treat her as a victim. Nothing would deter Vivian from reaching her goals, and now with Joe out of the picture, the Irish scrapper got herself back on track.

Albuquerque did not have a major entertainment center in the thirties. Its popular legitimate stages, the Crystal and the Elks theaters, were torn down in the late twenties. The KIMO Theatre, located downtown, had opened in 1927 featuring silent movies accompanied by a piano played by Vivian's older sister Venus. Occasionally, the KIMO invited touring companies to perform on its stage. In 1930, a new vaudeville show called *Cushman's Revue*, with its advertisements of "live flesh," came to town. "It was a cheap tabloid show that used to tour the south and midwest, playing as an extra added attraction in the movie houses," Vivian remembered. It featured comics, dance routines, and the proverbial chorus of scantily dressed women.

While Mae prepared that night's dinner, Vivian marched into the kitchen and announced, in her characteristically forthright manner, that she intended to get a job in *Cushman's Revue*. Not thrilled with the idea, Mae tried to prevent it. According to Vivian, "war was officially declared between Mama and me." Not knowing how to handle her headstrong daughter, Mae attacked in the only way she knew how. "Mama would recite all the dirty things that men must think when they saw me dancing," Vivian said.

In *Cushman's Revue*, Vivian got to do what she did best at this time, deliver a song with honesty and conviction. She sang popular torch songs while, much to Mae's distress, showing a bit too much of her body in what Vivian agreed were sleazy costumes. Considering the recent dissolution of her marriage, it is ironic that she opened her act with the song "After You've Gone."

One of Lou Ann's earliest recollections of Vivian "is when she was doing *Cushman's Revue* and I got to see her. I know I was old enough to go to the theater but not old enough to go by myself. I remember seeing her sing on the stage. She sang "My Man" quite a lot—that was one of her songs. I got to go backstage and got to see her sitting there in her dressing room." As a result of her appearance in *Cushman's Revue*, Vivian's popularity in Albuquerque blossomed overnight.

The initial excitement of performing quickly wore off for exactly the reason that Mae did not want her second-born in the show. Vivian never described those days with fondness. "Here I was, a horrible actress in a tawdry tab show which was close to the bottom rung of the ladder in show business. I got dosed with the thought of the dirty old men sitting in the front row. I put up a brazen defense, but to tell the truth I was embarrassed too."

The prospect of working for her father in the grocery store and living with her mother had no appeal. Mae's constant attempts to make Vivian settle down just increased the tension between mother and daughter. But since Albuquerque offered little opportunity for an aspiring actress, Vivian continued with the show, putting her reservations and feelings aside. Night after night, she belted out songs and showed her legs to dirty old men.

When the show moved on, so did Vivian. It continued on to Gallup, New Mexico; Bozeman and Butte, Montana; and every small town in between. Vivian's experiences with *Cushman's Revue* were never glamorous but they helped mold a person that, to this day, most describe as streetsmart and tough.

"I used to lie backstage at breaks during the evenings, listening to the hollow sound of the movie soundtracks and watching the giant, distorted figures on the reverse side of the screen," Vivian wrote. "I'd always been afraid of the dark, and now I had nightmares in strange rooms in strange towns where the only people I knew were the other members of the company and they weren't much more than strangers."

One night in a hotel in Butte, as she walked down the hall to the women's bathroom, a drunk with his pants at half-mast came barreling out, screaming, "You're the blond-haired son-of-a-bitch who sank the ship." He proceeded to chase Vivian until she hid in the lobby behind the clerk's desk. When her pursuer gave up and finally staggered away, Vivian looked to the clerk for reassurance and asked, "For Pete's sake, who was that?"

"His father runs a railroad. He bought this hotel. Figured he'd have a place to keep his son when he got to drinking."

By that time, Vivian had had enough of *Cushman's Revue*. She packed her bags and headed to Albuquerque preferring to deal with her mother and the uncertainties of employment rather than be chased by lunatics in the middle of the night. Years later, however, Vivian realized that the experience of touring with *Cushman's Revue* had been an important education. "I learned how you can push yourself out of bed in the morning no matter how you feel, how to memorize lines, how to walk on and walk off, how to go through a performance from curtain up to curtain down."

Back in cow town, a former Broadway actress named Kathryn Kennedy O'Connor had recently formed the Albuquerque Little Theatre. O'Connor's promising theatrical career had come to an abrupt end when she contracted tuberculosis in 1926 while on Broadway understudying Jeanne Eagels in *Rain*. She had moved to Albuquerque because of her illness.

With the help of the Works' Progress Administration (WPA), a program initiated by President Franklin D. Roosevelt to help boost employment during the Great Depression, O'Connor decided to build a theater. In addition to dealing with the logistical problems that usually arise while structuring a small theater, O'Connor had to face businessmen on the board of directors who thought it frivolous to spend money from the WPA on such an undertaking. But O'Connor argued that a community theater would surely lift the morale of the down-and-out citizens of Albuquerque while guaranteeing them construction jobs building the theater. The board hesitantly accepted her reasoning.

The construction of the Albuquerque Little Theatre took time, until 1936 in fact. Meanwhile, the acting troupe rehearsed in vacant buildings around town and used the KIMO theater and other places as temporary performing spaces.

When Vivian returned to Albuquerque from her time with *Cushman's Revue*, O'Connor invited her to join the acting company. She had seen Vivian in the revue and felt the young performer showed promise. Vivian eagerly accepted.

The Little Theatre had few amenities. Actors had to double as technicians, dressers, makeup artists, and office administrators. But Kathryn O'Connor's infectious excitement spread throughout the company and she demanded professional conduct from everyone. For her part, Vivian embraced the "let's-put-on-a-show-no-matter-the-obstacle" philosophy and did her share of backstage work.

O'Connor knew she needed to involve the entire town in the Little Theatre in order to assure her group's success. She regularly called on the Albuquerque newspapers to print tidbits about the goings-on of each production. Using her charm, she encouraged families with money and prestige to give parties and dinners on opening nights.

The Albuquerque Little Theatre opened its first season

with *This Thing Called Love*, a drawing room comedy written by Edwin Burke. It was purposely chosen to lift the spirits of the audience. At O'Connor's request, the local papers printed several articles about the production and its cast. Newspaper columnists repeatedly used the word "professionals" to describe the fledgling thespians while highlighting Vivian's appearances in *Cushman's Revue* to bait an audience. "Vivian Vance is preparing to give theatergoers a new thrill with her interpretation of the fiery vamp," one said, while another trumpeted, "Those who know Miss Vance are assured and confident that she will carry her role of *vamp* successfully. Miss Vance is an actress of wide experience."

Much to the delight of the board of directors and Kathryn O'Connor, this strategy paid off. A thousand people attended opening night and the show received high praise from everyone. Vivian played Miss Alvared, the vamp. Though not the star of the play described as "an amusing satire on marriage, abounding in clever lines and situations," Vivian got a lot of attention from reviewers. "Miss Alvared, the home wrecker deluxe, is portrayed with a professional touch by Vivian Vance," said one. "Two of the cast who went far toward creating high interest and excitement were Vivian Vance as the vamp, and Bruce Hanger, Jr.," said another.

The Cradle Song was the second production of the season. It was written by Spanish playwrights Gregorio and Maria Martinez Sierra and translated by John Garrett Underhill. It's a lighthearted comedy set in a Dominican convent in Spain where a baby girl is left abandoned at its doors. The sisters of the convent rear the child and twenty years later, the young woman marries and leaves. In essence, the play deals with the delicate balance of love between the young girl and the sisters in the convent. As a columnist noted, "The play was not written with dramatic climax but was primarily a study in subtle influences, calling for restraint and stage teamwork."

Eva Le Gallienne produced the show in New York while it simultaneously played in Paris. In order for the Albuquerque Little Theatre to do a production of the play, Kathryn O'Connor had to secure permission from Le Gallienne and the play's translator, John Underhill. In addition, the scope of the play demanded a great deal of detail work in the making of the costumes and construction of the sets. Dominican sisters from the area allowed the costumer to copy their habits and gave the set designer permission to sketch the inside of their convent. All in all, *The Cradle Song* was a real test for the novice theater company.

The hype for the Albuquerque production even reached New York. *Variety* reported: "A real comeback, Kathryn Kennedy O'Connor, who did an airing stunt [a turn on Broadway] here for a while, but now topping it off in Albuquerque. She directed and played the lead in *This Thing Called Love*, given by the Albuquerque Little Theatre. Now she will direct and star in *The Cradle Song*. Looks like Kath will see the big street soon."

Like Vivian's former teacher, Anna Ingleman, O'Connor believed that with proper training, Vivian would eventually graduate to Broadway. She lit Vivian's flame of desire and guided her on the road toward a career as a professional actress. Vivian, wanting to prove to her new mentor that she had what it took, worked hard to convey the conviction and truth that the part of Sister Joanna of the Cross required. Her portrayal in *The Cradle Song* of a nun who dedicates her life to an orphaned girl despite the dissonance it creates in her belief in God, carried the show.

Reviewers usually worded their unfavorable critiques carefully to avoid deflating any egos among the infant theater community but Vivian received critical attention of a different kind. She collected a steady stream of great reviews which placed her work at a higher level than the others and with each part she played, she received stiffer scrutiny. "As Sister Joanna of the Cross, a character of great depth and restraint within the convent, Vivian Vance twice brought scenes to a close with almost spectacular finish," wrote one reviewer in an almost-gush. Another noted that "many will be interested seeing Vivian Vance, so fine as the 'vamp' in the first of the Little Theatre plays, *This Thing Called Love,* taking the part of a nun with great finish in *The Cradle Song.*"

As director of the play, O'Connor kept a watchful eye on her performers and noted one close call Vivian had before the opening of *Cradle Song.* "Her lusty athleticism rewarded her with a black eye as she fell off a horse," O'Connor remembered. "That night, painful or not, she went on with the show. And when at the climax of the play she cried, and the tears washed away the makeup covering the black eye, the women in the audience never noticed, because were blinded by their own tears."

Now sixteen, Vivian's sister Dorothy joined the Little Theatre, appearing in minor roles. The two sisters shared a great deal of time together, giving them a chance to get reacquainted and allowing Vivian the opportunity to confide to her younger sister all the mishaps endured since leaving Independence. While Dorothy did not always endorse Vivian's survival methods, she did not reproach her older sister for her behavior.

Most of Dot's concerns centered on Vivian's relationship with Mae. "Viv lived life to the hilt and I'm sure that's what gave my mom some moments of worry. But, that's how Viv lived and no one could change her mind," Dot said. On several occasions, Vivian swore Dorothy to secrecy concerning her escapades. To this day, Dorothy still keeps many of these secrets, refusing to discuss certain episodes or feigning forgetfulness to avoid answering questions about them.

Like everyone beginning a life as an actor or actress, Vivian had a tough time making ends meet. But she flatly refused any financial assistance from her family and worked several jobs to provide for herself. When not performing at the Little Theatre, she made a living by singing with local bands, crooning love songs for the well-to-do at the Albuquerque Country Club. She also worked as a lifeguard at the community swimming pool and made fifteen dollars a week as a seamstress for Rosenwald's, a local dress shop. Vivian never allowed the failure of her marriage to interfere with her social life, dating any eligible bachelor who asked her out.

Even in her early twenties, Vivian's affable manner and unwavering sense of humor came across as a sign of strength and maturity. Joan Crawford of New Mexico remembers how her mother, who was a member of the Little Theatre, often invited Vivian and other members of the company over for gatherings. "Many of the members of the Little Theatre had tuberculosis and they'd rest all day and party all night," Crawford recalls. "Vivian used to entertain everyone after rehearsals. She'd straddle a chair and sing. She had a beautiful voice, and a wide range, she could sing as a soprano or she could sing the blues. When it got too late for her to drive home, she'd spend the night on our couch."

When she was still on Broadway, Kathryn O'Connor had starred in a production of *Rain* and perhaps it was her fond memories of the play that led her to choose this vehicle for the finale of the Little Theatre's first season. As Sadie Thompson, the "bad woman" of *Rain*, O'Connor

The cast of Rain *in 1931 at the Albuquerque Little Theatre. Vivian, in her costume as Mrs. Davidson, is seated second from left. The founder of the Little Theatre, Kathryn Kennedy O'Connor, is standing in the center holding a parasol.*

would again feel the adulation she had received on the Great White Way.

The "good man meets bad woman" theme of *Rain*, though simple in its conception, is too often delivered with melodramatic effect, thus making it a difficult play to stage. Even though the Little Theatre had triumphed in its two previous efforts, those following the growth of the theater were skeptical as to whether this production could attain the same success. No one doubted that Kathryn O'Connor would carry off the part of Sadie Thompson but some questioned whether anyone in the company could interpret the part of Mrs. Davidson, "the wronged woman." By now, other actresses with legitimate stage credits had joined the Little Theatre and competition for parts had increased. But Vivian won the part of Mrs. Davidson, the missionary's wife. One reporter in a local newspaper opined, "To be an actress of some finish is necessary to keep the part of a woman so directly opposed to the atmosphere of the South Sea Islands, where the action is placed. Miss Vance is expected to provide a great deal of the major interest in the play."

Vivian dove into the part of Mrs. Davidson with complete abandon. She changed her physical appearance so drastically that the audience found it difficult to recognize her when she walked on stage. To produce the effect of a dowdy housewife, she padded her body, wore a floral dress, a black wig, and donned horn-rimmed glasses. Vivian's physical changes and dramatic skill in the part of Mrs. Davidson left even Kathryn O'Connor stunned. Years later, she recalled, "Vivian played many types of roles while a young girl here, some glamorous, some comical, some sentimental, but one I remember in particular because it convinced me of her ability to make an audience respond as she wanted them to. It was the role of Mrs. Davidson, a pinched, frustrated character in which Vivian savored words and gave flavor and meaning to the character and completely obscured her own earthy personality."

According to Joan Crawford, "No one thought Vivian could do the part. Everyone criticized Kathryn for choosing her. Vivian was known for comedy and singing, but when she came out on stage in *Rain* she brought the house down in tears." For critics, *Rain* was the icing on the cake for the Albuquerque Little Theatre's first season. "Mrs. O'Connor playing the lead, Sadie Thompson, with a professional finish and ease, gratified the audience with her interpretation of the main character. No less gratifying was the character of Mrs. Davidson, the missionary's wife played by Vivian Vance with just the right amount of restraint to create great sympathy for the character. Spontaneous applause at one particular occasion showed that the audience appreciated her excellent portrayal of the role," wrote one reviewer. "An outstanding feature of the performance was the part played by Vivian Vance, who was the wife of the minister. A most trying part, Miss Vance played it well and achieved a role entirely new to her audience here," noted another.

The Little Theatre's first season came to a close after the third production. A press release boasted that the theater had made $856.16 in profit, a notable success during the Depression. The theater provided Albuquerqueans with the entertainment they needed and a hopeful feeling that things would get better despite present economic difficulties.

On April 20, 1931, two weeks after the success of *Rain,* Vivian received her final divorce decree from Joe Danneck.

Vivian was very grateful to the Little Theatre and Kathryn O'Connor for introducing her to the joys of ensemble work. At twenty-one, she began to get an inkling of how to reach true artistic excellence. Even when she attempted roles out of her range, written for older and more experienced actresses, Vivian's integrity and honesty gave credence to her interpretations.

Five months went by before Vivian would again have a chance to be on stage. Meanwhile, she took some time to enjoy her newfound success and continued to perfect the art of singing torch songs at local night spots. Whenever they could get their hands on a car, Vivian and Dot ventured away from Albuquerque on short road trips. They drove around looking at the incredible natural beauty of New Mexico. This became one of Vivian's favorite pastimes throughout her life, a way to relax whenever she felt tense or unproductive.

Kathryn O'Connor chose the play *Broadway* to introduce the Little Theatre's second season. Word quickly spread that "Vivian Vance, Albuquerque's principal purveyor of 'torch songs'—is expected to play the leading part." Instead of the lead, however, Vivian played the comedy role of Lil, "the big girl with the big heart," and Dorothy had a small part in the chorus.

To the public, the Albuquerque Little Theatre was touted as a friendly group of talented artists, rallying to each other's sides to put on a show, so no one suspected that behind the scenes, the ALT was hardly a cradle of congeniality. The troupe contained several refugees from failed theatrical careers, alcoholics, and those recovering from nervous breakdowns. Everyone had ambitions to use the Little Theatre as a springboard to the heights of success. As more and more attention was focused on Vivian, who flourished in each part she played, others who had acted in films and Broadway sat in limbo in the background with their anger and jealousies fermenting.

Vivian lent more than just her acting talent to the production of *Broadway*. Since she'd seen how a professional company handled the material, she took on the position of assistant director, orchestrating many of the numbers. Vivian enjoyed this side of the theater tremendously. She had impeccable instincts when it came to looking at a scene and determining what needed work to give it more impact. It was a gift that would both benefit and hinder Vivian later in her career.

The part of Lil did not require Vivian to sing, but to publicize the new show she sang on the KGGM radio station. Opening the season with *Broadway* was a wise move and audiences gathered to support their theater. Favorable reviews welcomed Vivian back for a second season. "Skillful acting on the part of Vivian Vance as the hard-boiled Lil who is too old to dance gave the performance a professional tone," one reviewer said.

Meanwhile, another alumnus of *Cushman's Revue*, comedian Rudy Wintner, planned on opening his own show in Chicago and offered Vivian a part. An article in the *Albuquerque Journal* noted that "Miss Vance plans to accept the offer because she feels that Albuquerque is a long way from 42nd and Broadway. She feels that once she reaches Chicago she may be able to go on from there." Up to this point, Vivian's lack of money made accomplishing this goal impossible.

Vivian had also planned to take another member of the Little Theatre along. But at the last minute she decided against leaving. This was partly due to her less-than-gratifying experience with *Cushman's Revue*. Also, O'Connor suggested that Vivian might be better off staying with the Little Theatre until she could think of some way to provide Vivian with the financial backing she would need to stay afloat. Vivian did not know what O'Connor had in mind but trusted her. She also felt relieved that, for a change, someone else had made a decision for her.

To make the offer of staying a bit more attractive, O'Connor decided to give Vivian the starring role in the comedy *See Naples and Die* by Elmer Rice, the second production of the season. Vivian played Nanette Dodge, an American heiress who marries a Russian prince shortly before his death. The farce takes place in a *pensione* in Naples and deals with blackmail, infidelity, and several love affairs. It also starred a handsome actor named Fred Ward, an actress named Una Baker, and a local singing star named Lucia Sanchez de Rael.

Little love existed between Vivian and some of the female cast members, especially Una Baker, whom the Albuquerque press likened to Greta Garbo. According to O'Connor, Ms. Baker had designs on becoming the next Little Theatre star. O'Connor tells this story about the rivalry between Baker and Vivian:

There was the occasion when Vivian was appearing happily and hilariously in one of our comedies, wearing a dress which had been provided for her by our costume mistress. The dress, a little blue silk number costing about $15.95, was pretty and set off Vivian's blond good looks. But trouble came to paradise with another blonde in the cast [Una Baker], who, incidentally, owned a dress shop. At the dress rehearsal I had carefully checked the blond store owner's pink dress, and concluded that though it was extravagantly elegant, it was no competition for Vivian's vital personality. Lo and behold, on opening night, here was the blond "second woman" standing in the wings waiting for her entrance cue in the splendid original of the cheap little blue copy that Vivian was wearing on stage. This was no sister act. I yanked the dress shop femme fatale toward me, and whispered menacingly, "You've one minute before you go on. You go back to your dressing room and change into the pink dress, or so help me, I'll slap you so hard, you won't be able to go on at all."

Whatever illusions Una may have had about replacing Greta Garbo or Vivian Vance vanished completely when the reviews for *See Naples and Die* came out. "It was Vivian Vance's show. *See Naples and Die* was one big laugh from the moment the Little Theatre star stepped on the stage. When the exigencies of the plot removed her a couple of times, the performance sagged and became thin after the manner of pie dough stretched against a tin." Another review stated: "It was Vivian Vance's play. But the little girl got plenty of support. As the unwilling bride of a Russian prince, Vivian was a star among a constellation that performed brilliantly. It was her night. Her entrance was marked by applause. She was stunning. Her gestures, her inflection of voice, her mannerisms—all Vivian Vance and all the business of a finished actress."

Vivian undoubtedly won the hearts of the people of Albuquerque but the comfort she found in their acceptance and reverence for her acting ability did not offset the amateur status of the Little Theatre stage. Yet Vivian's early experiences in the professional world had left her wondering whether to remain in Albuquerque, a town she loved, and simply enjoy her celebrity status and forego the hardships of reaching for stardom.

But the warnings from her grandmother years before rang in Vivian's ears. Don't get trapped in a conventional life, her grandmother Ragan had said. Don't get caught in a position of constantly asking "what if?" as Mae and, to a certain extent, her grandmother had done. For Vivian, Mae was always the prime example of what she did not want to become. As she saw it at that moment in time, Vivian's only alternative to a conventional life of husband, house, and a dog by the fire was Kathryn O'Connor and the opportunities at the Little Theatre.

As a public relations move, O'Connor offered the services of the Little Theatre for programs to benefit the Albuquerque Community Chest. The receipts from the plays would go toward funds for the poor. This admirable gesture justified the existence of the Little Theatre in the minds of its detractors who still believed it a folly to support a theatrical venture in the midst of a depression. The Railway Postal Employees was the first group to call upon the services of the Little Theatre. The theater troupe decided to perform *Ten Nights in a Bar Room* and the postal employees secured space at the National Guard Armory for the run of the play. Proceeds were earmarked for the unemployment relief fund.

Ten Nights in a Bar Room is a melodrama set in the gay

nineties and it seemed outdated by the 1930s. Director O'Connor and co-director Vivian instructed the players to use exaggerated gestures appropriate for the old-fashioned costumes and makeup. The only part of the play that they kept intact was its original message regarding the evils of drink.

The play was condensed into a one-act to be followed by solos and a finale of Vivian singing "Sweet Nell," "You Made Me What I Am Today," and "A Bird in a Gilded Cage." A reviewer felt that "Vivian Vance sang "A Bird in a Gilded Cage" with such a touching effect, and in such an old-fashioned gown, bustle and all, that the audience was convulsed with mirth when she made her exit [bringing] a roar of applause from the audience." After the performance, dancing and bridge continued onstage for the audience's pleasure. The evening was a great success, bringing three thousand people out for the celebration and raising more than $700.

O'Connor needed to keep the original intent of the ensemble going: namely, to have the talents of the community involved rather than spotlighting the abilities of a chosen few. Therefore, she decided Vivian should play a minor role in the ALT's next production, *Within the Law* by Bayard Veiller, because the blond actress's notoriety had prompted some to nickname the theater the Vivian Vance Playhouse. So O'Connor played the lead while Vivian played the comedic role of Agnes Lynch, "a con woman and blackmailer who has a weakness for the purses of susceptible old gentlemen who have a weakness for her." The play, which had a long Broadway run and made a million dollars as a movie, deals with a girl who is wrongfully accused of theft by her employer and jailed. Once out, her revenge is to marry the employer's son.

Taking this into account, it's not at all strange that little mention is made of Vivian and her part in this production. Still, according to one reviewer, "Vivian Vance made the most of a somewhat minor part."

Kathryn O'Connor set her sights too high for the final play of the ALT's second season. Leo Tolstoy's *Redemption* presented the overzealous director with insoluble problems. O'Connor tells this story about *Redemption:*

> Saints preserve us! I should have listened to the warning of my husband who declared: "For the love of Saint Patrick and His Holy Mother, you don't know anything about Tolstoy, much less about Russia! God forgive you and give you a little common sense." I replied, "Think of all the local people we can get into the big cast. It'll give them a chance to participate in this community endeavor. We can fill the house with relatives and make all the lovely money on tickets sold."
>
> I was mesmerizing myself. I should have been warned too by the heterogeneous crowd which came to try out. How to make actors, Russian aristocrats, lower-class bums, out of fresh-faced cowboys, consumptives, modish dames, and aspiring youths? No amount of prayers could perform that miracle.

In addition to the problem of integrating amateurs into the play, its costly costumes and elaborate sets pushed production costs up. Then some of the cast members were discovered drinking whiskey while on stage. And after all that, Tolstoy's contemplative themes proved too esoteric for the audience and the show flopped. Reviewers, careful not to blast the Little Theatre for its effort, avoided an honest critique. "For it wasn't jazzy, it wasn't snappy, it wasn't light, and it wasn't amusing. But herein lies the kernel of the matter—it was a play of proportions. Not light and airy, but somber and Russian. Full of the inevitable futility of life, of the Russian necessity for long conversations on life and love and why, why, why?" No member of the company received praise for their work in *Redemption*, including Vivian, who played one of the leads, a gypsy girl.

Though grateful to the Little Theatre and Kathryn O'Connor, Vivian wanted to move on. But the big questions remained—where to go and how to pay for it. Then O'Connor came through with her promise to help. In the spring of 1932, she went to New York and, in an effort to gain national prominence, she entered her theater in a nationwide little theater contest. While there, O'Connor asked Eva Le Gallienne to allow Vivian to audition for her Civic Repertory Theatre. Ms. Le Gallienne obliged but made no promise of acceptance.

Born in England in 1899, Eva Le Gallienne made her first appearance in 1914 on the stage of the Queen's Theatre in London. She debuted in New York in 1915 in *Mrs. Boltay's Daughters* and continued acting for the next six decades, delighting audiences around the world with her amazing range of classical and modern characters. Le Gallienne's extraordinary theatrical career included contributions as a director and author. She opened the Civic Repertory Theatre in 1926, successfully running its operations for several years. Acceptance in this high-caliber company meant prestige and affirmation in the New York theater community.

O'Connor, convinced that Vivian would certainly join the renowned acting company, thought of a way to fund her stay in New York. Banking on Vivian's popularity, she made a plea to the public to help one of their own by proposing to use the proceeds of an ALT production to send Vivian east. O'Connor picked *The Trial of Mary Dugan* by Bayard Veiller and cast Vivian in the title role. All the action of this play takes place in a courtroom and the character of Mary Dugan remains on stage the entire time.

Mary Dugan is a young mistress who is unjustly accused
of killing her benefactor. When her lawyer hesitates to grill
the murdered man's wife for details which would undoubtedly show the young girl's innocence, Dugan's younger
brother comes to the rescue and unravels the truth—
Mary's lawyer and the dead man's wife committed the
murder.

With the exception of *Rain*, most of Vivian's repertoire
had consisted of light or comedic parts. Everyone, including Vivian, saw the role of Mary Dugan as a departure. As
an article in a local paper pointed out, "It affords her an
opportunity to display her talents as an emotional actress.
Miss Vance has not had a great deal of opportunity to present this side of her histrionic aptitude in the past, many of
her roles being of the type that aroused mirth—from snick-
ers to belly laughter—rather than sobs from the audience."

Vivian later wrote of this experience, "They decided
that I would play the lead in *The Trial of Mary Dugan*.
Dear God! I couldn't handle it even today. Ann Harding
had starred in a movie version of the celebrated weepy,
and they figured if she could do it, so could I. With that
kind of confidence expressed for my abilities, I felt ready
to tackle anything. So long as somebody was pushing, I
was willing to give it a try. At this time, I hadn't learned I
really wasn't a star. That was something else I realized
later."

Everyone from women's civic groups to the mayor got
involved with making the play a success and bringing in a
large audience. Mayor Tingley urged Albuquerqueans to
pack the house, adding that Vivian is "probably one of the
most talented young actresses in the state." Even Mae is
reported to have aided her women's group in the sale of
tickets.

The rehearsal period put a great strain on Vivian

because she was simultaneously preparing for the role of Mary Dugan and constantly agonizing over the audition piece assigned by Le Gallienne. Vivian could not ignore the fact that every finger pointed at her and that the success of the play ultimately depended on her ability. By dress rehearsal, Vivian told a reporter that she couldn't wait for the show to premiere because she "couldn't stand it (the pressure) much longer."

On August 16, 1932, *The Trial of Mary Dugan* opened to a standing-room-only crowd. The structure of the play asks the audience to act as the jury for Mary Dugan. For this performance, they were also asked to judge whether Vivian was worthy of their contributions toward her future. Understandably, Vivian's nerves were stretched far beyond any point in her previous experience but she wouldn't exhibit the slightest inkling of insecurity to anyone.

Vivian gave her audience all they had expected. She hit the mark with her two wrenching scenes, one on the stand during a heavy-handed cross-examination and the other as Mary Dugan remorsefully reveals her sordid past to her brother. The reviewers raved about her performance. "Whether Vivian Vance can make good in New York will be decided next month, but the Albuquerque actress Tuesday night showed that she can make good before a hometown audience. Playing the emotional role, Miss Vance presented one of the finest performances she has ever given here. Miss Vance so steeped herself in the difficult role she portrayed that when she left the stage after her big emotional scene, she was still visibly moved."

Another reviewer called attention to the issue at hand. "Naturally the audience took in the play from the angle of 'Do you think she can make the grade?' Whatever the opinion formed, most of the audience will tell you that actresses on both the stage and screen with far less ability have made successes. It was a heavy, difficult dramatic role. She carried it off in a realistic manner, registering emotions of joy, fear, and sorrow in a manner to satisfy the most exacting director."

At a backstage going-away party given after the performance, Vivian floated from guest to guest as each one offered praise for her performance and support for her future endeavors. "Dozens of dear people came up to me to wish me luck, press a five- or ten-dollar bill into my hand, and say good-bye," she remembered. "The directors put all the money from the ticket sales into a bank account they opened for me. All I had to do when funds ran low in New York, they said, was to write and tell them so. The trouble was that they never mentioned how much was deposited in my name."

Vivian had but a few days before leaving the security of Albuquerque. She decided to take an offer made by Professor Herman Oliphant, a frequent vacationer in the area, to drive east with him as far as Michigan, where she would relax for a week before boarding the train to New York. This offer also gave Vivian an opportunity to see Oliphant's nephew, Newt, whom she dated while he attended the University of New Mexico.

Vivian had some trepidation about leaving Albuquerque. She wondered whether she would run into the same obstacles that had faced her after leaving Independence. She would miss her family terribly, especially Dorothy, her closest and dearest ally, but Vivian could not forgo this opportunity. She had no choice but to leave. At this point in Vivian's life, achieving stardom meant achieving acceptance. She had found some success at ALT where they lauded her talents but seemed hard-pressed envisioning her as a star. Instead, many, including Kathryn O'Connor, openly said they believed she would one day make a fine character actress. These words from her mentor and others in the theater group left Vivian feeling ambivalent, questioning the very abilities everyone so readily celebrated.

"I loved being part of the Little Theatre group, but what I had been told time and again by some of them was this: 'You're not pretty enough to be an ingenue. You don't have the style for a leading lady. You'll have to wait until you're old enough to play character parts. That's when you'll come into your own.' " This was unacceptable to Vivian. Although she felt indebted to the Little Theatre and Albuquerque, she felt the need to prove them wrong. As she left New Mexico, her complete focus turned toward achieving success as an actress. With this added pressure, she left for New York.

Vivian in a publicity shot, circa 1930s

Chapter Four

Vivian Vance—
the Girl of WINS

❖

In September 1932, wearing a tweed suit and carrying an oversized suitcase with all her belongings, Vivian made her second appearance in New York City. This time she didn't have Joe Danneck for guidance, just her own guts and instincts.

The train took her to New Jersey. After a ferry ride across the Hudson, Vivian walked three miles from 42nd Street and 10th Avenue to the MacDougal Street Girls Club in Greenwich Village. Not knowing how much money the ALT board had deposited in a bank account for her, Vivian thought it best to do without any kind of luxury, no matter how small.

Though not fully equipped to face the upcoming hurdles in her way, Vivian was hardly a wide-eyed, innocent girl.

She had traveled on her own at sixteen, worked with road companies, married and divorced. Armed with references from several Albuquerque bigwigs, Vivian was allowed to enter the reputable Girls Club but she had to appear, especially to the women she was going to live with, wet behind the ears, a naive and unsuspecting small-town girl whose dream was to make it on the stage. More importantly, Vivian had to appear respectable, something she had a difficult time believing of herself.

Several hours after her long trek across Manhattan began, Vivian finally arrived at the boardinghouse with sore feet and aching arms. The woman who ran the house greeted Vivian and quickly issued a list of rules: no visitors in the rooms (especially boys), and no cooking or laundering allowed on the premises. The ladies had permission to use the telephone downstairs "only if fully dressed," Vivian told an interviewer years later. Having grown up hearing all about the dangers of Sodom and Gomorra, the list of rules had a familiar sound to Vivian.

She also received the usual warning given to new arrivals at the Girls Club—avoid the bakery across the street. Vivian quickly learned why—the bakery concealed a speakeasy. Though her mother would probably have had a seizure at the thought of her child residing so close to a place of decadence and sin, Vivian felt a tingling of excitement and curiosity.

No one would have mistaken her room, furnished with a cot-sized bed and a four-drawer bureau, for the Waldorf. As Vivian described it "the walls stood so close together, there wasn't enough space to change your mind." Since the $11-a-week price of the room, paid for by the folks of Albuquerque, included meals, she'd put on her tweed suit and dine with the other girls at the club whether she was hungry or not. The debt she owed the people of her adopted hometown would not allow her to waste their money.

While she waited to audition for Eva Le Gallienne, Vivian re-rehearsed her audition piece while visions of stardom danced in her head. To pass the time, Vivian, like many other young hopefuls in New York, walked the streets of the Broadway theater district, longing to step onto one of its stages.

Finally the day arrived for the audition. Along with dozens of other would-be actors, she proceeded to the theater on Fourteenth Street wearing, as she put it, that "damned tweed suit."

No one but Vivian has ever really known what went on in that audition and she was always reluctant to talk about it because it was so disastrous. Eva Le Gallienne was slow to issue the results of the auditions so each passing day stretched into an eternity for Vivian. She couldn't sleep, couldn't hold down her food, and felt she had wasted the money the town had provided. Then the notice finally arrived. Relieved at having received the verdict but terror-stricken at the thought of rejection, she slowly opened the envelope. "So sorry to inform you," it said in part. "May we suggest you immediately return home."

Now she stood face to face with the thing she dreaded most—failure. Vivian's hopes collapsed. "A few formal chilling lines said I'd been rejected," she remembered years later. "It was all I could do to keep breathing. The whole town of Albuquerque was counting on me to make good. I was the only girl they'd ever sent to New York, and I'd failed them. I was the biggest, most catastrophic flop in the world. Maybe I could go back and face my family, but the whole town—*never!*"

Back in Albuquerque, her sister Dorothy received a letter from Vivian stating that, "upon her arrival in New

York, the school had closed." It was a fib, of course, that Vivian fabricated to buy some time until she could figure out her next step.

Ironically, Vivian's face-saving fib ended up having more reality than truth in it. Five years of running the lucrative Civic Repertory Theatre had taken its toll on Le Gallienne so she had decided to change the infrastructure of the theater. While convalescing from injuries to her hand suffered in an explosion, Le Gallienne decided to downsize the group by reducing "the acting staff to a dozen of the major players, who had agreed to hold themselves ready for the resumption of activities at a minimum weekly salary." But despite her efforts to resume normal operations, the theater eventually closed. Vivian did not know that Le Gallienne had not accepted anyone that year but the information may not have lessened the blow to her self-esteem.

Even though she had no job and no prospects for a job, Vivian refused to go back home. Instead, she decided to stay in New York and create her own luck. But a new Vivian Vance had to emerge. She'd tipped the scales at 154 pounds on her arrival in New York and was hardly able to compete with the willowy showgirls of Broadway. So she shed thirty-four pounds within the first three months of her stay. She created a whole new look by changing her makeup but could do little to camouflage a hump on her nose. (In the early days of her career, columnists admired Vivian for her kidding on the subject. But years later, with money no longer an issue, she opted for plastic surgery.) Out came the "damn tweed suit" again but this time altered to be more fashionable. Determined to pay her own way, Vivian gathered all her strength and set out to get a job.

The story goes that Vivian aimlessly wandered around

New York until she reached the theater district and noticed a group of people outside the stage door of the Alvin Theatre waiting to audition for a new musical, joined the queue, auditioned, and was chosen. The reality is a bit different, however. The producer of the show at the Alvin was none other than Peggy Fears, who had also produced *Peggy Ann*, the show Vivian toured in with Joe Danneck. It stands to reason that Vivian heard of the audition through an acquaintance made on her first trip to New York. Her sister Dorothy tells this story about the audition at the Alvin. "Viv had never been to a Broadway call before. These people were singing all these arias and Viv got up and belted out 'After You've Gone,' real loud, in the smokiest Sophie Tucker manner." Convinced that her ploy had backfired, and afraid they'd boot her out when her number was cut short, she was preparing to leave when the stage manager approached her and asked "if she'd take ensemble work." Sitting in the darkened theater, Oscar Hammerstein II and Jerome Kern found Vivian's display of chutzpah so incredible, they hired her on the spot. Vivian had made a move worthy of a seasoned performer.

The play was *Music in the Air* starring Al Shean, Walter Slezak, Kathryn Carrington, and Natalie Hall. The action of the play involves two songwriters and a girlfriend who live in a small Bavarian village who set out for Munich to find success. After lessons learned the hard way, they return to their small village to live in uncompromising bliss. The vehicle did not and could not provide Vivian with the star status she enjoyed at the Little Theatre, a rude awakening for a girl who'd been the center of attention for two years. But she had a job on a Broadway stage.

Vivian quickly made friends and attempted to enter the

inner circle, taking the time to study the other women in the company and learn the ins and outs of Broadway theater, consciously absorbing what she could use later. Physically, she took on a more glamorous look by copying the makeup and hairstyles of the girls in the basement of the Alvin Theatre. Having lost a significant amount of weight, she finally retired the tweed suit, and chose a wardrobe in primary colors which projected a cheerful and confident image.

Some of the women Vivian tried befriending strolled in nightly covered in jewels and furs. Since Vivian knew that a $35-a-week paycheck couldn't buy such frills, it didn't take her long to deduce what extracurricular activities were necessary to buy such finery. "There was an alternative to hard work that I'd already rejected," she said. "The sophisticates of the Alvin's basement had said enough down among the steam-pipes, to convince me that most of the beauties that paraded the stage in the *Follies*, the *Vanities*, and George White's *Scandals* were kept women. It was taken for granted that rich men set them up in apartments—three rooms on Park Avenue went for more than $125 a month, brand-new—and drenched them in furs and jewelry. That I didn't want, and that I didn't choose. It struck me as another kind of bondage. So far as I was concerned, a girl had every right to move in with a keeper if she decided to, but not this girl. I was a singer, a qualified professional now. I could handle an audition. It was time to get going."

Vivian immediately found work singing in two nightclubs, one in a hotel called the St. Moritz and the other in a speakeasy called the Simplon Club. Though choosing to be a kept woman or singing in an illegal speakeasy would, in her mother's eyes, reserve her a place in hell, Vivian saw her choice as the nobler of the two. "If it wasn't so sinful, it would have seemed extremely tame. I was never arrested and the closest sound to gunfire I ever heard was the popping of champagne corks."

While working in a nightclub, Vivian befriended a young brunette named Dolores Reade. One night after their final show, Dolores told Vivian of her date with a comedian working in the show *Ballyhoo*. The following day Dolores confided in Vivian that she had met the man she planned to marry. True to her word, the following year Dolores married the now legendary Bob Hope.

Vivian kept herself real busy over the next seven months. She'd perform a matinee at the Alvin, run to the hotel for a dinner show, zoom back to the Alvin, and afterward head to the speakeasy for a supper show. She moved out of the Girls Club and leased a one-room cold-water flat in a four-story walk-up, paying her own rent and stashing every other dollar to buy what she considered a necessity in life, a car. When she'd saved enough money, she bought a second-hand Packard convertible. Once she had the car, Vivian began taking day trips to small towns surrounding New York in search of land to buy. Later in life, she stressed to young actors the importance of investing in property, a commodity which she believed could only appreciate in value.

Vivian made up her own rules of survival. She ingratiated herself with Jerome Kern by bringing him an apple a day, an act which the other chorus members found suspiciously orchestrated to score points with the top brass. She also had a fling with the star of *Music in the Air,* Walter Slezak. The relationship did not offer the copious material benefits some other girls reaped, but Vivian did gain access to theatrical professionals.

On a whim, she entered and won a radio contest. The *Albuquerque Tribune*'s Society Flashes announced that

"Vivian Vance began broadcasting Monday at 3:45 o'clock eastern standard time over station WINS, New York City . . . a Hearst station . . . and she is featured as Vivian Vance the girl of WINS . . . all in addition to her work in the *Music in the Air* show company." The radio job was a publicity stunt by the station and it did not last. However, it did get Vivian's picture in the New York papers, showing a smartly dressed young woman sitting coquettishly, with just enough leg showing, holding copy and microphone ready to deliver the news.

The stunt generated enough attention for Vivian to be invited out to Astoria, New York, for her first screen test. Though she was complimented on her husky, sexy voice and her physical resemblance to Jean Arthur, no one offered Vivian a contract. She attributed the rejection to the bump in her nose. In theater, the illusion created by light, makeup, and distance easily transforms an actor's appearance. In film, however, the lens is unforgiving to those with the slightest imperfections.

Feigning indifference to the rejection, Vivian expressed disdain for the medium of film. "Movies? No! I had a taste of the Hollywood glamour treatment and frankly I wasn't impressed. They wanted to pull out all my teeth, and put new ones in, of course, and straighten this nose of mine, but I balked. I like my face just as it is, and the parts I'm playing now and the parts I'll be playing at forty," she continued unyieldingly "won't require one of those beauty masks they put on actresses in Hollywood." Her protests to the contrary, Vivian was sensitive about her appearance. In addition to the plastic surgery she had on her nose later in her career, she had caps made to camouflage her crooked teeth. Whenever she was faced with a camera, she promptly popped them in.

In the midst of her singing and stage work, Vivian took a detour in her life which no one expected. She called her sister Dorothy and told her that she'd become engaged. "Vivian, who was quite popular in the night clubs of New York, had a real intimate way of singing and was very pretty," Dorothy said. "She had quite a following. That's how she met George Koch."

This Brooklyn-born Jewish man studied classical music at Erasmus Hall High School and eventually made his living playing violin in popular bands. A rather short, stocky, and unattractive fellow, Koch attracted little attention with his quiet and unobtrusive personality. But his excellent musical abilities often attracted the attention of the opposite sex. Though George seemed sweet, he did not impress those he met and no one could explain his relationship with the lively Vivian Vance. He obviously did not share the same outgoing, prankish personality as Vivian. "I can see where they wouldn't have a very natural relationship," her sister Lou Ann said, "because he was an entirely different person. I don't remember him having much of a sense of humor."

Though they seemed to have less than nothing in common, Vivian Vance became Mrs. George Koch on January 6, 1933. This union seems to have been a business deal more than a marriage. Vivian may have rejected the idea of being a kept woman but for a struggling actress seeking an extra security blanket in the midst of a depression, a second paycheck would definitely come in handy. She continued with her professional and personal pursuits as if this marriage of convenience had never taken place. Years later, Vivian would not publicize her first or second marriage, instructing family members not to acknowledge or mention the existence of either union to the press.

In the thirties, New York supper clubs overflowed with good and sometimes exceptional singers. While Vivian's voice was not unique, she had a natural gift of believability that made listeners empathize with her. Her repertoire consisted of popular tunes of the day delivered in a style that fell just short of imitating the singers who had already made the tunes successful. This formula guaranteed a winning performance but not steady employment.

When *Music in the Air* came to a close after a seven-month run, Vivian went on her first tour of the nightclub circuit. Billed as "the former star of *Music in the Air*," she brought her act to the Palmer House in Chicago and sang with the Abe Lyman Orchestra at the Coconut Grove in Los Angeles. Reviewers agreed that Vivian Vance "was both beautiful and a good singer."

In New Orleans, Vivian appeared in the Blue Room of the Roosevelt for a six-week engagement, singing with the Smith Ballew Band which featured Harry Goodman, brother of legendary orchestra leader, Benny Goodman. The hotel was owned by Huey Long who was infamous for his wildcat politics. The Roosevelt served as Long's sanctuary and sometimes his private pleasure trap.

After seeing Vivian perform, he invited her to a party in his hotel suite. Believing that every contact could further her career, Vivian accepted the invitation. But when she arrived, there were no other guests. When she started to question Long, he locked the door and quickly undressed. Wearing only his shorts and socks, he chased Vivian around the rooms of the suite. After a marathon run, he cornered her. Looking him square in the face she said, "Mr. Long, you're a big shot in the Senate, aren't you?"

"Damn right," he panted.

"Well, you're a big shit to me!" Vivian retorted. Those simple words must have dampened his mood because Long put his clothes back on and ordered dinner for two. After a lengthy political discussion, Vivian excused herself and said she had a show to do. "When the time came to go down to sing, he escorted me to the door like a southern gentleman," Vivian said. Long died a year later when he was shot on the steps of the Louisiana state capitol.

After her nightclub tour, Vivian returned to Albuquerque. She felt defeated but the folks in Albuquerque were excited about the news of her work in *Music in the Air* and her stint as the WINS Girl. They greeted her at the train station with a hero's parade, complete with brass band. The adulation did little to help Vivian's morale. In fact, it convinced her to return to New York as quickly as possible.

There was a new musical production getting underway in the city just about the time Vivian returned. *Hard to Get* was written by the newly formed team of Howard Lindsay and Russell Crouse and was backed by producers Vinton Freedley and Alex Aarons. Cole Porter had collaborated on the score. Today we know this play by its revised title, *Anything Goes!* Most people can hum a bar or two from this musical's most famous compositions— "I Get a Kick out of You," "You're the Top," and "Anything Goes!" Vivian auditioned for the chorus and landed a job.

This famous musical had its share of problems coming together. The last scene remained a mystery right up to its Boston tryouts. Before the final dress rehearsal, Lindsay and Crouse emerged from the men's room with the last lines written on toilet paper.

On November 21, 1934, reviewers greeted the opening of *Anything Goes!* with lots of praise. Most, if not all, of the attention went to Ethel Merman, the woman who would forever be associated with this vehicle. Born in 1909 in Astoria, New York, Ethel Merman's powerful, brassy voice quickly catapulted her to the top and secured her place as the queen of musical theater. She belted out hit after hit in such classic musicals as *Annie Get Your Gun* (in which she introduced the show business theme song "There's No Business Like Show Business"), *Call Me Madam*, *Gypsy* (which contains her signature song, "Everything's Coming up Roses"), and scores of others. It is evident that Vivian studied Merman's voice inflections and mannerisms since several who described Vivian's style after her time in *Anything Goes!* note similarities between the two.

During the run of this show, Vivian graduated from the chorus to a speaking role. "During the writing of the musical comedy, Howard Lindsay and I had been forced two or three times to throw lines to chorus girls," Russell Crouse said. "This we are always reluctant to do because while chorus girls, as chorus girls, are perhaps the most efficient and hardest working and even most charming element in the theater, they rarely know how to read lines. Give a chorus girl a line and she will become Kathryn Cornell overnight in her own mind . . . So Mr. Lindsay and I began to look around for a chorus girl who could say a few lines in *Anything Goes!* I can still hear [Vivian] saying all of them because she meant them."

Vivian's four lines eventually turned into the small part of Babe and gave the girl from Albuquerque her first billing in a Broadway theater program. It also won her, according to Crouse, "the unenviable task of understudying Ethel Merman" in the role of Reno Sweeney. The star, known for her incredible stamina, rarely missed a performance. If necessary, she would have crawled to a theater in order to perform. However, Crouse remembers that on at least two occasions Vivian did get the opportunity to go on for Ms. Merman "giving surprisingly good performances." This did not convince the management to turn the role over to Vivian once Ethel Merman left for Hollywood, however. They wanted a name and the part went to Benay Venuta, known for her stage and radio work.

Vivian developed a relationship with Russell Crouse during the run of *Anything Goes!* Although Lindsay and Crouse both expressed interest in Vivian, she later revealed that "Buck was the one I was moon-eyed about. He did have a wife though which turned my relationship with him into one of those wonderful, suffering love affairs. I clutched to my bosom every word and every smile he threw in my direction when he and Howard decided it was time to show me a whole new side of New York City." Vivian, it seems, completely forgot about her own marriage to George Koch.

Through Crouse, Vivian was able to join the inner sanctum of the literary and theatrical intelligentsia of New York. She frequently found herself among the likes of George S. Kaufman, Marc Connelly, and columnists Frank P. Adam and Frank Sullivan when they gathered for regular poker games with Crouse. "My appearances weren't made at the Algonquin for lunch but sixteen blocks uptown at the St. Moritz on Central Park South as a kibitzer for poker," Vivian wrote years later. "It was understood that every so often each man was allowed to bring a friend. It was pretty heady stuff. I'd never been close up to people with this style before, and me no more than a high school graduate. I'd sung for them in speakeasies, and I'd seen them on the other side of the footlights. But now I was accepted as an ornament at their poker games. It was good for morale and I was too crazy over Buck to start asking myself whether or not I fit there."

Technically, Crouse wasn't really married. He had divorced his first wife, Alison Smith, in 1929 though they continued to live together off and on for the next fourteen years. This arrangement gave Crouse the freedom, when he chose, to have relationships with other women. Throughout his relationship with Vivian, Crouse remained devoted to Smith while helping to further Vivian's career.

Vivian invited her sister Dorothy to New York for a long visit during the run of *Anything Goes!* Fresh out of high school, Dot made a beeline to the big city which made Mae worry even more. Having her younger sister near provided Vivian with a confidante and the support system she had been lacking. When Dot moved to New York, she moved in with Vivian and George on West 55th Street. They later found a larger apartment at the Parc Vendome on West 57th.

Dorothy recalls those days fondly. Vivian, who always loved animals, owned two Pekingese dogs. "I used to walk them while Viv was doing the show [*Anything Goes!*] and then I'd meet her," Dot remembers. "Sometimes we'd take in a midnight movie or have a late supper. Manhattan was a beautiful town in those days."

Vivian continued her supper club gigs, appearing with Jack Denny's orchestra at the Hotel Biltmore, and with others at the Mon Paree, House of Lords, and Marlborough House. In those days, parking in New York wasn't quite as bad as it is today but Vivian's insistence on arriving for her gig in her Packard still created a problem. There was a parking garage racket on the city's streets then. In an attempt to convince motorists to park in their garages, mobsters punctured the tires and broke the windows of cars parked along the curb. They warned Vivian, who refused to oblige, that if she insisted on parking outside the club, she would have to leave the lights on at all times. Knowing all too well that the battery would go dead if she followed this rule, Vivian found a solution. Upon arriving at a club, dressed to the nines and ready to perform, she'd produce two gas lanterns from the trunk of her car, light them, and place one in front and one in the back. The gutsy move paid off and the hoodlums left her alone.

Eventually *Anything Goes!* went on the road with Benay Venuta and Irene Delroy and settled in for an indefinite run in Chicago. A second touring company was assembled in late 1935 to bring the play to smaller cities, and this time Vivian played the role of Reno Sweeney. Instead of returning to New York when the tour ended, Vivian began the nightclub circuit again. Miami's Roney Plaza Hotel engaged Vivian's husband George and his band, including Vivian, for a five-week run. A young Cuban band leader, Desi Arnaz, also headlined at this club around the same time. There is no record, however, that the two met at this time.

Once the Florida run was over, Dorothy joined Vivian and George for a drive to Albuquerque. The trip gave Vivian an opportunity to introduce George to her family. He impressed them with his musical talents but most of all, he won over Vivian's little brother, Robert, by giving him several Fifth Avenue dress shirts and ties out of his wardrobe. "I really thought I was big time wearing these things from New York City," Robert recalls.

During the three-week visit, Vivian made an appearance in the Little Theatre's last production of the season, *One Viennese Night*. George Koch helped the orchestra arrange the music and played in the violin section. After the curtain fell on closing night, Vivian, dressed all in white and looking like a million bucks, came back on stage and sang several songs from *Anything Goes!* The audience was visibly proud of their hometown girl, the one who went to New York and made it on Broadway.

Vivian represented a true success story to the people of Albuquerque. But in New York, she was still just a chorus girl with possibilities. But Lindsay and Crouse had prom-

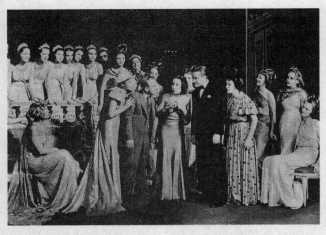

Vivian and the cast of Red, Hot, and Blue! *in 1936. Standing in the center are, from left to right, Vivian, Jimmy Durante, Ethel Merman, and Bob Hope.*

ised her a part in *Red, Hot, and Blue!*, a new musical starring Ethel Merman, Jimmy Durante, and a hot new comedian named Bob Hope. According to Crouse, "We firmly intended to reward Miss Vance with a small role. [But] in the rewriting, the part became smaller and smaller. By the time the show reached New York, it was infinitesimal. It consisted of one line. The line was in fact one word. The word was 'who?' "

So Vivian's career took a step back, a course not uncommon in the theater. She had regressed from four lines and understudying Ethel Merman to one word—and understudying Merman. Even though Merman's excellent health stifled opportunities for understudies to perform, Crouse remembers that "Vivian went on several times and made good," in the title role of "Nails" O'Reilly Duquesne.

Red, Hot, and Blue! reunited the same writing team from *Anything Goes!* But when the show opened on October 29, 1936, its overworked plot about the search and ultimate discovery of a woman with a waffle iron imprint on her behind did not excite reviewers. Even the show's Cole Porter songs did not deliver the same impact as those in *Anything Goes!* But the popularity of Merman, Durante, and Hope carried the show and it ran for 183 performances. Vivian's close friends Grace and Paul Hartman, a famous dance team of the thirties, rounded out the stellar cast.

Comedian Jimmy Durante was the focus of Vivian's fondest memories of this show. Durante, who had a long career in show business and was much beloved, began by playing piano and singing to drunks and whores in Coney Island's saloons. He later achieved stardom in films, radio, and television. Well-known for his generosity, he regularly treated people to dinner. This is one of Vivian's favorite Durante stories:

> In those days when the show played New Haven, policemen had to escort girls from the stage door across the street to the restaurant, for the Yale men were not gentlemen. They were rude, ill-mannered, and pests. One night after the show, when Jimmy took all of us over across the street to supper, a group of Yale men drew chairs, sat down, ordered drinks and started their usual unfunny, not at all amusing and rather insulting conversation. Jimmy rose and invited them all to the bar to have a drink.
>
> When he returned sometime later, the Yale men were not with him, so I asked how he got rid of them. He said, "I told them if they wanted drinks I'd buy them, but I couldn't allow them to stay at the table and use such language in front of the ladies I'd brought in for supper,

and said when I was your age I didn't have any money and had to play piano in a whorehouse and I never heard one man who came into that house use the kind of language you were using tonight—don't ever come to my table again."

Red, Hot, and Blue! did not meet the public's expectations in the same way as *Anything Goes!* and it did little for Vivian's career or anyone else's reputation. However, it did teach Vivian an important lesson. "None of us were in *Red, Hot, and Blue!* as long as we'd expected. There was so much kidding around during performances by some of the cast that the impact [of the show] got lost and the audiences dwindled away. As a result, the show had to close way ahead of time, thrown out the window by the people it was paying to pull in the crowds. In my mental notebook, I underlined [the] lesson. I'd never be guilty of joining in games like that."

Yip Harburg's contributions as a lyricist forever guarantee him a place in musical theater and film history. He wrote the lyrics for over five hundred songs including "Brother Can You Spare a Dime," "April in Paris," and "It's Only a Paper Moon" as well as all the song lyrics and the dialogue that integrates the songs into the script for *The Wizard of Oz*. In 1937, he had an idea for a new musical, *Hooray for What!* Eventually, Ed Wynn, Kay Thompson, Jack Whiting, Paul Haakon, and Hannah Williams signed up to star in Harburg's latest venture with music by Harold Arlen and direction by Vincent Minnelli.

Howard Lindsay and Russell Crouse were hired to write the book for *Hooray for What!* They wanted to reward Vivian with a part but "there was nothing for Miss Vance," Crouse said. "We didn't think of her for the [lead] part of

Stefania Stevanovich because we knew a 'name' was wanted. We were a little ashamed to talk to her because we felt we had let her down. But she wasn't afraid to talk to us. 'All right,' she said, when she heard the bad news. 'I'll go into the chorus again.' "

Once again Vivian became an understudy, this time for Kay Thompson. For Thompson, *Hooray for What!* was supposed to be the musical that would give her recognition as a Broadway star. Thompson had worked constantly from the age of four on her career in show business. By sixteen, she was performing on the piano with the St. Louis Symphony.

No one ever described Thompson as a beauty. In fact, early newspaper stories cruelly referred to her as an ugly duckling. But Thompson became famous as a singer and later went on to coach such stars as her goddaughter Liza Minnelli, Judy Garland, and Lena Horne. Perhaps Thompson's greatest achievement was her creation of the popular character of Eloise, a lonely, whimsical child whose escapades Thompson chronicled in several best-selling children's books. Thompson never spoke to anyone about her ordeal in *Hooray for What!* And she never appeared in another Broadway show after the play closed.

The behind-the-scenes story of *Hooray for What!* would make a better show than the actual musical itself. The play's long trek to Broadway produced its share of casualties. In her autobiography, Agnes de Mille, who was hired by director Vincent Minnelli to choreograph *Hooray for What!*, recalls in detail the nightmarish events during rehearsals. It was chaos. Producers and business cronies gave late-night parties and invited chorus girls to attend as a reward for their investments. Because of their dalliances with the producers, the chorus girls felt they didn't need to devote their energies to learning dance rou-

Vivian picks Ed Wynn's pocket in Hooray for What! *in 1937.*

Vivian in a publicity photo taken in the late 1930s shows off what she considered one of her best assets, her shoulders.

tines because their jobs were guaranteed by other activities. And the business manager encouraged this belief because he felt the way to treat dancers was "Thirty-five dollars a week, twenty dollars for rehearsal, and a little loving on the side," recalled de Mille. "For every one of these chorus girls, I had to let a trained dancer go. I had to take them and I couldn't fire them. Great limousines with liveried chauffeurs fetched them and delivered them at the stage door. They didn't know their left knee from their hair dye."

Though still married to George Koch, Vivian found protection by dating E.Y. Harburg. "I thought she might be having an affair with Yip Harburg because they were dating a lot, pretending it was platonic," remembers chorus member and songwriter Hugh Martin. However, Harburg, who was as well known for his libido as his songwriting, did not involve himself in platonic relationships.

Hugh Martin became a legendary songwriter with hits such as "The Trolley Song," "Have Yourself a Merry Little Christmas," and "Pass the Peace Pipe." Like de Mille, he remembers problems with *Hooray for What!* but adds that "it was at the top that it was rotten. Down where we were, it was sweet and wonderful. We loved each other and worked our asses off. There was no Equity ruling about how long they could work us. We worked around the clock."

Over the course of rehearsals the hierarchy of the production systematically crumbled. No one saw eye to eye on anything. Harburg argued with Minnelli, Minnelli turned on Wynn, the business manager harassed Crouse and Lindsay, and it all left Hannah Williams in tears. It was all somewhat resolved by the firing of Agnes de Mille, who was replaced by Robert Alton. June Clyde took over

Hannah Williams's role and then Minnelli took to his bed as did Harold Arlen, both declaring ill health.

De Mille got a bit of sweet revenge when she received a phone call from Kay Thompson with details of how the business manager fell off the stage and broke his back. De Mille, who was elated by the news, never mentioned the business manager's name in her book but according to Arlen's biography, *Happy with the Blues*, the man who fell off the stage was Harry Kaufman, the producers' right-hand man.

Somehow the show managed to glue itself together and opened out of town for previews. After one of these performances, the stage manager tapped Kay Thompson on the shoulder and told her, according to Martin, "that will be your last performance, Miss T." Vincent Minnelli recalls in his memoirs that Kay Thompson left the production of her own will. But Hugh Martin remembers differently. "She was fired because she was angular and bony and wasn't sexy enough," he said. "I know, I was there. I was outside her dressing room and I never heard such sobbing in my life."

On the other hand, the management found Vivian, as Martin describes, "voluptuous, what the Shuberts [the producers] considered sexy in the thirties. Vivian was very much like a Joan Blondell type, blond and plumpish, but in an attractive way. She was curvaceous and vivacious." They turned the part over to her but, continues Martin, "Vivian did not want to replace Kay. She almost had a nervous breakdown over that. We were all shell-shocked because we loved this woman. The Shuberts had been grossly unfair to her."

Guilt-ridden and unsure of her capabilities, Hugh Martin remembers Vivian telling him that "she couldn't do this to this wonderful woman." Vivian turned to her idol for advice. Martin recalls Thompson reasoning with Vivian and telling her, "You must do it. It won't help me if you refuse. They'll just get someone else and you need the break. You're a gifted person."

With Thompson's encouragement, Vivian started rehearsing, going over dance routines and practicing her big numbers—"Moanin' in the Morning," "The Night at the Embassy Ball," and "Down With Love." Vivian opened in Boston in a matinee performance.

"In view of what happened, I thought it best to pop in the dressing room and steady a girl who had every right to be completely shaken," wrote Russell Crouse. "The curtain was about to go up and she was about to go on. It was probably the most important moment in her theatrical life. Suddenly she reached over and patted me on the shoulder. 'Now, Russell,' she said, 'don't you be nervous.' " Hugh Martin recalled of Vivian's performance, "She was wonderful. She wasn't as good as Kay but then Kay was kind of a genius."

Now Vivian's singing voice had to sustain the rigors of performing every night along with the pressure that came from having a major role. On the road, Vivian asked Martin for help with her singing, and paid five dollars for each lesson. Vivian told him, "I know I'm not a great singer, but I know I could do well in musical comedy if I sang a little better. Will you coach me?"

Vivian's singing lessons were the start of a new career for Martin. Over time, he developed into the premier coach for several musical performers and later, Judy Garland's musical director. He remembers fondly, "I never would have thought to try it if Vivian hadn't come to me. She was my first pupil and I owe her a lot for that. Viv began to get a little bit more acceptance on her singing as a result. I told her at the start, 'You don't have a great singing voice but

I like your style and I think you'll do well.' And indeed she did."

The Shuberts' offer of the lead role came with a major caveat—Vivian would take over the part only until they could find a "name." Potential substitutes studied her role at every performance. Two days before the Broadway opening, Vivian learned that the Shuberts had finally picked her name to blaze on the marquee of the Winter Garden Theatre. But the moment she had waited for since leaving Independence had come with its share of compromises. She was filled with self-doubt and emptiness where she should have felt fulfillment and pride instead.

In *Hooray for What!*, Ed Wynn plays a scientist who, in an attempt to concoct a pesticide to rid his garden of fruit flies, invents a gas so terrible that whoever gets hold of it could conquer the world. Vivian played a sexy spy from a foreign country who tries to entice the scientist to give up his secret. While Wynn stands behind her, she uses the reflection in the mirror of her compact to copy the formula. Unfortunately, the formula in the mirror image produces laughing gas.

When the show opened on December 1, 1937, the reviews were all over the map. Some critics said that Vivian "has beauty and did her big number 'The Night of the Embassy Ball,' with impressive naughtiness." One reviewer urged theatergoers to "take an especially long look at the blonde with the accent who plays the part of the international spy. There, in the elongated person of Vivian Vance, you will see a dream walking and singing." Another found her to be "a blues singer of the Ethel Merman school, handsome and lively as a beautiful international spy."

Others, however, were not impressed. "A young lady named Vivian Vance heads the rest of the troop moaning

Vivian, Ed Wynn, and other members of the cast of Hooray for What!, 1937

out numbers in what can only by courtesy be called a voice." Another said, "June Clyde and Vivian Vance sing as well as they can, which is nothing remarkable." John Mason Brown, a critic for the *New York Post*, was particularly harsh. He wrote, "I understood from the program that Miss Vance came from nightclubs, where she might be at home, but I personally would not stay up until four in the morning to hear her." Vivian confronted him at a party demanding to know why he made such mean-spirited remarks. He replied that as she performed it, "The Night at the Embassy Ball" came across as vulgar and offensive. Vivian was quite hurt that someone would pass a moral judgment on her work, describing her as a two-bit barroom floozy rather than a professional actress. Her head reeled with the familiar sounds of her mother's words.

In spite of all its problems, the show was considered a hit by 1930s Broadway standards and it made the most of Ed Wynn's popularity. Wynn's illustrious career ran the gamut from vaudeville to television. He entertained in both world wars and had the distinction of participating in the opening of the famed Palace Theatre in 1913. He received scores of awards, for his work not only as an entertainer but also as a humanitarian. Thousands tuned into his successful radio show. As her friend Anne Denove Farleigh recalls, Vivian "became friendly with Ed Wynn. She figured he was a star and people kind of kept their distance. She felt he was lonely and would like some company so she latched on to his coattails. Also, he could help her in show biz." The twosome regularly saw each other before the show. They once attended a matinee performance of *Our Town* that so affected them, they found it difficult to perform in that night's performance of *Hooray for What!* After their curtain call, Wynn apologized for their lack of enthusiasm.

Our Town came to mean a great deal to Vivian. She cherished the wisdom of the author's words and throughout her life tried to abide by its lessons. A young Martha Scott played Emily in the cast of the original production. She went on to appear in films such as *Ben Hur* and *Sayonara*. She also earned an Academy Award nomination for her portrayal of Emily in the film version of *Our Town*. Vivian later developed a close friendship with Scott and the two eventually lived next door to each other in Connecticut.

Vivian developed a series of physical ailments during the run of *Hooray for What!* Even though she slept ten hours every night and took naps during the day, she was constantly fatigued. She also lost her sense of taste. "Everything I ate and drank seemed to be pulp or plain water," she said. During the day, her tongue would swell and she'd have to wrap it in gauze. Sometimes she would lose her voice just before going on stage. Vivian never spoke to anyone other than her sister Dorothy and her physician about these peculiarities. Dorothy felt Vivian's condition was the result of stress while her doctor chalked it up to anemia and prescribed vitamin B_{12}.

Vivian went along with the diagnosis but intuitively felt that the symptoms pointed in another direction which neither she nor anyone else understood. In an attempt to keep everyone at bay, she always presented a fun-loving and life-affirming Vivian to the public, appearing, as Martin said, "full of laughter and good humor. Laughing at herself a lot and always just wonderful company, never aloof. Anything but."

By this time, the United States found itself on the threshold of another world war and audiences no longer thought that a musical about nations vying for control of the world through chemical warfare was funny. *Hooray for What!* closed after two hundred performances. But Vivian continued to benefit from her newly found fame. Albuquerqueans were impressed by her favorable reviews, especially a two-page color spread in *Life* magazine, and Rudy Vallee invited Vivian to guest star on his radio program on NBC.

At about this time, Vinton Freedley, who produced *Anything Goes!,* called Vivian to offer her a small part in his new show. The role consisted of only one song written by Cole Porter, and it was choreographed as a quasi-striptease. Vivian felt she'd had enough bashing by the critics with *Night at the Embassy Ball* and that taking the part would put her back in the chorus, so she turned it down. So Freedley offered the part in *Leave It to Me* to a young Mary Martin who made the song "My Heart Belongs to Daddy" an instant hit.

Vivian decided to accept an offer for a screen test with Warner Brothers, taking the opportunity to drive cross-country in her Packard. Her brother Robert joined Vivian in Albuquerque for the drive to California. Robert remembers the trip and the screen test well. "One of my duties was to take care of Vivian's fur jacket, carrying it in a pillowcase. To keep cool we bought a cake of dry ice, put it in a pan and directed the little fan on the Packard's dash onto the dry ice and onto our bodies. It was a very primitive air-conditioning system and not too efficient, but psychologically it helped."

Vivian's screen test did not result in an offer of a contract because producers felt that her eyes were too wide apart. But while in Los Angeles, Vivian stayed in Beverly Hills with a trumpet player who worked in Eddy Duchin's band. On the day of her arrival, she received a call from Ethel Merman inviting her to dinner. Merman had just cashed in on her Broadway success by accepting offers to make movies. She found the Hollywood lifestyle lonely and missed the excitement of New York.

With no other prospects to keep her on the west coast, Vivian returned to New York and another round of night-clubs, singing "Danny Boy," "What'll I Do?", and "After You've Gone." Things looked dry for prospects of a new show but Vivian had put a few dollars away to cover the spell. And even though George and Vivian had grown apart, he still provided financial support.

A talent agent saw Vivian performing at a club and referred her to the top theatrical agent of the day, Sarah Enright. Enright thought Vivian might be right for a part in a touring production of the hit Broadway show *Kiss the Boys Good-bye* written by Clare Boothe and directed by Antoinette Perry. Enright suggested Vivian meet Brock Pemberton, a highly regarded and successful producer.

Over the course of his long career, Pemberton brought playwrights such as Maxwell Anderson, Preston Sturges, and Sidney Howard their first taste of fame, and he introduced audiences to the talents of Fredric March, Walter Huston, Miriam Hopkins, and Claudette Colbert. Pemberton had heard about Vivian from Lindsay and Crouse during their weekly poker games and agreed to see her. After listening to Vivian relate her story of getting drunk on laced beer in Emporia, Kansas (Pemberton was from Emporia, Pennsylvania), he felt her personality and humor suited the part of Myra Stanhope. A playbill from the Detroit production describes their meeting this way: "Vivian walked into the Pemberton office and vamped everyone in sight."

During the rehearsals of *Kiss the Boys Good-bye*, director Antoinette Perry became Vivian's new mentor, teaching her speech, stage decorum, and the mechanics of playing comedy. Perry is widely known for her many contributions to the theater. She is the namesake of the Tony

Awards (Antoinette Perry Awards) which are handed out annually by the American Theatre Wing which she helped to develop. She started acting in Chicago in 1905. After marrying, she gave up the stage only to return after her husband's death. In 1928 her career focus shifted to directing and producing with Brock Pemberton. Her many successes include *Harvey*, *Lady in Waiting*, *Going Home*, *Personal Appearance*, and *The Barretts of Wimpole Street*. Perry was widely known for her attention to detail, her skill in analyzing scripts, and the respectful manner in which she treated actors.

The touring production of *Kiss the Boys Good-bye* opened in Chicago in January, 1939, after a trial run in Buffalo. Meanwhile, the New York company still played on Broadway. There was a young actor in the New York company, Philip Ober, whom Perry felt would have a promising career. Perry, somewhat of a matchmaker, introduced Phil to Vivian prior to Vivian's leaving on the tour. Though married to others, they began a long-distance affair. After her initial meeting with the tall, debonair, upper-crust New Englander, Vivian phoned her sister Dorothy (now married to a music publisher), and told her "that she had met the man of her dreams." Phil Ober, much like her father, possessed all the qualities she admired in a man: intelligence, good looks, humor, and talent. After his birth in Fort Payne, Alabama, in 1902, the family moved to New England where Ober attended private school and later enrolled in Princeton University. After graduating, he worked successfully as an advertising executive for *Liberty, The Spur,* and *Collier's* magazines but harbored a secret desire to act.

He joined a local theater group, the Beechwood Players, where he performed for six seasons before making his Broadway debut as Jo Fisk in *Animal Kingdom.* Ober's interpretations of Henry Broughton in *She Loves Me*, Chester Norton in *Personal Appearance*, and Horace Rand in *Kiss the Boys Good-bye* gave him a reputation as a dependable and efficient leading character actor. His military bearing and balding scalp gave him a stately and aristocratic appearance on and off the stage while his earthiness and offbeat sense of humor let him easily hobnob in the penthouses of Fifth Avenue to the basements in Greenwich Village and everywhere in between.

David O. Selznick's highly publicized search to find the perfect actress to play Scarlett O'Hara in *Gone with the Wind* had inspired Clare Boothe to pen *Kiss the Boys Good-bye*. She found the saga of young actresses willing to sell their souls in exchange for the part of Scarlett so absurd, she wrote a play based on those characters. Vivian played Myra Stanhope, a Brooklyn-born self-made gal who will go to any lengths to play the heroic southern belle, Velvet O'Toole. The one-liners written for the character of Myra are filled with double entendre and were tailor-made to match Vivian's comedic abilities. Ironically, the description of Myra Stanhope's character— a ruthless, blasphemous woman who serviced anyone who could help further her career—echoed Mae's predictions for Vivian.

Anne Denove Farleigh was a young actress from Alabama then. She was hired to understudy the female roles and remembers the tension of opening night. "There was a blizzard and most of the critics didn't get there." But Cecil Smith, critic for the *Chicago Tribune* (he would later marry Lucille Ball's cousin, Cleo) did make it to the theater. His favorable review pointed out that "Vivian Vance is excellent as an outworn cinema glamour artist endeavoring to win the coveted movie role for herself by saying 'Take my mouth, it is yours' to every man she can fasten onto." Farleigh described Vivian as "a tall, beautiful blonde who had a shape to kill for and made a stunning appearance in the part of Myra. She'd mainly been a show-girl until then and she really wanted to succeed in this show because it was her first legitimate job."

The role of Myra gave Vivian the chance to play a resilient, humorous, hard-nosed woman who refused to abandon her fight to succeed. Obviously, Vivian found Myra's plight close to her own and identified with her. Because of her role in *Kiss the Boys Good-bye*, producers pegged Vivian as a second female lead and she became typecast for similar roles.

While in Chicago, Anne and Vivian roomed together in a small, two-room apartment. Vivian felt close enough to Anne to suggest sharing expenses. Anne tells this story about their time together:

> Vivian was very careful with a dollar. I remember her being very housewifely. She'd wash her hose and bras every night and go marketing every day. She thought we could save money if we ate at home. That was fine with me but I had grown up with a cook who would not let me into the kitchen. One day, however, I saw a recipe for quick rising rolls and told Vivian I was going to cook the meal. I wanted to surprise her, and I got it all together when the phone rang. It was a friend of my mother's from Kentucky and she talked and she talked. When I got off the phone and went into the kitchen I could hardly get in. Those quick rising rolls were climbing up the refrigerator. Vivian came in and saw the mess. We cleaned everything up and she told me never to walk into the kitchen again!

During their meals together, the women confided in each other. Farleigh says that "the Vivian you saw was not the real Vivian. You saw what she wanted you to see. She covered up the sadness, unhappiness, the insecurity," and placed great importance on how she came across to others. "Before leaving for Chicago, Vivian had gone to Gimbels Department Store. She asked the salesgirl where the dresses were. 'Oh, you must want the basement,' the sales-girl said. Vivian told her, '*Look*, I have two hundred dol-lars in my pocket. I was going to spend it here and *now* I'm not gonna do it.' Vivian's front definitely covered up a basic insecurity that she had."

By this time, the relationship between George and Vivian had all but disappeared. Farleigh remembers Vivian writing to George asking him to send her favorite blue sweater. He wrote back, "What drawer is it in?"

"I guess that's how George was," Farleigh said. "Vivian didn't say anything derogatory about him but also she didn't say anything nice either. Men and marriage didn't seem important to her, only as a means to an end. Her whole focus was on becoming successful."

Earlier in life Vivian had wanted nothing more than to have a good time. But by the time she reached Chicago, Farleigh said, "Any partying she did was with the idea of it helping her career. She'd go anywhere, be nice to anybody in order to get ahead. 'You never know who can help you,' she'd say." In Chicago, there was a businessman who had struck up an ongoing business deal with Vivian. Vivian told Farleigh that a man would eventually call their apart-ment after seeing her name in the papers. Thinking *Kiss the Boys Good-bye* a musical, he would ask Vivian to bring some chorus girls to his penthouse at the Drake to entertain business associates.

"Sure enough he called, and so Vivian turned to me and said, 'Anne, you've got to go.' I didn't know whether they slept with them or what they did," Anne said. Vivian assured her friend that the party involved a few men who liked having pretty girls around to help them relax. "Not only that, when you leave, they'll press a hundred-dollar bill in your hand," Vivian told Farleigh. Farleigh remembers a gathering filled with music and fun but no hanky-panky. Perhaps that's the reason why Farleigh didn't walk out with a hundred-dollar bill pressed in her hand as some of the other girls did.

It was clear to Anne Farleigh that Vivian had developed her own survival techniques through the years. Farleigh says that "Vivian knew the score completely. Everything was a stepping-stone to further her career. She once told me, 'Anne, if you don't succeed, you have just disappointed your family and your friends. But if I don't succeed I've disappointed a whole town.' She took that very, very seriously."

Once the Chicago run closed, Anne Denove Farleigh headed up a newly formed touring company of *Kiss the Boys Good-bye* and headed west to play Myra Stanhope. Vivian, meanwhile, headed to the east coast with yet another company. Vivian's run on the road lasted for over two hundred performances.

When Vivian's tour ended, a new cast of *Kiss the Boys Good-bye* was assembled for the Spa Theatre summer season in Saratoga, New York. It included Phil Ober, Sheldon Leonard (who would later produce such television classics as *The Dick Van Dyke Show*, *The Danny Thomas Show*, *The Andy Griffith Show*, and *I Dream of Jeannie* among many others) and Marjorie Lord (who later played Danny Thomas's wife on the television sitcom *Make Room for Daddy*). Only two members remained from the original touring company, Vivian and Lucia Lull.

While in Saratoga, Vivian continued her affair with Phil Ober. During the play's run in the Spa Theatre, Dorothy received two calls from Saratoga, one from a

Vivian and Marjorie Lord, who later appeared on The Danny Thomas
Show, *backstage getting ready to appear in* Kiss the Boys Good-bye
*at the SPA Theatre in Saratoga, New York. The woman who is
standing is unidentified.*

dejected George who had discovered his wife's infidelity
with Ober, and the other from Vivian sharing the news
that she had called it quits with George and planned to
marry Phil.

But Vivian's relationship with Phil introduced a whole
new set of problems. Ober had a child and the state of New
York did not readily grant divorces. Meanwhile, Vivian
filed for divorce from George through the District Court of
the County of Bernalillo in New Mexico.

After *Kiss the Boys Good-bye* closed, the second production of the Spa Theatre was *Springtime for Henry* with Vivian, Edward Everett Horton, and Marjorie Lord. Edward Everett Horton, a Brooklyn native, made his Broadway debut as a walk-on in *The Man Who Stood Still* in 1908. He appeared in scores of Broadway shows and is readily recognizable in such films as *The Gay Divorcée*, *Top Hat*, the 1937 version of *Lost Horizon*, and *Pocketful of Miracles*. He was the original Mr. Dewlip in *Springtime* and went on to perform this role almost three thousand times throughout the country.

The talents of Mr. Horton pleased the critics and Vivian's streak of good notices continued. "Vivian Vance went from the hard-boiled actress role of the first show to an English wife last night. She continued to be slightly hard-boiled—and she continues to be very good." Horton so enjoyed working with Vivian and Marjorie Lord that he asked them to join him on tour. Lord accepted but Vivian declined, saying that she needed to attend to personal matters in New York once the Saratoga season ended.

Gypsy Rose Lee starred in the next play of the Saratoga Players, a vehicle appropriately named *Burlesque*. In the 1930s, Lee's burlesque act made her the most famous stripper in the country. In fact, Arthur Laurents's musical *Gypsy* is based on Lee's memoirs of the same name.

Burlesque deals with the backstage gossip and private lives of burlesque actors. Vivian played Mazie, the best friend of Gypsy Rose Lee's character. Lee's notoriety pulled in huge audiences but her charisma and hard work could not sustain her performance. As this review points out: "It is unfair to compare (Miss Lee's) acting ability with that of the veterans who supported her—Vivian Vance provided in generous quantity and superb quality

*Vivian and Glenn Anders in the 1939 production of Skylark
at the Morosco Theatre*

any acting ability which may have been needed to balance the show. We like Miss Vance better every time we see her, and we thought she was excellent the first time."

When Vivian rejoined the *Kiss the Boys Good-bye* company on Cape Cod, the producers of another show, *Skylark*, were vigorously searching for an actress to play the part of Myrtle Valentine. This comedy revolves around the character of Lydia Kenyon and her husband, an advertising tycoon, whose drive for success renders him useless at home. The story deals with the wife's rebellion and a redefinition of the relationship between the two people. The play starred Gertrude Lawrence and the company needed a place to work out the kinks before its fall debut on Broadway. An earlier version of the play had been tried out in Boston but had little success. Richard Stoddard Aldrich, managing director of the Playhouse on Cape Cod, invited the inimitable actress to try out her new vehicle at his theater.

Gertrude Lawrence made her debut on the stage in 1908 as a child dancer and made her way to the American stage in 1924 acting with such notables as Beatrice Lillie. Along with a handful of other theater stars from the 1930s, Lawrence is considered a legend, a diva of her time. She had full approval of the cast of *Skylark* which included Glenn Anders, Donald Cook (later, John Emery, then married to Tallulah Bankhead, took over his part), and Ann Driscoll. A young Hollywood actress had originally played the role of Myrtle Valentine in the Boston company but Lawrence thought her too pretty and convinced the producer to let her go.

Actor Glenn Anders had spotted Vivian in *Kiss the Boys Good-bye* but at the time, didn't think much of her as an actress. Nevertheless, he introduced Vivian to Gertrude Lawrence. Vivian never tired of recounting her first meeting with the *grande dame* of the theater. "When we walked into the pine and chintz living room, Miss Lawrence was in the shower. She made her entrance naked except for a miniature bath towel that provided more coyness than coverage as she held it across her front. I did all my talking to this gorgeous, glamorous Englishwoman while she toyed with her doily." Ms. Lawrence took a liking to Vivian immediately. She appreciated Vivian's upbeat humor and approved her to play the part of Myrtle Valentine, the ex-chorus girl and beauty queen married to a rich advertising executive to whom she freely gives her opinions even though she "knows as little about advertising as she does about virtue—but certainly knows which side of the bed her husband sleeps on."

Opportunity was now pounding on Vivian's door. Antoinette Perry, who felt Vivian could go far in the theater, offered to sponsor her if she would go to England and study at the Royal Academy of Dramatic Arts. Perry told Vivian, "Once that personality of yours gets some polish over there, there'll be nothing to hold you back." This appealing offer may have given Vivian an advantage over her peers but remembering the debt she felt to her Albuquerque sponsors, Vivian rejected the idea of traveling to England. One I.O.U. was enough for a lifetime, Vivian thought. Besides, she didn't want to spend any more time away from Phil.

After Cape Cod and another try-out in Chicago, where it finally received some critical approval, *Skylark* opened on Broadway at the Morosco Theatre on October 11, 1939. Seven days later, just a few blocks away, a new musical produced by George Abbott also opened. Making his Broadway debut in the cast of *Too Many Girls* was a handsome, Cuban bandleader named Desi Arnaz. Both shows ran approximately two hundred and fifty performances.

Skylark received enthusiastic reviews thanks in large part to the talents of its star, Gertrude Lawrence. The notices focused mainly on her and the playwright but even given the competition from Lawrence, critics still noticed Vivian. "Vivian Vance serves the hell-cat admirably, standing up to her impulsive star bravely." Critic Brooks Atkinson wrote "Vivian Vance plays the unpleasant part of a blond harpy with sleek venom." Vivian's old nemesis, John Mason Brown, brought out his sharp pen to say that "Vivian Vance is worthy of at least a red ribbon as a female candidate for the Dog Show."

Though no one ever doubted Gertrude Lawrence's professionalism and commitment to the theater, the actress was still a bit insecure. Because of Vivian's positive reviews, Lawrence started a silent feud between the two which carried onto the stage. Though she would never admit it, Gertrude Lawrence was an expert in upstaging, a method by which actors draw the attention away from one player and redirect it to themselves. Vivian understood that Lawrence did not appreciate anyone standing in her spotlight. And it's possible Lawrence would have preferred to play the saucier, attention-grabbing role of Myrtle Valentine. "Some nights," Vivian remembered with frustration, "she might as well have been. She had a way of never quite finishing her lines when she was supposed to. She'd add little lilts and gurgles and flourishes to her words and trail her long white gloves to the point where I couldn't decide whether I should come in with my next line without seeming to be cutting her off. When she wasn't gurgling, she was fiddling with props, moving the chair I was supposed to sit on so that my back would be turned to the audience for my biggest scene. It got so bad after one performance I telephoned Tony (Perry) to pour out my complaints.

Perry advised Vivian to "stand very still while she's turning your chair around. Don't say a word. Let her have her way, then put that chair back where it belongs, sit in it and face the audience."

"The next evening I did what Tony advised," Vivian said. "This was the solution. Miss Lawrence didn't bring up the subject, and she restrained herself in the future from furniture moving. But she did have little bells put on the slippers she wore in one scene. Every time I opened my mouth to speak, she wiggled her feet. Oh, what the hell!"

Though less experienced, Vivian was just as competitive as Lawrence and refused to give up her own spotlight. The veteran thespian ultimately won the war but not without escaping criticism from the reviewers. In many ways Vivian came out on top when one wrote, "Vivian Vance is known among producers, actors, and critics in New York as a 'good trooper.' She isn't temperamental, she works hard and attends rehearsals faithfully, and she doesn't use the tricks of the trade by which an actor or actress can steal the stage from other members of the cast, or at least spoil the effect of the other actor's line by a movement at the wrong moment or some other such tricks."

While Vivian was appearing in *Skylark*, Antoinette Perry and Brock Pemberton were casting their new play, *Out from Under* by John Walter Kelly. They rounded up players familiar to them including Margaret Douglass, John Alexander, Ruth Weston, and Phil Ober. Perry thought the part of Claire James perfectly tailored to Vivian's successful run playing the "other woman" and invited her to join the company. In light of the shenanigans happening on stage at the Morosco, Vivian accepted the offer with excitement. The added bonus of working with Phil Ober clinched her decision to give notice to the producers of *Skylark*.

Vivian had high hopes that this Perry-Pemberton venture would give her instant name recognition. She told a newspaper columnist, "I hope what they say about Brock Pemberton having discovered so many famous actors and actresses is really true. Brother, if it is, I'm on my way up right now."

In that same interview, Vivian elaborated on some of the ups and downs of her career. "Practically everything went wrong. Almost everything I counted on failed me. Things I never thought would happen turned out to be a winner. I guess I did it the hard way." When asked about the parade given in her honor by her Albuquerque fans, she said "That did something to me. I had to turn right around and go back to New York and really make good. I had to go through all the dismal business of plying managers with requests and being auditioned and never getting a job. Then came *Anything Goes!* But believe you me, I did not feel I had won stardom through that short experience."

In *Out from Under*, a small-town newspaperman writes a scandalous bestseller under an assumed name to escape his humdrum existence. The book creates havoc in his life as scores of shady characters come to town after someone exposes him as the novel's author. Vivian played a New York bombshell who arrives in the small town to lure the author into a life of fun and excitement.

The comedy opened at the Biltmore on May 4, 1940, to less than glowing reviews. Critics felt the premise, though promising, used too many stereotypes, making it stale and predictable. Brooks Atkinson of the *New York*

Times felt that "it is one of the emptiest comedies of modern times and the performance, at high speed and raised voices, is one of the hollowest." Vivian, however did receive some favorable mentions. "Vivian Vance, the blond armful who made trouble for the heroine in *Skylark*, is the homewrecker in this one and works enthusiastically at it," said one. Another noted that "Vivian Vance is both ornamental and assured as the blond menace" while a third said that "Vivian Vance, G. Albert Smith, and Philip Ober—they are all of them agreeable performers when given half the chance," and "Philip Ober and Vivian Vance did what they could under the circumstances." *Out from Under* was one of the few failures for Pemberton and Perry, closing after only nine performances. By this time, tensions between Lawrence and Vivian had eased, so she returned to *Skylark* as it finished out its run on Broadway.

Though still married and by all accounts still content, Phil Ober frequently joined Vivian after the show for supper and then escorted her to an apartment she had recently rented at One University Place in Greenwich Village where he would spend the night. For Vivian, this affair was different. She did not hide the fact that she loved Ober and hoped to have a future with him.

With Gertrude Lawrence in the cast, *Skylark* was guaranteed a successful and sold-out tour after the Broadway run and Vivian decided to stay with the company. A royal welcome greeted the company in each of the thirteen states they played, as well as Canada. In public, Lawrence never failed to display the *grande dame* everyone expected to see. On shopping sprees, Vivian would stand behind Lawrence, holding her sable coat while Gertie bought everything in sight, only to return the unopened merchandise after leaving town.

At times, Lawrence's upstaging bravura went beyond the stage. In Vancouver, British Columbia, Vivian wanted to buy a coat:

> I made the mistake of telling her [Lawrence] that I spotted a wonderful camel hair coat that I was going to buy right after the matinee. "I ought to go with you, darling." Gertie smiled. You shouldn't have opened your mouth, I told myself. You know what's going to happen to you and your shopping if she comes along. Sure enough, when we got inside the little store, she played the star. Everybody surrounded her, and I couldn't get anyone's attention to help with the coat. So while she was twirling around in a dozen different coats and hats, I slipped away to the rack, unhooked the camel hair job I wanted and carried it over to one of her admiring salesmen. "I'd like to buy this one," I said. Miss Lawrence found just the right lines for her second act curtain speech: "Darling, darling, don't buy *that* coat! I have one at home exactly like it. I'll *give* it to you."

While Lawrence and Vivian did not see eye-to-eye on anything, their private feud never escalated into a shouting match. Looking out for her own interests, Vivian chose diplomacy over threats when dealing with the *grande dame*. Instead, Vivian directed her frustrations toward others in the cast, especially Ann Driscoll, who played a small role as a maid the entire run of the play. Driscoll felt that Vivian behaved suspiciously like Lawrence. "Miss Lawrence was unkind on stage, but she was a hard worker and a star. Vivian was considered to be what today is called a bimbo. Therefore, I could not understand why she was so condescending and judgmental of others." Vivian seemed to have a superiority complex and treated Driscoll unkindly both on and off the stage. "We shared a hotel room in San Francisco and I could tell she was an egocentric. I had a favorite suit which I had bought in New York and liked wearing a lot. One day Vivian yelled to 'stop wearing that, it looks shabby!' You could see a breakdown was coming on because she exaggerated everything."

In July, 1940, Vivian received her divorce from George Koch. She told her family that "George drove off in my car and took my best camera." Now at the end of the *Skylark* tour, Vivian returned to her Greenwich Village apartment and a future with Phil Ober. However, there was someone standing in the way. Phyllis Roper Ober would not allow her husband to leave her and their daughter Emily without a fight.

Vivian and Phil Ober

Chapter Five

The Blond Menace

❧

When the tour of *Skylark* returned to New York toward the end of 1940, Vivian decided to take some time off. While on hiatus, she and Phil spent much of their time together, making no attempt to hide their relationship. During the day they took long drives in Vivian's new car. In the evenings after Phil finished his performance in *Mr. & Mrs. North*, the two headed back to One University Place for late-night suppers. Though she enjoyed this romantic and passionate affair, Vivian wanted to marry as quickly as possible because she knew it would not take long before the news of her entanglement reached Albuquerque and her mother's ears. George Koch had granted her an uncontested divorce but Phil's wife was another matter entirely.

Phyllis Roper Ober, who came from an influential and wealthy Westchester family, had married Phil in 1923. At first, the socially conscious Phyllis had wanted her husband to succeed as an advertising executive but when he started to succeed in the theater, she grew to enjoy the spotlight. She had known of Phil's frequent nocturnal rendezvous for some time but she didn't think his relationship with Vivian worthy of concern. But once Phyllis realized that their illicit affair had grown into more than a mere fling, she plotted her revenge and swung into action.

On February 6, 1941, Vivian drove to the Belasco Theatre to meet Phil. After buying a couple of sandwiches from a deli, they headed to their Greenwich Village hideaway. At about 2 a.m., they retired for the night. The following morning, someone rang the doorbell of apartment 7B and Vivian heard a woman's voice demanding to see her husband, Philip Ober. Vivian replied that he wasn't there. The woman continued ringing the bell for the next 25 minutes. Finally Ober opened the door to see his wife, three detectives, and a newspaper columnist standing on the doorstep.

The next day the headlines blared "Linked to Blonde by Drop of a Pin!", "Actor's Wife Sues: Names Blonde Star!", and "Lights Went Out but Ober Didn't!". For the next month, newspapers printed more salacious details about the affair between Phil and Vivian for the public to read, and most of the stories defamed Vivian's character.

Phyllis had planned her coup very carefully, instructing the detectives to follow Phil and report his every move. Inevitably, he led them to Vivian's apartment. After several nights, Phyllis joined the stake-out in front of One University Place. To make her case against Phil stronger, should he decide to argue his innocence in court, Phyllis wedged a hairpin in Vivian's front door "in such a fashion that it would fall if the portal were opened." In court, this would prove that he had spent the entire night in Vivian's apartment. Then Phyllis went home and waited for a phone call from the detectives. At 7:30 in the morning, they informed her that the raid was ready to take place.

Phyllis knew her actions would get Phil where it counted most, his pocketbook. Once the case reached the court, Phyllis complained to the judge that her husband had not supported his family over the past ten months, leaving her unable to pay for her daughter's schooling. As a result, Phyllis had sent Emily to live with Phil's parents in Florida. Adding insult to injury, she claimed Phil squandered their livelihood on Vivian's rent and payments on a brand-new car. With the evidence gathered by the detectives, the court had no other recourse but to find in favor of Phyllis awarding her 35 percent of Phil Ober's income for child support and custody of their daughter.

Vivian could do little to change anyone's mind about her depiction in the papers as a calculating, gold-digging floozy whose only accomplishments in the theater had been as a chorus girl in the musical *Red, Hot and Blue!* She made an attempt to discredit Phyllis's story in a small article printed on the back page of one newspaper, denying that she had shared an apartment with Phil or that he had bought her a car.

But Vivian's immediate concerns were not about the views of the New York public but of her hometown of Albuquerque. She called the Albuquerque newspapers pleading, "I've been headlined as a co-respondent. Please don't print that. Oh, please! My mother would die!" The reporters, protecting their favorite daughter, never ran the story.

Still, Vivian had no guarantee that her family would not get wind of the news. Anticipating this, she called home and told them that the strict New York state laws and Phyllis's refusal to grant Phil a divorce had driven the couple to stage the scandal in order to put Phyllis in an awkward position where she had no choice but to concede. Her family accepted Vivian's explanation without question and made no mention of it from that moment on.

Even though Vivian had avoided a confrontation with her family, the incident had left her in a quandary. As a member of a sophisticated bohemian society, she believed in its unconventional rules, including a tolerance for unorthodox lifestyles. But the tongue lashings received from her mother had seeped into Vivian's consciousness and put her in conflict with these free-thinking principles. When she was branded a whore on the front pages of newspapers, Mae's visions of her daughter's ultimate downfall seemed to come true.

At this time in her life, Vivian had no confidante or support network nearby. Her sister Dorothy was now married to musician Armand Klein and traveled around the country with the Ramon Ramos band. When Dot heard the news she called Vivian from Florida. "It was a very bad period for Viv," Dorothy said. "She didn't know how to handle all the bad press she had received." Marjorie Lord, who had met Vivian and Phil in Saratoga the year before, recalls Vivian's struggle. "I knew that she fell madly in love with him and he was in love with her. We all thought it was a great love affair. They were both married and the divorce was very unpleasant on Phil's side. The only ground for divorce in New York at the time was infidelity, and you had to have a witness. It was awful for her, but because they adored each other, Vivian went through it. I know that Vivian was terribly distressed over the divorce and all the problems that Phil's wife Phyllis gave her. She didn't take those things lightly and didn't want to hurt anybody, but she was hopelessly in love with him."

To make matters worse, Vivian's hiatus had now become a self-imposed exile. Because of the rumors circulating in New York about her life as a femme fatale,

Vivian had avoided auditioning or singing in nightclubs. But with funds running low, she needed to get back to work. The answer to her problems came by way of a phone call from her friend Edward Everett Horton. He wanted Vivian to join him and Marjorie Lord in a production of *Springtime for Henry,* which he planned to stage in San Francisco in early May. Eager to get out of New York, Vivian accepted. The spring tour would give her time for the gossip to die down until the final divorce papers came through. Then she would be able to make plans for her wedding. When Vivian left for California, Phil accepted an offer to appear in a summer stock tour of *Mr. & Mrs. North.* The couple decided they would meet in Albuquerque in June.

Horton owned a large estate in Encino, California, with several guest houses. Marjorie Lord and Vivian moved into a guest house where F. Scott Fitzgerald had lived and written many of his books. Once again, Vivian's survival mechanism kicked in. She joked and laughed, showed no outward sign of anxiety, and seemed to forget the distressing affairs back in New York. "Whenever she spoke of Phil, she referred to him as her husband, and all she could think of was getting back to him," recalls Lord.

After three weeks of rehearsals, the troupe moved on to San Francisco where Marjorie Lord and Vivian shared an apartment in the Alexander Hamilton Hotel. Newspapers printed the obligatory feature articles for publicity but no mention was made of the events which took place in New York. In one of those articles, Vivian explained the reason for her recent absence from the stage this way. "I decided to take some time out for a little studying, and was deep into it when Eddy called me for the western production of *Springtime*."

In a second article, Vivian revealed that she had suffered a strange physical malady during the tour of *Skylark*. "It was a very funny thing. I was lying on a couch backstage, when all of a sudden a radio, or what sounded like a radio, went off inside my head and the darn thing's been playing there ever since." These symptoms occurred during the same period that her relationship with Phil began to get serious. While in *Hooray for What!,* the pressure to perform well had produced similar symptoms. In fact, each time Vivian underwent emotional stress, her body reacted by manifesting some kind of physical malady.

In addition, Vivian began to have erratic mood swings which worried those closest to her. In public, she rarely exuded anything other than high energy and good humor, but in private she suffered deep depressions triggered by unknown causes. Unable to fully recognize or define her problem, Vivian grew more dependent on Phil and retreated into this new relationship. She relinquished her individualism and reverted to an old survival pattern by reinventing herself. This time, Vivian became what Phil believed and stood for.

The ten year-old comedy, *Springtime for Henry,* written by Ben W. Levy in 1941, had already enjoyed a certain amount of acclaim. As the character of Henry Dewlip, Horton abandons his *bon vivant* existence for a very young and moral secretary played by Marjorie Lord. Vivian played yet another wise-cracking, street-smart character, Julia Jelliwell. She continued her string of successes playing this type of role, receiving favorable reviews. "Vivian Vance, who had the thankless part of the other woman in Gertrude Lawrence's *Skylark* last August, plays a sulky blond enchantress with wit and style, and her acid badinage with Lord is one of the best scenes in the play."

During the two-month run of the show, Marjorie Lord came to know Vivian on many different levels. "Vivian had wonderful taste and could make anything look beautiful. Though I grew up in San Francisco and had been living in New York and was aware of what was fashionable, Vivian was much more fussy. I once forgot to put on white gloves before going out to lunch—and Vivian said, 'You don't go out without your white gloves!' "

Vivian appeared shocked at Lord's lack of etiquette. Lord believes that Vivian constantly struggled between her true self and what she desired to project. "On the surface Vivian didn't appear to be afraid of anything or anybody, but how does anyone know what's inside of someone? She was very quick and humorous, deep, and very sensitive, strong, direct, and honest. She had no phoniness or artificiality. She knew what she wanted, but if she didn't get it, she was not the type to yell and scream about it, but would hold it in. She desired to be a major star."

It had been ten years since Vivian left Kansas to follow her dream, and although she could claim to be a working actress who was able to support herself financially, she still had not reached her ultimate goal. Vivian had all the attributes to become what she desired but her insecurity held her back. She struggled against these feelings for many years.

Once the show closed in San Francisco, Vivian left to meet Phil in New Mexico where she planned to appear in the title role of the Albuquerque Little Theatre production of Eugene O'Neill's *Anna Christie*. Kathryn Kennedy O'Connor's initial plan to develop the ALT into a renowned regional theater had worked. Finally in its permanent facility, the ALT had earned a reputation for producing quality plays. This enticed noted actors from nearby Hollywood to appear there between film commitments. The ALT had wooed actor Pat O'Hara, then enjoying a fair amount of success in the movies, to play the part of the sailor Matt Burke in *Anna Christie*.

To show her gratitude to the ALT, Vivian offered her services free of charge. She did not, however, make a big splash in the role of Anna. Instead, most of the attention went to a local actress, Marie Wallis, who critics described as superb in her part. The *Albuquerque Tribune* wrote, "Her [Vivian's] great moment came in the climactic first scene of Act III, when she tells her father and her lover of her past errors. But it was hardly an unmixed triumph, because the play's star tended to become eclipsed in the few scenes she shared with Marie Wallis." Still, another review conceded that Vivian "had an ability to give every break to other members of the cast at the same time that she extracts full value from her own lines."

Years later, Vivian described the events on the opening night of *Anna Christie:*

Jimmy O'Connor [Kathryn's husband] insisted on having only the best of everything for our production, sending to MGM Studios for fog like they have in the movies. Day after day, I kept asking if the fog had arrived. I had a strange intuition that things might go adrift if we hadn't a chance to rehearse with the mysterious cone of chemicals. Every time I asked, he grew a bit more belligerent. I didn't want to be anything but darling Viv who went to New York and made good, so I bit my tongue and shut up.

The cones were delivered just in time for opening night. At curtain time, the row of cones were lit. Within a minute, the cast and crew were choking and coughing in a cloud of acrid smoke. The draft from the back of the stage pushed the stinking stuff out over the audience. My opening line was something about how much I enjoyed it there in the fresh sea air. Nobody heard it, theater lovers were hacking their lungs out, groping toward the aisle. The next thing I was aware of was the scream of the engines' sirens and the clamor of their bells. The entire Albuquerque fire department answered the call. After about an hour, the suffering ticket holders returned to their seats. The curtain rose again with

not a wisp of mist in sight. A local actress stole the
show and was singled out in all the reviews.

Vivian did not take this less than triumphant return to
the ALT much to heart. She had more important details to
contend with, including introducing Phil to her family. He
made a striking first impression on all. Using his good
looks and savoir faire, he charmed the entire Jones clan in
spite of the fact that he had little in common with this mid-
dle-class family.

When the couple returned to New York to await Phil's
divorce, producers greeted them both with offers to appear
in Broadway shows slated to open in the fall, just weeks
apart. This good news was followed by the final divorce
decree from Phyllis. Vivian anxiously wanted to get a ring
on her finger before starting rehearsals on her new show,
Let's Face It!

Although Vivian had wanted a more elaborate ceremony, her marriage to Phil was an intimate occasion which
took place on August 12, 1941, in Marblehead, Massachusetts, where Phil was completing a run in *Mr. & Mrs.
North*. Neither of the couple's families attended the ceremony. While honeymooning, they visited Phil's family in
Maine. Mr. and Mrs. Frank Ober received Vivian with a
New England coolness. Though hospitable, they did not
exude the same warmth that the Joneses had demonstrated
to Phil.

Vivian noticed several differences between the privi-
leged Obers and the more practical Joneses. In fact, Phil's
behavior toward her seemed to change whenever they
were in his parents' company. He became judgmental and
corrected her conduct. Thereafter, whenever Vivian visited
her in-laws, she always felt ill-at-ease. "If we went to dinner at his parents, the shades were always pulled down
before the soup was served, blotting out magnificent sun-

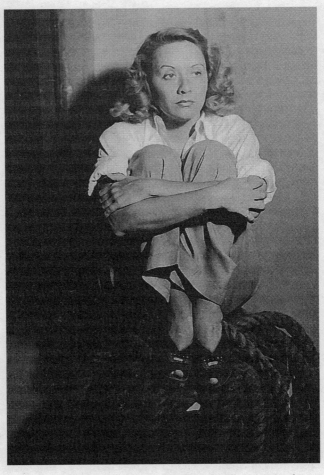

Vivian as she appeared in Anna Christie at the Albuquerque Little Theatre, 1941

sets, making a house that always seemed dark to me even gloomier," she said. "One time, I fell into the error of exclaiming with delight over a dish that had been cooked and got a kick from Phil on the ankle. One did not discuss food at mealtime in that house."

The newlyweds returned to New York and settled into a spacious apartment on West 9th Street, between 5th and 6th Avenues, just blocks away from their former love nest. For the first time in her life, Vivian had a place she could call home. She took great care in decorating it, blending Mexican style furnishings with antiques given to them by Phil's parents and using red, yellow, and blue, her favorite colors, in wallpaper and accent pieces. Vivian proudly told a columnist, "We have a whole floor with fireplaces in both our living room and bedroom. There are big double windows in the bedroom where the sun comes in." Trying to change her image as a blond home wrecker, Vivian asserted that instead of glamorous parties, they opted for quiet evenings at home. For fun, they enjoyed watching baseball games and "seldom entertained, except very informally. Most of the time we like to stay at home with a pile of magazines and newspapers to read."

Vinton Freedly signed Vivian to play the part of Nancy Collister in *Let's Face It!* The cast included Eve Arden, Edith Meiser, Mary Jane Walsh, Nanette Fabray, and a fast-rising star named Danny Kaye. The musical is about the lives of three young wives who invite three soldiers over from an army camp while their husbands are off on a hunting trip. The wives suspect that their spouses are after something livelier than just deer in the way of game.

The book, written by Herbert and Dorothy Fields and based on the 1925 play *The Cradle Snatchers,* had music and lyrics by Cole Porter. Kaye's wife, Sylvia Fine, saw the musical as a launching pad to propel her husband to super-stardom and wrote special material in the play suited to his talents. Sylvia controlled all aspects of Kaye's career and everyone knew that if they wanted Kaye, Sylvia was part of the package.

Danny Kaye had last appeared on Broadway in the musical *Lady in the Dark* starring Vivian's old nemesis, Gertrude Lawrence. In that production, the *grande dame* and the brilliant young performer had vied for control of the audience's attention by continually upstaging each other. Each time Kaye produced a new piece of business, Lawrence would simply and confidently supersede him with another. Unlike Vivian, Kaye had given Lawrence a run for her money.

Vivian told this story about how far Kaye would go to keep others from shining on stage:

We were all in one big number called "Baby Games" which had the nursery rhyme "London Bridge Is Falling Down" woven into its lyrics. Nobody could think of how to provide a slam-bang finish for the dance we did. The dance director asked everyone to chip in ideas. Danny suggested, "Let's make a bridge of our hands and the girls can go under while we sing, falling down, falling down." Eve went through and as she stooped, the boys gave her a polite goose, giving her the chance to demonstrate one of those wide-eyed Eve Arden doubletakes. Next came Edith, a tall, elegant Vassar girl, who responded to her touch with a look of cold hauteur. On my turn, I bent over, got my dues, then giggled and backed up for more. Laughter all around. We'd found a climax for the dance.

Show business being as competitive as a ping-pong game, it must be reported that the next time we rehearsed, Edith and Eve each tried to be last girl under the bridge so that she could do the backing up bit. Eve especially wanted that moment of reverse gear to be hers. They were both bigger names than me so it was time to call in the Irish when I spoke to Cole Porter. "I thought that up myself," I said, "and I'm going to be the one. It's my kind of comedy." Agreed. Justice triumphed.

After the show opened at the Imperial, that beautiful, wonderful laugh got lost. This is something else that can happen in show business when you are dealing with a product as fragile as comedy. Danny decided that at every performance he would give the biggest goose that ever laid an egg. By now, he'd become a star, and there was no holding him back. Comedy had to look spontaneous, handled with care so that it seemed to the audience that we'd never done "Baby Games" before. Danny's big fat goose obviously had been around the farm yard quite a while. I resented it bitterly when that bird turned into a turkey.

Despite her insecurities, Vivian was confident of her abilities and she did not allow those around her to distract her from giving a good performance. However annoyed she was with Kaye, she said little, knowing that the show would run for a while and give her the opportunity to stay in New York and be close to Phil.

While Vivian was performing in *Let's Face It!*, the producers of a new musical, *Oklahoma*, offered Vivian a part in the show. But Vinton Freedley refused to release Vivian from her *Let's Face It!* contract. Forever after, Vivian always wondered how her life might have changed had she taken a part in this now American classic.

Meanwhile, Phil opened in Jerome Chodorov's new play, *Junior Miss*, in the role of Harry Graves. Both *Junior Miss* and *Let's Face It!* became instant successes and settled in for long runs. Nanette Fabray, who played the role of Jean Blanchard in *Let's Face It!*, fondly recalls that evenings after the show, a group from the cast would meet

The cast of Let's Face It! *Starting at the top and working left to right, Danny Kaye, Eve Arden, Edith Meiser, Vivian, Benny Baker, and Jack Williams.*

at the Howard Johnson's on West 46th Street for hot fudge sundaes or take walks in Central Park where Phil would often join them.

Fabray had studied dance under Bill "Bojangles" Robinson and made her stage debut as Baby Nanette in vaudeville. She went on to star on stage, film and television, winning the Tony and several Emmy Awards. "Vivian was very close to Phil," Fabray said. "They were inseparable. I never saw her with anyone else. I figured that they were in a marriage of the ages. They were equal, both young, and life was wonderful. Both talked endlessly about their ranch in New Mexico."

Their steady employment had given the Obers an opportunity to buy a small ranch in Cubero, New Mexico. For fifteen hundred dollars, they had purchased four and a half acres of land with a well and a windmill, all enclosed by a three-strand fence. When she wanted an adobe house built on the property, Vivian called her brother-in-law Ralph Bowyer. "We hired guys from Cubero to do the work," he said. "They dug down and made the adobe right there in her front yard and put it up ten feet high for only $75.00."

With war raging in Europe, Phil and Vivian wanted to have a place of their own where they could feel secure, and that was in Cubero. Vivian began to think of their future and hoped to retire to the ranch some day, raise cattle, and live their lives happily ever after. The austerity of the place left friend Dorothy Konrad wondering how anyone could possibly consider living there. "She used to talk about it all the time as a place to retire," Konrad said. "Retire where!? The ranch was just a little hut you could hardly turn around in—with beds built in the walls—you could stand in the middle of the room and touch all four sides. And this was their great hacienda."

Until the time came that they could retire, Vivian enjoyed New York and a small group of friends such as Paul and Grace Hartman who had appeared with Vivian in *Red, Hot and Blue!* Paul Hartman, best known for the role of Emmett in the 1960s *Andy Griffith Show,* owned a summer home in Kings Point, Long Island. "Entertainers who could afford it," Vivian said, "gravitated to Long Island to buy a place to spend those wonderful show business weekends that began after the Saturday night performance and lasted through next Tuesday morning. That was a Broadway tradition which went back way beyond the time when Beatrice Lillie and Gertrude Lawrence were whisked off to the island to play alongside the young man who became the Duke of Windsor. Later on Saturday nights, the houses lit up when the cars rolled up the driveways with the weekend guests. There were parties and music and laughter, and you'd never guess that Gatsby was dead and the war was on." Phil and Vivian, whom many dubbed the life of the party, gladly accepted the many invitations that came their way.

To those on the outside, the Obers' relationship seemed nothing short of perfection. But Vivian felt otherwise. Years later, she wrote about her relationship with Ober:

> I had suspicions, that some of the forecasts had been right all the time, but that was about the best that could be said. Our natures and our needs were basically too far apart for this to be a perfect match. I couldn't pretend I was the greatest of wives, but I was neat as a pin as a housekeeper. But I overreacted to the prickly things that are hard to avoid but bound to irritate in so many relationships. In our case, there was no shortage of irritations, available in all sizes. At home, after I'd set the table, he would carefully rearrange the knives, forks, and spoons in accordance with his ideas of a proper place for everything. The feeling began to dawn on me that he considered he'd married beneath himself. To him I'm a peasant, behaving the way peasants do because they don't know any better. I halfway believed him. I must have or else I wouldn't have stayed. He looked a lot like Daddy, but his affect on me was the same as Mama's. He was strong on discipline, and I'd grown up on being disciplined. He liked to dominate. I was used to being dominated.

The hostility that kept bubbling up inside must be

> repressed because otherwise the world would count me
> as a failure. I had to rise above a sea of trouble and
> make myself superhuman, a goddess in disguise.

No matter how she felt inside, Vivian never let on to friends about her unhappiness with Phil. Those who witnessed them together describe a loving relationship, especially about the way Phil catered to his wife, looking after her needs and sharing her goals. While differences between the two did exist, the degree to which they affected Vivian didn't surface until years later.

Since she had been married twice before, Vivian considered it crucial to make this one work. Vivian clearly felt she bore much of the responsibility of keeping the marriage together because of the scandal of their affair and the fact that Phil lost custody of his daughter. But in the same way that she suppressed issues concerning her parents, Vivian did not speak of her discontent with Phil to anyone.

Danny Kaye didn't stay to complete the run of *Let's Face It!* Instead, he left New York to star in such classic films as *Up in Arms, The Secret Life of Walter Mitty,* and *Hans Christian Andersen.* He later devoted his energies to UNICEF, the United Nations Children's Emergency Fund, as its Ambassador-at-large.

When Kaye left for Hollywood, José Ferrer replaced him in the role of Jerry Walker. Since the media had touted *Let's Face It!* as Kaye's show, sales fell when he left. The musical closed on March 20, 1943, after 547 performances. Not long after that, Phil's show also closed.

Working for nearly two years in successful Broadway shows gave the Obers a semblance of normalcy in their lives. But with the country at war and the fear of air raids, Phil and Vivian worried about living in a major U.S. city. Whenever an air drill exercise sounded in New York, Vivian hid under a bed, terrified. Since it always took her a long time to recover from these drills, no one expected her to accept an offer to perform in wartorn Europe for $200 a week.

By the mid-forties, the energies of the United Services Organization (USO) had lifted the morale of thousands of service personnel at home and abroad through its financial support of Camp Shows, Inc., a civilian organization which brought entertainment to the GIs. Many Hollywood and Broadway entertainers joined in this effort and offered their services, telling jokes, singing, and dancing as they traveled through the various war zones. Ruth Gordon's *Over Twenty-one* was the first theatrical production to tour the war zones of North Africa and Italy. She had written the play while her husband, Lt. Garson Kanin, completed his tour of duty in Washington, D.C. The comedy is a simple story of a man trying to get through officer's training school with his wife helping him in his darker moments, and it closely resembled the dilemma Gordon faced as the wife of an officer.

Katherine Cornell toured in the first full-length play, *The Barretts of Wimpole Street*, staged in Europe during the war. Complete with period costumes and scenery, the show ran successfully in various surviving theatrical houses.

In March, 1944, while *Over Twenty-one* was enjoying a successful run on Broadway, the head of the New York USO gathered a company of actors together to take the play to Europe. Erin O'Brien-Moore headed the group, which included Vivian, Phil, Adele Longmire Franz, Harry Bellaver, and Judson Laird. In April, the company took a train from New York for Newport News, Virginia, where they boarded a carrier to take them to Algeria. "Vivian, Erin, and I were placed in the WAC's section and the men with the male troops," Adele Longmire Franz recalls.

Everyone in the cast suffered seasickness during the

eleven-day trip from the States to Africa. The voyage seemed to especially drain Adele, who could not keep anything in her stomach the entire trip. "Vivian was particularly solicitous of me, as if I were her little sister. Because I couldn't get in for meals, she'd bring me soda crackers."

Once they reached the city of Oran in Algeria, the actors went through briefings and automatically received officer's status, which meant that they would be treated better in case they were captured. During the voyage, Vivian lost eleven pounds and when she reached shore, she caught a violent case of dysentery. Despite her illness, she and the other players traveled on a truck from city to city, performing *Over Twenty-one* sometimes twice a day in any available open area. They would pin up a backdrop painted to resemble the inside of an apartment and without any additional scenery, costumes, or props, would perform the entire play.

"People believed what was given to them," Longmire Franz said. "There was no alternative. If the generators providing power for the lights went on the blink, the headlights of Jeeps were used so that the performance could go on." Longmire Franz is positive that many directors used this impromptu lighting scene in their movies. "I suspect that it must have happened more than one time, in more than one company."

After a month in North Africa, the company flew to Naples where the Seventh Army had just gained control of the region. Over the next five months, the theatrical troupe played in Rome, Florence, Siena, Bari, and Foggia where Adele Longmire met Arthur Franz, her future husband. "We were all deeply and emotionally affected by our troops and their situation," she said. "The tour was a life-changing experience. It was horrifying to see the deplorable conditions under which people lived."

To Vivian, the company's own circumstances seemed

The cast of Over Twenty-one in Europe on the USO Tour. Seated from left to right, Vivian, Erin O'Brien-Moore, Phil Ober, Harry Bellaver and standing, Judson Laird, Adele Longmire Franz, and Bob Allen. This is one of the rare photos saved from Vivian's bonfire of 1960.

Vivian and Harry Bellaver visit wounded servicemen during the USO Tour of Over Twenty-one.

trivial and sometimes humorous compared to the condition of the Italians. "In Naples, we were given one helmet of water per day and that had to be for everything. 'How do you bathe with one helmet of water?' we asked. We were told, 'From the head down.' "

At one point in Naples the cast of *Over Twenty-one* crossed paths with the cast of the musical *This Is the Army.* Marc Daniels, stage manager of the musical, had met and worked with Vivian in New York. Along with Phil and Adele, they gathered in a makeshift outdoor restaurant where they ate oven-baked pizzas and shared the details of their travels. That night they laughed, enjoyed good food, and talked about what each would do when they returned home.

While in Florence, Adele and Vivian took a side trip by bus and went to see a variety show put on by GIs. "We were terribly impressed by one strapping, hollow-cheeked young man who did an Al Jolson act, singing 'Climb upon My Knee, Sonny Boy' to a much smaller soldier. The singer was sexy-looking, and we spent some time telling him that when he got out of the army he certainly ought to go see Maynard Morris, a big talent agent. We'd be happy to write him and help him in any way we could. Years later, I often sat across a bridge table from that handsome ex-GI. I never did mention 'Sonny Boy,' and neither did Burt Lancaster."

As the tour went on, Vivian began to visibly suffer. "I had become an old soldier—hadn't had a bath in six weeks. I'd often flown in the belly of C-57s and I had tried and failed to figure out a way to strap on a parachute while wearing a skirt. I was terrified on the rides up and over the Italian mountains with drivers so young you'd guess they hadn't finished grade school. I couldn't force myself to accept those blacked-out drives, which brought me closer to a personal blackout. I'd been in and out of every air-raid shelter in our side of Italy, and I'd invariably slept in all my clothes with my helmet at my side so I could get there first when the sirens screamed. I'd gone into hospitals to exchange a smile and a few words with hundreds of servicemen who'd always carry a souvenir in the scars on their bodies or in their minds. I couldn't get accustomed to it or hardened by the sights and smells of war. I felt anger beyond belief at the useless waste, to the point where it seemed certain my mind would explode."

Longmire Franz says that "Vivian was definitely beginning to show some signs of being disturbed. I don't know if that was because of the pressure we were under—not that we were ever exposed to any danger. You could hear bombs falling in the distance but nothing ever came near the hotel. Still, the whole experience was very unsettling. You never knew where the Germans had planted mines, but compared to the danger where the men were fighting, our danger was a mere bagatelle."

After six months, everyone had had enough and wanted to get back home. Phil had begun to be concerned about Vivian's behavior and started guarding her very closely. During the tour, Erin O'Brien-Moore shared Adele's concern over their mutual friend's behavior. Longmire Franz says, "We could tell Vivian was panting to get out. When two seats became available on a plane heading back to the States, Vivian jumped at the chance to leave. Before she left, she said to me that I must never see Arthur ever in civilian life if we ever met again. I can remember exactly how she said it. Terror was on her face. 'He will kill you, he will kill you!' And I said, 'Vivian, what are you talking about?' I thought she meant that he might break my heart. 'No!' Vivian continued. 'No! He will physically kill you!' "

Arriving home emotionally drained and physically exhausted, Vivian's inexplicable physical pains returned, this time in her wrists, arms, and ankles. During a vacation on their ranch, now named the Lazy B-O, her symptoms worsened. When she returned to New York, her doctors theorized that since they could not locate the origin of her pains, they must be psychosomatic. So Vivian gave up trying to find the source of her problems and pressed ahead, never realizing that these symptoms were only a preview of what lay ahead.

Chapter Six

The Breakdown

Vivian faced a major disappointment and a huge success on her return to New York. Producers Theresa Helburn and Lawrence Langner had chosen *Carousel* as their next Broadway offering. Richard Rodgers and Oscar Hammerstein II had adapted the musical from the book *Liliom* by Ferenc Molnar. Rouben Mamoulian auditioned Vivian and assigned her the role of Mrs. Mullin. But during the first week of rehearsals, Theresa Helburn inexplicably fired Vivian.

"When Miss Helburn returned from the coast, I was promptly called into the office by Mr. Mamoulian," Vivian said. "Great apologies and then: 'I'm sorry, Vivian, we have to let you go. Miss Helburn doesn't want you in the play.'"

The only other time Vivian received a pink slip was when a director didn't like the sound of her voice. This time, no one offered an explanation. But considering who was involved in the production, the reason for her dismissal seems obvious, though Vivian may not have wanted to contemplate it. Agnes de Mille, who Helburn held in high esteem, was the choreographer for *Carousel*. She believed that Vivian had been a participant in the backstage shenanigans during *Hooray for What!* De Mille may have told Helburn about the problem-plagued play and carefully arranged Vivian's firing from *Carousel* in retaliation for de Mille's firing years earlier. Vivian, who had always gone to great lengths to ingratiate herself with those in power, may not have taken into account those hurt along the way. Understandably, the success of *Carousel* left Vivian bitterly resentful about having lost the role of Mrs. Mullin.

However, *Voice of the Turtle*, by John Van Druten, was playing to packed houses on Broadway and producer Alfred de Liagre had assembled a touring company which included K.T. Stevens and Hugh Marlowe. Vivian joined the company in Chicago, replacing Bette Lawford in the role of the opportunistic, feisty but all-around good gal, Olive Lashbrook. This play was very important in Vivian's career and would have a great impact on her personal life. Its benign plot is predictable—two out-of-work actresses pining for the same man, a soldier on leave. But when it opened on Broadway, critics were unanimously pleased.

Since two other actresses had already played Olive, Vivian dove into the role, searching for untapped places to make the part her own. Among other quirks, she chose to exaggerate the enunciation of certain words and to wear a huge hat made of layers and layers of pink netting complete with two roses, one on the hat and one on her shoulder.

Claudia Cassidy of the *Chicago Tribune* said that producer de Liagre "could relax where Vivian Vance was concerned. Miss Vance is a tall comedienne with the upswept outburst of curls and a rangy bounce that takes laughter in its stride. The audience took to her on sight and whooped with such glee at the sight of her outrageous pink mousseline headpiece that the management wrote off its cost with a sigh of relief. Give her a performance or two to dovetail her timing to audience reaction and there's an expert Olive for you. I suspect Mr. de Liagre's notes held firm injunctions to K.T. Stevens and Hugh Marlowe to do a little relaxing on their own account and slip back into the ease of unforced performance."

In Chicago, Vivian's name regularly appeared in the society columns, making her the toast of the town. Marshall Field & Company advertised that copies of the dresses that Vivian and her co-star K.T. Stevens wore in the play could be purchased at their store. Theatergoers mimicked Vivian's unique delivery of the line "Hello . . . Is that you?" making it the gag of the day.

While Phil appeared as Judge Wilkins in the San Francisco production of Norman Krasna's *Dear Ruth*, Vivian settled into her successful run. She moved into the Canterbury Court Apartments on North State Parkway, a long way from the Michigan Avenue "two-room apartment looking out on nothing" which she had shared with friend Ann Denove Farleigh while in *Kiss the Boys Good-bye*.

Shortly after the opening of *Voice of the Turtle*, Vivian found herself constantly tired and sleeping twelve hours a day. Dorothy, who now lived in Chicago, moved in with Vivian. She describes how Vivian would just lie around not doing anything. Doctors assured her that rest and vitamins were the cure and they prescribed vitamin B to help with the lack of energy. It didn't.

Unable to understand the source of Vivian's condition, Dorothy tried consoling her sister on long walks in Lincoln Park. She'd known how deep Vivian's depressions had been through the years but had always attributed these mood swings to what she considered to be her sister's histrionic personality. "When Vivian did anything happy it was wonderful, but when it was sad, it was sad!"

Those around Vivian noticed an obvious change in her behavior. Marjorie Lord remembered that "Vivian had always been fussy about everything being neat and lovely in her dressing room." Now, however, everything degenerated into chaos. Vivian had always greeted her pets with affection but now she began to hug and fuss over her dogs with obnoxious and nonsensical baby talk. She later agreed that this behavior "had begun to shock rather than amuse onlookers."

One night on stage, while reaching for a prop, she found herself unable to move. "The brain ordered but the arm declined. It was one of the most sickening moments I have ever gone through," she said. Her voice failed her once again as it had in *Hooray for What!* Memories of her mother losing her voice in front of the church congregation terrorized her. And Mae's words, "If you don't mend your ways, Vivian, you will lose your voice and have a nervous breakdown just as I did," haunted her.

She continued working through her exhaustion. Now, instead of sleeping twelve hours a day, Vivian found it impossible to rest because of paranoia. She had conflicting fears of leaving her room and of staying in it. In the early hours of the day she would sometimes slip a note in her pocket, "with name and address so someone would know who I was if I went crazy," and wander aimlessly around the streets of Chicago.

One morning, her symptoms overpowered her completely. Unable to maintain her equilibrium, she could not go on with the show. Hugh Marlowe called Alfred de Liagre and told him about Vivian. Patricia Neal, who had been hired to understudy Vivian's role, telephoned K.T. Stevens and was told that "Vivian was leaving the show and that I was playing that night, New Year's Eve."

But Vivian did not leave. Somehow, she gathered enough strength to continue performing and adamantly refused to contact Phil. "I could not bring myself to be a burden to him or to anyone else," she said. "In some people that is a noble reflex. In me it was just another neurotic symptom."

Then she had a second acute attack. "I was lying in bed in my hotel room, my hands shaking helplessly, in violent nausea, weeping hysterically from causes I did not know, unable for a long while to move," she said. "I was positive I was losing my mind."

The producer took it upon himself to call Phil. When he arrived, Phil convinced his wife to return to San Francisco with him. When the *Voice of the Turtle* company arrived in San Francisco, Vivian returned to play Olive at de Liagre's request. Once again, she received favorable notices. "Miss Vance, completing the cast as the girl who stands up to the sergeant, is a born comedienne who plays with a deftness of touch that is wonderful to behold."

Meanwhile, no one in Vivian's family, with the exception of Dorothy, who seems to have forgotten details of this period, knew about Vivian's afflictions. "My family knew I'd quit the play in Chicago, but no more than that," Vivian said. "I was scared to write the truth. At last, I got up the nerve to send Mama a letter, telling her that I'd had a nervous breakdown . . . the reply arrived air mail, special delivery at the hotel. 'No matter what you've done,' she wrote, 'come home and I'll forgive you.'

"As I read her words, I was listening to her voice, the same old voice that sounded through my childhood. The suspicions were as plain as if she'd spelled them out. The only reason I'd cracked up was that I'd done something that would reflect on her sanctity, maybe had an illegitimate child that I was hiding someplace so she wouldn't hear about it. No performance of Olive Lashbrook by me that night. Beautiful, talented Pat Neal had to step in again."

Vivian tried to see the show through to the end of its run but after fifteen weeks, she had a crippling relapse. The Obers returned to New York and their Ninth Street apartment. Though it cannot be confirmed, there are reports which indicate that Vivian entered a private sanitarium for emotional stress. Later she did admit that during this difficult period she had often contemplated suicide as a solution to her problems. Vivian worked little and spent most of her time "waiting and thinking about myself and the way I was and nothing else." While before she wouldn't discuss problems with her friends, Vivian now shared them with anyone who would lend an ear. "Shirley Booth, who'd had more than a spot of upset herself, would sit and try to cheer me over an endless succession of lunches at Sardi's," Vivian said, "driving in again and again with the affirmation that this too would pass."

Before she had her complete breakdown, Vivian had investigated every kind of doctor and analyst suggested by friends. In psychology books and magazine articles, she tried to identify the cause of her symptoms. While on the road, she consulted psychiatrists but she never remained in a city long enough for it to do any good.

During the run of *Voice of the Turtle*, Vivian attended a party in Philadelphia where she met a psychoanalyst. After a long conversation, the doctor suggested that Vivian give her a call when her tour ended. Once back in New York, Vivian contacted the young woman and began seeing her several times a week. The analyst encouraged her to speak openly about her childhood recollections by using free association. The memories which gushed forth were about her parents, especially her mother. Years later, Vivian chronicled the events that had impaired her life. It's no surprise that Mae's constant censure of Vivian emerged as the cause of her daughter's guilt and shame.

Sadly, Vivian realized how truly estranged her relationship with her mother had become through a memory of a brief moment of togetherness. "I could remember but once finding happiness in her company. It was winter and there had been heavy snow. It was night, we went walking together wrapped up against the cold. She must have been in one of the upswing moods that came in between the series of nervous breakdowns she suffered. She was laughing and I laughed with her as we scooped snowballs to toss against the trees and ran side by side. The thought went round and round in my head, 'My mother and I are having a good time. We are really happy in this very minute.' The experience was never repeated."

In an article printed years after her initial therapy, Vivian tried to explain the origin of her problems. "The beginnings of most psychiatric difficulties go back to childhood, and mine were no different. But few case histories can be, or should be, made fully public because their complexities must touch on other persons who are essentially innocent of wrongdoing. Hence I can only say here that I was beset by a sense of wrongdoing, actually of sin.

"On the one side I had a compulsive, an irresistible urge to act. I could no more have fought it than I could have willed myself not to breathe. On the other, there was the deepest, unshakable conviction on the part of my mother and father, splendid folk, but tempered in inflexible religious and moral dogma, that the stage was a sinful business."

After this article was printed, Vivian remarked, "The intention [to explain her problems] was there, but the prose was rose tinted." Still, her words plainly communicate that, contrary to what some family members now say, her parents played a major role in the shaping of her psychological difficulties.

It's curious—and inexplicable—that Vivian included her father as someone "tempered in inflexible religious and moral dogma." In later material written by Vivian, she describes her father this way. "My wild handsome father had more than an eye for other women. Maybe that was inevitable when Mama turned him off the way she did. Daddy ran around. The two of us kept the secret. When he went to visit his girlfriend, I used to ride with him and wait in the car while he went into her house. He was always wearing a big special smile on those occasions. I didn't blame him. I'd be a mistress when I grew up because seeing Daddy so happy made me certain this was the kind of woman that men liked. Much more fascinating than a wife or mother."

Vivian's therapist diagnosed her as having anxiety neurosis, a disorder believed to develop in individuals who suffer from early childhood trauma, a lack of nurturing, and a distorted view of their sexual role in society. Vivian was a woman with a hearty sexual appetite. She had had affairs with several men but each affair left her with an unshakable fear. Growing up in the Jones household, no one had spoken to her about sex except in veiled expressions. And she'd been warned as a young girl that if she ever touched a boy, she would get pregnant and this unwanted pregnancy would result in her father shooting the boy and her mother's suicide. "Hellfire and damnation were served to us three times a day," Vivian explained in her later years. "Everybody was going to be punished, especially me."

The anxieties Vivian experienced in the mid-1940s had haunted her throughout most of her life in the form of blackouts, swelling of the tongue, pains in the joints, loss of voice, constant fatigue, hearing impairment, and paralysis. Analysis enabled Vivian to begin to understand the causes behind the physical maladies but it did not provide her the means to settle the obvious differences she had with her parents. It is evident from interviews and her writing that she placed the bulk of the blame on Mae. She found it easier to accept her father's behavior but was not inclined to forgive her mother's actions.

After months of therapy and several thousand dollars, Vivian pronounced herself cured but later confessed it was a mistake to stop the analysis so soon. "Out of the memories of childhood, I began to make sense of the mysteries of my predicament," she wrote. "Fancies, fears, and motives I'd never suspected swam up into sight. I gained an insight into the emotions underlying them and the struggle made to repress them. Okay, I had reason to hate my mother and worship my father. I was ambivalent about being an actress because she had told me it was a sin to show my legs. I was terrified of dying because I believed I'd drop straight to hell. Knowing this much convinced me that I was cured. Vivian Roberta Jones was out of psychiatry and on her way to health. It was such a glorious feeling that I took off like a bird. No more tremors. No more vitamin shots. No more blackouts. What I didn't realize was that the treatment had only just started. Waiting down the road was a different kind of conflict—between my yearning to get well and the desire to avoid what that involved."

Since leaving *Voice of the Turtle,* Vivian had kept a low profile. Though her need to act still existed, her obsession with stardom had waned. This was partly because of her analysis and partly because of the realization that at age 38, those goals did not hold the same urgency for her as they once had. Ironically, Mae had correctly predicted one outcome of her daughter's mental collapse—the breakdown caused Vivian's singing voice to falter. Because of this, she shied away from musicals and instead focused her attention on working in straight plays.

In early 1947 she began rehearsals for the part of Bee Clark in *It Takes Two*, a new comedy directed by the legendary George Abbott. Martha Scott (whom Vivian had seen years earlier in *Our Town*) and Hugh Marlowe starred. The show also introduced John Forsythe, of television's *Dynasty* fame, to the stage. The show opened on February 3, 1947, but soon flopped. Vivian, however, received favorable mentions. "Vivian Vance and Anthony Ross are in there fighting. Despite George Abbott's energetic directing efforts, I'm afraid *It Takes Two* is a troublesome evening on both sides of the footlights."

The show did little for Vivian's career except to reaffirm her talent as a dependable actress who could deliver comedy despite bad material. Internally for Vivian, though, certain things had changed. She had always loved the rehearsal process but now found it difficult. She lost control only once on stage but the possibility of an anxiety attack made her hesitant about stepping out in front of an audience.

Luckily, George Abbott was sensitive to Vivian's plight and helped guide her efforts while she tenaciously pressed ahead, determined to give a good performance. Yet in spite of all Abbott's help, she constantly questioned her timing and seemed ill at ease. Later, she remembered:

> George Abbott helped tremendously during one comeback I attempted, by handling me with a sort of brisk non-sympathy, that is, with neither more nor less sympathy than he would have shown a stable person. In the time I spent taking direction from him, he taught me the way of playing comedy that I've employed ever since. He prepared a specially marked script. Lines

marked in green had to guarantee a chuckle from the audience, lines in blue called for hearty laughter, and lines in red had to bring the house down. I had a lot of laughs in my lines, and I was eager to bust britches. "Vivian," he kept telling me, "you're being funny in a funny part." I had no need to overplay it. He'd make me rehearse a scene so many times I'd go home at night to weep and throw up in the bathroom. That went on until the moment came when I knew just what he was saying: "If the lines are funny all you have to do is speak them. Keep it crisp, and stop right there."

In the summer of 1947, the North Shore Players in Marblehead, Massachusetts, hired Marc Daniels to direct *Counselor-at-Law*. It starred Paul Muni, Jack Hartley, Adele Longmire Franz, Pat Harrington and featured a young Sydney Lumet who later went on to direct scores of classic films including *Twelve Angry Men, A View from the Bridge, Long Day's Journey into Night, Serpico,* and *Network*. Daniels asked Vivian to play the role of Bessie Green. Vivian accepted with reservations. "I'd heard so many tales about what a horror Paul Muni was to work with in Hollywood that I fancied we might just as well be starting in on *Frankenstein*."

Muni began his career in the Yiddish theater stock company in New York in 1908 before going on to perform on Broadway in several dramas. His film career took him to Hollywood in 1929 where his artistic integrity gave him a reputation for being a difficult star. His films include *Scarface, I Am a Fugitive from a Chain Gang,* and *The Story of Louis Pasteur* for which he won the Academy Award for best performance by an actor.

In the month-long engagement in Marblehead, Vivian developed a fascination for the dedicated and conservative star as well as a romantic crush. Vivian later told her sister,

Lou Ann, that Muni, a devoted husband who always traveled with his wife, Bella, flatly refused her advances. It appears that Vivian's infatuation with Muni stemmed more from his brilliant acting techniques rather than something physical. "At every performance after we opened," Vivian said, "he'd spot me standing in the wings when I wasn't on stage, studying him. 'What do you do there, making all those motions with your hands and arms?' he asked me after one show. I fumbled to tell him. 'I've always had such trouble with my hands. They're like two drunken sea cows when I try to make a gesture. I watch and practice what you do.' That pleased him."

Once she got over her initial attraction for Muni, Vivian began a close relationship with him and his wife. At the end of the run, the actors all contributed money for a plaque in honor of director Marc Daniels who would soon leave the stage for television.

Vivian made another attempt to conquer Broadway in *The Cradle Will Rock* by Marc Blitzstein. It opened on December 26, 1947, at the Mansfield Theatre. Brooks Atkinson wrote that this show was "the most vivid proletarian drama ever written in this country. At the moment it is impossible to recall another musical drama so candid, so original and so fresh in stage conception."

In *The Cradle Will Rock*, Vivian played a part originated by Shirley Booth, that of Mrs. Mister, the rich wife of an industrialist. Alfred Drake played Larry Forman, Will Geer played Mr. Mister and Leonard Bernstein, who was the show's musical director, assigned himself the small role of a clerk. Howard Da Silva staged the show and the musical drama opened on the night of the worst snowstorm of the century, mostly to critical praise. The praise, however, did not help ticket sales. *The Cradle Will Rock* closed after five weeks.

Disappointed when the critically acclaimed show closed

so soon, Vivian began to reflect on the years she'd spent struggling. With the magic of show business beginning to wear off, Vivian questioned her devotion to the industry. During 1948 and 1949, while Phil appeared in a few successful shows including revivals of *Craig's Wife* and *Light Up the Sky!*, Vivian spent a great deal of time traveling between New York, New Mexico, Los Angeles, and Chicago where Dorothy had just given birth to her second daughter, Martha. At that time, Dot's marriage showed signs of strain so Vivian stayed to lend her sister a shoulder to lean on. Later, after her divorce from Armand Klein, Dot moved back to Albuquerque, then eventually settled in Carlsbad. Vivian followed to help her sister settle in a new life.

Vivian's sister Lou Ann remembers that this period was also not a happy one for the Obers. She recalled a disturbing event on a visit to the Ober homestead in Kennebunkport, Maine. "Phil's father had recently died and Phil was chopping up a tree to use up anger and remorse," Lou Ann said. "One night at the dinner table, I was spouting some optimistic plan of something about my brother when Phil said something that really put it all down. Vivian was furious with him. She really told him off. He quickly left the room. I knew at the time that Viv was having problems, but I didn't know how serious they were. She covered up those things."

During her travels, Vivian spoke to several therapists because it hadn't taken her long to realize that the seven months she'd spent in analysis had not cured her of a lifetime of mental anguish. In New York, she spent a great deal of time with friend Jane Sebastian and her family. Sebastian wrote several radio and television plays and wanted to write a show specifically for Vivian. She later asked Vivian to be the godmother of her sons, John and Marc. When John grew up, he became a songwriter, starting the Lovin' Spoonful band, and wrote such hits as "If You Believe in Magic." Marc followed suit with the song "Summer in the City."

While in New York, friend, actor, and director Mel Ferrer called the Obers with the news that he had been signed to direct a movie, *The Blind Spot*, for RKO Studios. He offered them parts if they'd come out to Hollywood. Since they were both in a lull in their theatrical careers, Vivian and Phil wondered whether it wouldn't be wise to try a new road. They left Kennebunkport where they had been visiting Phil's parents, and headed west.

In Hollywood, the couple moved into one of the bungalows at the Garden of Allah on Sunset Boulevard and Crescent Heights, a favorite spot for yet-to-be-discovered contract players, screenwriters, and directors. They quickly went to work on the now retitled movie, *The Secret Fury*. The characters played by Claudette Colbert, Robert Ryan, and Phil directly affected the plot of the movie. Vivian plays Leah, a streetwise chambermaid whose blackmail attempts get her killed early in the film. Though it was a small role, she still received a small mention in one of the reviews. "Dave Barbour and Vivian Vance are credited feature players who are expert in small footage."

Right after *The Secret Fury*, Vivian landed a role in the tear-jerker *The Blue Veil* starring Charles Laughton and Jane Wyman, who was fresh from her Oscar-winning performance in *Johnny Belinda*. The supporting cast included Joan Blondell, Agnes Moorehead, and Natalie Wood. The combined talents of the newly formed producing team of Norman Krasna and Jerry Wald created an atmosphere of surefire success for the film.

Vivian had recently gained weight and her more rotund, matronly look was perfect for the role of Alicia, Laughton's wife. Her performance once again elicited the

Vivian in one of her rare appearances in film with Charles Laughton and Jane Wyman in the 1951 production of The Blue Veil

attention of reviewers. "Glimpsed briefly but registering importantly are Everett Sloane and Vivian Vance as Laughton's selfish wife," wrote one critic, while another opined, "Lost in all the moisture is the pert but significant suggestion of Vivian Vance, as a nimble-minded newly-wed, that Miss Wyman stir herself and make a home of her own." About the movie itself, however, critics held a different opinion. "The picture is well-calculated to please the kind of audiences who confuse a good cry with a good movie."

During this stay in Hollywood, Vivian's agent told her "you will never be a star. You don't have the stuff in you. You're just not mean enough." Given all the survival skills she learned during her years as an actress on the stage and the different methods by which she found work, it is unlikely that Vivian didn't have what it takes to survive in Hollywood. But Vivian tended to agree with her agent. She had little interest in filmmaking and because of recent events in her life, Vivian's focus had shifted from her career to personal concerns. But above all else, Vivian feared the possibility of a second breakdown.

She escaped from Hollywood back to Cubero and planned to tour with Phil in the play they had previously appeared in in Europe, *Over Twenty-one*. Then another call came from Mel Ferrer. He wanted her to reprise the role of Olive Lashbrook in *Voice of the Turtle* at the La Jolla Playhouse in California. At first Vivian flatly refused. She didn't want to have anything to do with that part or that play. It was frightening to think of the possibilities of what might occur if she reexperienced this particular role. But Ferrer insisted and Phil counseled her to accept.

When Vivian opened in *Voice of the Turtle* with Mel Ferrer and Diana Lynn, she once again received accolades from both the critics and the audience. One reviewer wrote of a performance that took place on July 26th, Vivian's forty-second birthday, "Miss Vance is excellent as the thick-skinned but essentially tenderhearted actress who summons brave laughter to cover the disappointments of her love life."

That weekend, producers Jess Oppenheimer, Desi Arnaz, and Marc Daniels drove from Los Angeles to see Vivian on Daniels's insistence that she'd be perfect for the role in a television show based on the radio program, *My Favorite Husband*. After that night's performance, Marc Daniels entered her dressing room and after he introduced her to his guests, Desi Arnaz offered her the part of Ethel Mertz.

Forty-year-old Lucille Ball had come up with the idea of working with her husband, Desi Arnaz, as a way to keep an

eye on him. Desi had a reputation much like Vivian's
father. For years the two had struggled to stay together and
out of divorce court. Since Lucille Ball's career required
her to remain in Hollywood while Desi Arnaz made his
living traveling with his band, he had ample opportunities
to stray, and the goal of a steady marriage had eluded the
couple. They thought that doing a television show together
would help their personal lives and their faltering careers.

From its inception, however, the show presented the
Arnazes with several obstacles: CBS's hesitancy to cast
Desi Arnaz, finding sponsors, locating a studio equipped to
film the show, and the logistical problems of shooting a
television series in Los Angeles instead of New York. A
move to the east coast would have resolved many of these
issues but the Arnazes adamantly refused to budge.

On top of that, the task of finding an actress to play the
role of Ethel Mertz had taken longer than expected. Bea
Benadaret, Lucille Ball's first choice to play her next-door
neighbor, could not accept the offer because of a previous
commitment to another show. Contrary to popular belief,
Lucille Ball did not see Vivian's performance at the La
Jolla theater that evening because she was in Chatsworth
nursing her newborn child, Lucie, born only eleven days
before. Desi Arnaz made the choice to cast Vivian without
consulting his wife.

Vivian had made quite an impression on Desi in the part
of Olive, so much so that Daniels went backstage during
the intermission to tell Vivian he was certain that Arnaz
and Oppenheimer would offer her the part of Ethel Mertz.
When she showed no interest, Daniels blasted her. "You
goddamned idiot, take the job! It's going to be a great
series. I've seen six or seven scripts already and the pilot.
It's going to be terrific!" But Vivian would not budge.

Desi Arnaz later described the first time he saw Vivian
perform. "She was such a wonderful actress, so honest.

Every line, every move she made was just perfect. I couldn't wait to go backstage and talk to her."

Though he made the decision to hire Vivian on the spot, he worried about how Vivian and Lucy would get along. "Oh, my God, what have I done? Suppose Lucy doesn't like her? What the hell do I do then? I got home early Sunday morning and told Lucy we had found the perfect actress for Ethel. 'Who?' she asked. 'Vivian Vance,' I answered. 'Who the hell is she?' 'No one you would know. I saw her at the La Jolla Playhouse and she's such a good actress, that I'm sure she will be wonderful with you.'" Perhaps Lucille Ball's less-than-gracious behavior at their first meeting was prompted by Desi's solo decision to hire Vivian.

Still, Marc Daniels's offer did not entice Vivian in the least. She had just completed two movies and had plans to tour New Mexico in *Over Twenty-one* with her husband. What's more, the idea of working in the precarious new medium of television didn't excite her. Daniels knew every effort was being made to produce a high-quality show so he cajoled Vivian into reading the script for Arnaz and Oppenheimer. Phil was appearing in *Come Back Little Sheba* with Una Merkel at the La Jolla Playhouse so Vivian went to Los Angeles to audition before returning to New Mexico.

Her reading convinced Oppenheimer and Arnaz that they had found their Ethel and they offered her the part. Hesitantly, Vivian told them she would think about it:

"Nobody in their senses would choose to go into television. In 1951, it was a silly new third entity that attracted little attention," she said later. "I'd tried my hand at television once before in New York, and I didn't like the taste of it. The memory was sharp and clear. The director of the *Playhouse Ninety* show for

Westinghouse in which I appeared with Zasu Pitts had impressed me as a hard-bitten character. Like all the plays in that series, this would be done live, and rehearsals continued almost up to air time. The voice of the director, out of sight in the control booth, began to get to us as it rasped out over the loud speakers. Zasu, who was a trembling soul, broke down in tears an hour before we went on. I could usually stick up for other people when that was impossible on my own account. I shouted for everyone on the set to hear, "I can't see you, but if you don't stop being rude to Miss Pitts, I'm going out on Route 66 and open a chili parlor."

Television? Not for me, thank you. It had been hard enough to come out of hiding and play *Voice of the Turtle*. Take on a full-time job in a medium that didn't amount to anything? The strain involved wasn't worth it. Besides, what could it lead to? No series anything like this *I Love Lucy* had been successful so far.

In New Mexico, the Obers performed in *Over Twenty-one* in Albuquerque and Santa Fe where they celebrated their tenth wedding anniversary. While in Albuquerque, phone calls poured in from Daniels regarding Arnaz's offer. Finally, Vivian reluctantly accepted and signed a contract which would pay her $450.00 a week for thirteen weeks. Lucille Ball had included the stipulation that Vivian could be written out of a script at any time.

So it was that Vivian headed to Hollywood against her better judgment to give the "silly new third entity" a try.

Chapter Seven

"Ethel, I've Got an Idea!"

❖

I n late August 1951, Vivian reluctantly left behind the security of her small ranch in Cubero. Uncertain about whether her new job would continue past its original thirteen-week contract, she rented a furnished apartment at the Shoreham on Sunset Boulevard instead of looking for more permanent quarters. On Monday, September 3, 1951, she waited anxiously for director Marc Daniels and his wife, Emily, to arrive and accompany her to the studio for the first reading of an *I Love Lucy* script.

There was chaos on stage 2 of the General Service Studios located on Romaine Street in Hollywood. The studio, unequipped for the technical problems of television, bustled with the activities of technicians in the midst of renovations. In spite of all the confusion, rehearsal was still scheduled to take place in Desi Arnaz's office.

Maury Thompson, the script clerk, along with others on the production staff, waited for the actors to arrive.

Thompson never forgot that day nor the impact of those first meetings. William Frawley, who would play the role of the penny-pinching landlord Fred Mertz, arrived first. Shortly thereafter, Lucille Ball and Desi Arnaz made their entrance. All eyes were fixed on Ball. "It was the first time I'd ever met her," Maury remembers, "and I thought— 'My God! What are they going to do with her?' She was just . . . ugh! She was wearing a big dark coat, flat shoes, she was in a babushka and great big glasses. [Lucy] comes scuffling in and I thought, 'Oh come on, this is a gag' because I expected Tallulah Bankhead, only younger."

Producer Jess Oppenheimer had advised Maury Thompson on the dos and don'ts of behavior around Lucy. He was told "not to cause a disturbance, and fit into the family." After introductions, Ball dispensed an "Oh, hi" in Thompson's general direction and brusquely asked, "About ready to go to work?" Before the script clerk could respond, Desi jumped in and assured his wife that they would as soon as the others arrived.

Then Vivian and Emily and Marc Daniels walked into the studio. Lucy continued working on her script and paid little attention to Desi as he made another round of introductions.

"Honey, I want you to meet Viv, Vivian Vance," Desi said.

Lucy glanced up and then returned to her script saying, "Oh, hi, what part are you here for?"

Vivian, her hair still pink from the *Voice* production, did not answer. Instead, Desi chimed in, "For Ethel Mertz, honey."

"Ethel Mertz! You don't look like a landlady," Lucy said.

"What did you have in mind, Miss Ball?" Vivian asked.

"I want a dumpy, fat woman in a chenille bathrobe and furry slippers with curlers in her hair," Lucy shot back.

Lucille Ball, Vivian, William Frawley, Desi Arnaz, and with her back to the camera, Joan Banks, in the I Love Lucy *episode entitled "Fan Magazine Interview"*

Ball had envisioned the character of Ethel Mertz as a one-dimensional prop put there to feed her lines. Thompson is convinced that "Lucy's idea was for Ethel and Fred to stick their heads in the door every script for a couple of lines and they'd be gone, then she'd carry the show. It shocked her when she saw how much was in the script for Ethel Mertz."

Lucy tapped her pencil on the table as she waited for Vivian's next move. Vivian, who still had not sat down, quickly assessed the situation. She knew that this project was very important for Ball, who had a reputation as a hard-working actress. She had followed Ball's career in the movies, first as the queen of B pictures for RKO, then as a glamorous showgirl in the MGM Technicolor extravaganzas, and on the radio. Remaining calm, Vivian decided to handle the redhead as she had other *grande dames* by accepting the idiosyncrasies and adjusting to them.

Ball continued, "Well, I don't know. You're not what I had in mind."

At this point, Desi interjected. "Honey, let's read it through. Let's get the feeling of the script anyway. See what happens."

That suggestion suited Vivian just fine. All the lessons she'd learned from Merman, Lawrence, Perry, and Abbott came together to serve her in this moment. Thompson, seated next to Lucy, wondered if Vivian could deliver the goods. His doubts soon faded. "Boy, ol' Viv just read those cold notes like a stevedore. She *rammed* it to her. And she spoke just as loud as Lucille did, she didn't whisper. I could feel Lucille dying. I could see her toes in her shoes wiggling, but she loved the reading."

Although Lucy appeared pleased, she made no attempt to boost anyone's ego. Just about the time stomachs started grumbling, the Arnazes' housekeeper produced fried

Vivian and Desi Arnaz sing Christmas carols in the seldom-seen holiday episode of I Love Lucy.

chicken brought from home. As the meeting continued, Lucille and Desi feasted, never skipping a beat. Ball did not offer a piece to anyone, prompting Bill Frawley to ask, "When do the peons eat around here?" Ball, feigning innocence, answered, "What do you mean, haven't you had your lunch?" Frawley barked, "Hell! I don't eat at ten o'clock in the morning, that was my call time for Chrissake! You've got enough chicken for the whole goddamned group!"

Everyone broke for lunch.

Maury Thompson's engaging recollections of that first day have appeared in other books, with slight variations. For example, in *Desilu: The Story of Lucille Ball and Desi Arnaz*, Thompson says that Vivian agreed with Ball's description of how a landlady should look by responding, "You got her. I look just like that in the morning when I get out of bed." And she went even further, assuring the star that she would dye her hair and that she did "photograph dumpy," since, as Vivian explained, "I'm round-shouldered."

Emily Daniels, who worked that first season as camera coordinator, has read all the varying interpretations of the same event. She feels that the only other person besides Arnaz who thought that Vivian would work perfectly as Lucy's sidekick was her husband Marc. She also remembers that "Lucy's only concern was that Vivian's hair color was too close to hers and she wanted Vivian to change it and that Vivian didn't want to." Ball, as Daniels points out, "Won out. After all she was the star of the show." The shade of Vivian's hair color gradually grew darker as the show progressed through the first season. Vivian said, "As soon as the series began to be screened, I'd get people telling me, 'Your hair wasn't the same this week.' Not exactly surprising when I spent days at a time with my

Ethel contemplates her revenge in "No Children Allowed."

Ethel reacts to Lucy's absurd plan in the I Love Lucy *episode titled "The Mustache."*

head in a bucket of cold water in the makeup department while they tried out different colors."

Desi Arnaz had been very concerned about the blending of this odd foursome and he breathed a sigh of relief after that initial reading. "The chemistry which ignited at the first meeting of Lucy and Vivian and the rapport and understanding Bill and I had was somehow naturally transferred to the characters of Lucy and Ethel, and Ricky and Fred," he explained later. "No one, including me, could have visualized that it would turn out so perfectly. We could have never found anyone to play Ethel any better or even as well as Vivian Vance did. She was great in the part. She was Ethel, or maybe I should put it this way—she was such a good actress that she made herself become Ethel."

In hindsight, it's interesting to note that some of Lucille Ball's concerns about casting Vivian were legitimate. Since she'd always portrayed the "other woman," Vivian did not come across as an old dumpy housewife and she herself admitted that "from what they had told me about Ethel, I couldn't figure out how they connected her with slinky Olive Lashbrook."

Wearing a pair of black slacks and white blouse, Vivian hardly looked the part of a frump on that first day of rehearsal. Though it is difficult now to think of anyone else as Ethel Mertz, it stands to reason that if time had not been of the essence, and production of the show did not have to begin immediately, the search for Ethel Mertz would have continued and perhaps someone else would have played the role.

Vivian had not wanted to accept the job but once she was committed to doing it, she had to see it through. There may have been times when she wanted to walk away, especially with the problems that developed later, but leaving would have meant failure, something she couldn't possibly deal with at the time. Vivian had to convince Lucille Ball she was capable of playing the role of Ethel Mertz.

There are those who, because of their loyalty to Lucille Ball, will not go on record but will privately admit that during the early days of the show, the Queen of Comedy tried everything within her power to have Vivian fired. According to Vivian, even Ball's agent chimed in. "Her eyes are bigger than yours," he said to Lucy. "You'll have to let her go." Later, when Lucy passed this story on to Vivian, she told Lucy, "If I had your looks or your talent, I'd fire that agent, not me!"

Along with Marc Daniels, Arnaz insisted that Vivian

could transform herself into an Ethel Mertz the audience would buy. "He believed her in the play at La Jolla, and that's all you had to do with Desi," says Thompson. Lucy might have gotten her way if Desi hadn't finally persuaded her to give Vivian a chance. He agreed that if after a couple of shows Vivian hadn't made the grade, they'd write the character out of the program.

After the minor skirmish over lunch, Thompson, Vivian, and Frawley decided to dine together in the studio commissary. No one commented on the events of the morning or on the star of the show. The co-stars had a pleasant and lively conversation, one of the rare times the duo displayed any camaraderie.

William Frawley and his wife, Louise, had made a name for themselves in vaudeville but their marriage did not last. He moved on to a career in Hollywood in 1916 and by the fifties, Frawley had appeared in nearly a hundred films. Considered a fine character actor, he was well known to audiences for his gruff exterior and gravelly voice. By the time *I Love Lucy* came along, however, he considered the craft of acting a chore. His real love, baseball, consumed more of his time.

Bill Frawley's personality baffled those who knew him. Known for frequently making crass comments about people's color, religion, and ethnic origin, he also gave generously to acquaintances and family members who needed help. Desi Arnaz took a gamble when he hired Frawley. There were rampant rumors about his drinking and Frawley was having real trouble finding work. When Frawley heard of the search for someone to play Fred Mertz, he phoned Ball at home requesting a meeting. Lucy had known Bill from her studio days and wanted to help the down-and-out actor. Desi agreed to hire Frawley with the understanding that if his drinking posed any problem on the set, he should immediately consider himself unem-

*Vivian and William Frawley in a rare moment of truce for
publicity purposes*

ployed. Frawley promised sobriety while working and the
character of Fred Mertz quickly found a place in the hearts
of the audience.

Desilu executive Martin Leeds notes that Frawley's
promise did not stop him from finding a way to enjoy his
favorite pastime. Once the series was underway, "Bill
would leave the show after filming on Thursday night, go
over to his favorite restaurant, the Musso & Frank Grill,
drink all night Thursday night, Friday, Saturday, and Sunday. Sunday night he'd stop drinking to be up for rehearsal
on Monday morning."

After five days of intense rehearsal, two sets of neighbors named Ricardo and Mertz made their debut in front of a live audience on the sound stage of the Desilu Playhouse. Vivian had terrible stage fright for that first show and could not find a way to calm her rattled nerves. "I was scared to death when we did our first show," she said. "After all, I had done only two movies and wasn't accustomed to working with one camera, much less four of them. Lucy sensed that I was scared and went out of her way to set me at ease. She got me laughing so hard before my entrance that I didn't have time to remember that I was so frightened." (Subsequent episodes were filmed with three cameras instead of four.)

Originally, the episode called "Lucy Thinks Ricky Is Trying to Do Away with Her" was scheduled first but was put on hold until some technical mishaps which occurred during filming could be ironed out. So the first televised episode of *I Love Lucy* was "The Girls Want to Go to a Nightclub." It aired on Monday night, October 15, 1951, on CBS Television.

The cast and crew gathered at Marc and Emily Daniels' house to watch that first broadcast. As Emily Daniels watched everyone's reactions, she noticed that "Phil Ober, who was the only one who had not seen it, sat there and just screamed from one end to the other. He loved it!" Everyone else thought it was "awful and no one felt it would go."

Most critics saw the show's potential but said that "*I Love Lucy* will have to come again before it can qualify along with some of the others of the same stripe. The writing and plotting should be more inventive and less contrived, just for the sake of laughs." Critics felt that Vivian had "ably abetted Lucille Ball."

That night, the Obers returned to their newly rented apartment at the Chateau Marmont on Sunset Boulevard

Vivian and Lucy in the episode "The Seance" with Vivian as Madame Raya

where Phil assured his wife that the show would certainly last. Vivian seemed pleased with her work but felt distant and apathetic toward the character of Ethel Mertz. She also balked about having to play opposite the sixty-four-year-old Frawley who seemed unenthusiastic about performing on the show. Vivian, however, felt that if this series succeeded, it might give her everything she had always wanted. Still, she wondered whether she could handle the hectic pace of the show and Ball's at times dictatorial manner.

"We worked so hard that we never traveled much farther than to make the trip between home and studio," she said. "It was all so new and the pressure was so much that in my mind I quit every Thursday night after we'd wound up one more performance. Every Monday morning when we started another week, I'd get as far along Sunset Boulevard as Schwab's Drugstore then I'd have to pull over and talk myself into making the rest of the ride in. I told myself, 'Contract or not, you can't keep it up. You'll be sick. You'll get the shakes again . . . but do you want to prove to the world that you're a quitter? Are you going to fail again? I'd rather be dead than that.' "

Vivian dreaded going through another experience like the one she had undergone while in *Voice of the Turtle* in Chicago in 1945. So this time she didn't wait to become

From "Lucy and Ethel Buy the Same Dress"

incapacitated but headed straight to a new analyst, scheduling several early morning sessions each week.

When Vivian arrived on the set on a Monday morning, she'd grab for that week's script and read it carefully, hoping *not* to find a scene requiring her to hug or kiss Frawley. Afterward she headed to rehearsals, thinking of ways to bring up ideas regarding changes to the script without getting an objection from Lucy. "I wasn't bashful about making suggestions," she said. "Everyone else had come straight from radio except me. That showed in some of the early scripts, and I'd pick holes in them during the Monday conferences that began the week. Someone would be given a line like, 'The phone is ringing.' I'd make the point,

Ethel Mertz's moment of fame in her hometown of Albuquerque, New Mexico, is upstaged by Lucy, Fred, and Ricky in "Ethel's Hometown."

'That's the way you're used to writing it for radio. It's out of place now that you're seeing the person.' Sight is different from sound."

William Asher, who directed the second season of *I Love Lucy,* maintains that "Vivian had tremendous work ethics and her instincts were incredible, but she was never difficult about having her ideas rejected."

On one occasion, however, Vivian adamantly insisted that the word "crazy" be written out of a script. Lucy felt they needed to use that particular word in order for the scene to work. It intrigued Ball that the use of the word affected her supporting player so much. Vivian tried to explain that "there are people who are confined and that word could destroy two years of their treatment."

Then Lucy found out that Vivian had indeed suffered a breakdown and had undergone analysis. Maury Thompson observed that Lucille Ball had a way of getting people to their boiling point by pestering them verbally. She'd target a person's weak spot and relentlessly drive them to the edge. Vivian, however, would not allow Ball to see her irritated. "Vivian did not expose her hand, she was too smart for that, she'd suffer it out. From then on, Lucille used the word [crazy] at every opportunity, because it was digging to Viv. She hated herself for doing it but she'd do it anyway."

During those early days, Thompson frequently drove Vivian home. He recalled that on a particularly trying day, "Lucille had been just terrible to Vivian all through the rehearsals." When he asked Vivian how she planned to deal with Ball's unyielding behavior, Vivian answered, "Honey, listen, if this show should be a hit, it could be the biggest thing that ever happened to my career. So I made up my mind, I'm going to learn to love that bitch!"

Vivian still found refuge from her problems by taking

long drives. On the weekends, Thompson would escort her as they explored the out-of-the-way towns of California. "Her car was a big Lincoln. When I saw it I said, 'My God, Viv! How much gas does this thing use?' She replied, 'If you have to worry about that, don't buy one!' She'd want to get out of the house but she didn't want to drive so I'd drive with her. The drives were her moments of refuge, of peace and quiet. There was only one agreement made—not a word spoken about the show."

As always, Vivian scouted opportunities for land investments. One weekend, she fell in love with the beauty of Solvang, a town just forty miles from Santa Barbara. Before leaving, she'd made arrangements to purchase land on which she hoped to eventually build a house.

The character of Ethel Mertz appeared in twelve of the first thirteen shows. The only episode in which Vivian did not appear, "The Audition," featured Lucy and Desi in a nightclub act they had done several times on stage while touring the country. In "The Audition," Ricky sings "Babalu" while Lucy saunters on stage and proceeds to create mayhem.

Of the remaining twenty-two episodes in the first season, Vivian did not participate in "Lucy Does a TV Commercial" in which Lucy creates her unforgettably hilarious Vitameatavegamin routine, "The Young Fans" which featured a very young Richard Crenna, and "Lucy Plays Cupid." This third episode was the one which Vivian must have regretted not working on most since it featured her friend Edward Everett Horton. Bea Benadaret, Ball's original choice for the role of Ethel Mertz, played Horton's love interest.

In the initial scripts, the writers focused their attentions strictly on the character of Lucy Ricardo, leaving Ball's supporting players to do just that, support. But as the sea-

son progressed, Ethel's entrances, frequently made through
the back kitchen door, slowly increased. In fact, at one
point Mrs. Mertz passed through the Ricardos' doors an
average of five times per show. Evidently, Vivian
impressed the writers and most importantly, Lucille Ball.

Still, the character of Ethel Mertz could not come across
as beautiful or young. The makeup department had to
apply a lighter base to Vivian's face to make her skin look
older, and had to follow strict instructions against applying
any eyelashes. Hairdresser Irma Kusely tried several hairstyles that first season to find one which gave Mrs. Mertz
an older, bedraggled look. *I Love Lucy* writers Bob
Weiskopf and Bob Schiller agree that "Lucy came from
the old school and she learned fast that you don't have any
younger, prettier people around. That was a lesson you
learned early on."

When Vivian worked on *I Love Lucy*, everyone thought
her much older than Lucille Ball. Years later, several
books tried to change this perception by declaring Lucy
two or three years older than Vivian. In reality, Vivian,
born in 1909, was indeed two years older than Lucille Ball
who was born in 1911.

Max Factor makeup coordinator Hal King had a close
friendship with Lucille Ball for years and understood the
rules of Hollywood divas but could not make sense of
Lucy's reluctance to allow Vivian to look even the slightest bit more appealing. "Lucy wouldn't let Vivian or anyone else look better on the show than she did," King said.
"Not that she hated anyone, she was just jealous. If anybody complimented anybody else but her, Lucy would get
furious. I remember once, she came over to me and said,
'What did you do to Vivian?' I said, 'Nothing. Why? What
do you mean?' She said, 'Well, she looks beautiful today
and I told her to take those eyelashes off.' I said, 'Oh for

Chrissake, you're Lucille Ball to Vivian Vance. She isn't going to take anything away from you just because I put false eyelashes on her and made her look a little nicer!' "

Maury Thompson also tells the story of the day that "Lucy spotted the makeup and the eyelashes and went over to Vivian, saying, 'You're wearing eyelashes?' And Vivian says, 'Yes! I've been wearing them for six months—so just leave me alone!' Lucille left her alone. She knew what she had in Vivian, especially after the show was successful."

Swirls are the name for the plain cotton housedresses tied around the waist that served as Vivian's wardrobe. "She hated those swirls the first year. But, she had to wear them. They eventually got away from that and allowed her to wear more flattering costumes," remembers Emily Daniels. However the terry cloth bathrobe which Ball insisted would delineate the character of Ethel endured from the first episode until the end of the series.

Stories have circulated for years that Vivian's contract required her to gain significant amounts of weight for the role of Ethel Mertz. It is true that Vivian put pounds on but this had occurred naturally over the years. She dieted constantly, hoping to lose the extra weight. Her size does fluctuate noticeably over the course of *I Love Lucy* and Ball may have asked Vivian to stay hefty when her weight increased. But it is unlikely that Lucy demanded Vivian remain plump.

Vivian's opposition to a plump Ethel Mertz had more to do with what she believed funny rather than her own vanity. When asked to pad her body to make it look fatter, she reasoned that "If my husband in this series makes fun of my weight and I'm actually fat, then the audience won't laugh . . . they'll feel sorry for me. But, if he calls me 'Fat old bag,' and I'm not heavy, then it will seem funny."

If Ball had initially visualized a heavyset actress for the role of Ethel, she probably would not have asked lean Bea Benadaret to play the part but would have settled on a friend from her days at RKO, hefty, peroxide-blonde Barbara Pepper. Despite a drinking problem, Pepper eventually cashed in on her rotundity as Mrs. Ziffel on *Green Acres*.

The combination of bedraggled hairdo, aged skin, unflattering housedresses, and weight gain astounded those who knew Vivian before the show, particularly Anne Denove Farleigh who had not seen Vivian since the early forties. "I was shocked when I saw her on *I Love Lucy* because I did not think she would ever let herself get fat and appear on television looking so homely."

What fuels the rumors of Ball's supposed demands on Vivian stems from a fictitious contract written by Ball and given to Vivian at a party. In the bogus contract, Ball outlines certain requirements—that Vivian gain five pounds a week, that she not wear eyelashes, that she not dye her hair within five shades of Ball's, and that Vivian never get more laughs than Lucy. These exaggerated conditions do bear some resemblance to the truth but by bringing these demands out in the open in the guise of a joke, Ball probably thought that everyone would have a hearty laugh and it would all be forgotten. However, the joke backfired. This mock contract took on a life of its own and through the years has become more fact than fiction.

Nothing that Vivian learned in the theater went to waste and she used all her lessons during the run of *I Love Lucy*. She drew from all the female types she'd known growing up, including her mother Mae, to flesh out Ethel. "Mama set her lips in a special kind of hard line whenever she was about to take someone apart," Vivian said. "I used that set-mouth expression a dozen and one times as Ethel." She once described the character of Ethel Mertz as one "who wasn't even a person to me, just an old frump with a technique for stirring laughter. It had never been my ambition to be that kind of female. Ethel was made up of bits and pieces of women I'd known but never admired."

After wrapping up that first season, Vivian left Los Angeles to vacation in Cubero with Phil. As she waited for the call from Desilu regarding the new start date, she had mixed feelings about going back to work. The prospect of steady employment for a second season had induced her to sign another contract. Now, however, she had second thoughts about returning to the frantic and stressful pace of the daily routine. A few weeks after they finished filming almost forty episodes, Vivian received a call requesting her immediate return to work.

The hectic pace of that first season continued well into the second year of the show. Lucille Ball was pregnant for the second time and the writers and actors cut their vacations short and returned to work in order to enable Ball to take a suitable maternity leave. Desi Arnaz decided to incorporate the event into the premise of *I Love Lucy* though the sponsor, Philip Morris, and CBS strongly opposed the idea. In 1952, pregnant women did not readily parade on television but after Desi Arnaz threatened to pull the show off the air unless they agreed to his terms, CBS and Philip Morris conceded. During the first season, *I Love Lucy* had taken its place as the number one rated television show and neither Philip Morris nor CBS wanted to lose out on the revenues the show would generate.

The company worked from July to November nonstop. The frenzied pace placed a great strain on everyone. At times, common courtesy gave way to rudeness. One observer tells this story:

> Because of her condition, Lucy's dressing room was right next to the set and she had two or three dressers to help her with costume changes. One particularly quick

scene called for a very fast change. Vivian had to run clear to another sound stage, which housed her dressing room, in order to change her outfit while Lucy obviously had no problem with her change. Vivian made her costume change, raced back to the stage, over cables and props, and took her place beside Lucy so they could both make an entrance together. Waiting calmly, Lucy snapped, "You almost missed your cue. You're late." Taken aback, Vivian took a deep breath, turned to Lucy, and said, "I'd tell you to go fuck yourself if Desi hadn't already taken care of that!"

Hairdresser Irma Kusely agrees that "some days on the set were terrible but it would always end up okay. There was a lot of combat in order to be understood. Lucy couldn't always have her way and Vivian couldn't have hers, but a day never ended in dissension. They were always forgiving of whatever happened."

Everyone had their own method of venting their frustrations. Arnaz yelled, Frawley slept, and Ball retreated to her dressing room, while Vivian paced the studio, fuming, trying to find a way to let out her anger. Thompson would usually watch as everyone disappeared from the set. "I remember one day I was at my table which sat up high, looking down on the floor. I had this big apple, it was icy cold and it was a hot day. I had taken one bite out of it—it tasted so good. Viv walked by [agitated] and said, 'Can I have a bite of that apple?' I said, 'Sure.' She took it, walked away, and ate the whole goddamned thing! She didn't apologize or say I'm sorry. She'd eat right out of your hand—she was very earthy!"

When filming for the second season took a break for a four-month hiatus, Vivian and Phil traveled to Albuquerque then on to Rome for a well-deserved vacation.

When Vivian told her mother that they had chosen the Italian capital as their getaway, Mae responded, "Why would you go there? It's so old!" Later, in the episode "Ricky's European Booking," Vivian has Ethel spouting, "Who wants to go to Europe anyway . . . it's so old."

During the break, Lucy rested, waiting to give birth. On January 19, 1953, the arrival of Desi Jr. coincided with the airing of "Lucy Goes to the Hospital" in which Little Ricky is born. Now the *I Love Lucy* phenomenon took hold and there was no going back. After the long break everyone returned to finish filming the final shows of the season.

With the success of the show, Vivian renegotiated her contract, demanding more than her initial $450 a week. Every year, Vivian's agent threatened pulling her from the show, saying that the stress put on his client would impede her from continuing. Johny Aitchison, Desi Arnaz's administrative assistant, suspects that "Vivian learned her negotiating skills from Lucille. Whenever it came time for renewal, Lucille would always say, 'Oh, I don't know if I want to come back,' just to get the price higher."

Citing overwork as an additional concern, Vivian's agent would say that Vivian may be tempted to renew if the Desilu offer met her standards. "She needs this kind of appreciation and incentive to prevent her from having a nervous breakdown," the agent would confide to Arnaz. Vivian informed Stanley Bergerman, who negotiated her first contract, what she would like to have included in her new contract. "She wanted to continue to have an active part in Desilu Productions," Bergerman said, "but demanded of us to improve her financial situation, since she had signed as an exclusive player with Desilu."

As producer of *I Love Lucy*, Desi Arnaz and his executives would sit at the bargaining table every year to negotiate new contracts. "Vivian's agent was another cup of tea,"

Arnaz remembered. "He represented many big names in the business and was considered quite a power in negotiations, which we always seemed to be in with him. We always managed to meet his terms because Vivian was worth everything she got."

But Martin Leeds, who worked for CBS before Arnaz hired him to run operations at Desilu, insists that Vivian and her agent did little negotiating. Leeds states that annual raises were given automatically based on a ten percent scale. "I never had Desi nor Lucy ask how much money Bill or Vivian made. I had made the original deals for CBS because it was going to be our (CBS's) show and Lucy and Desi were not involved with that. Frawley got to be the luckiest man alive. His agent cut a deal with me and said whatever happens on the show, whatever you give Vivian you have to give Bill. It was the normal contract for them with options for seven years. About a year later I left CBS and joined Desilu. Then we felt we had to do something for them. What Vivian and Bill got after the first year .was a little bit above fair—not a lot but above."

The first year they made $450 a week. The second year $1,000 per episode and by the third season they were making $3,500 per episode. By the time the show ended its run, the two supporting actors were pulling in $7,500 per show.

During the show's second season, the Obers left their apartment in the Chateau Marmont in West Hollywood and moved into a Spanish-style house previously owned by Lionel Barrymore located at 629 Frontera Drive in the Pacific Palisades section of Los Angeles. When Vivian asked her brother whether he thought the $23,000 price was fair, he quickly said he did. When he heard about the acquisition, Bill Frawley went to see the house before the Obers moved in and gave his stamp of approval.

Vivian's niece, Vivian Wilkison, described the manner in

which her aunt chose to decorate this home. "It was a beautiful home. She had a way of decorating which created a homey and elegant atmosphere." As in her first home with Ober in New York, Vivian chose earthy hues for the interior walls of the house which formed an L shape around the walled patio. The Mexican and Indian ceramics and paintings which the Obers had collected through the years easily blended into the Spanish design of the house. A guest house over the garage always welcomed needy actor friends. Glenn Anders, who had known Vivian for several years, not only made himself a permanent fixture in the guest house but grew dependent on the Obers for financial support.

Phil worked in some important films during this time but never quite made the impression he had made on stage. Although he was regarded as a competent actor, he did not have the qualities of a star. In Marjorie Lord's assessment, Phil Ober "was not someone who walked on stage and you got excited about. With his good looks, he should have been a bigger star. Something was missing. He had a lot of niceness about him but not a lot of excitement." His quirky looks and distinguished bearing made it difficult to think of him as a leading man.

When Johny Aitchison told Ober that he'd seen the film he'd made with Vivian, *The Secret Fury*, Phil quickly mentioned that he had top billing over his wife. "Phil had a much stronger theatrical background and he now felt envious of Vivian," Aitchison said. On stage, Phil often played the lead as he had in *Come Back, Little Sheba*. But when he auditioned for the movie version, he landed a small supporting role. A press release for the film said that Phil worked only on those occasions when he chose to and that "he had the world by the tail."

Vivian later pointed out that she brought home the bacon while Phil reaped the benefits. In his turn, Phil blamed her for his lack of productivity. He made these petty and egotistical complaints only in private, however. In public, he never ceased to play the supportive husband. Irma Kusely believes Ober's hamminess got in the way of his true feelings and he behaved the way he believed an actor should when in public. "Phil always appeared happy," Kusely said. "He used to come to the taping and root for her. He was a good laugher, but I think he just enjoyed hearing himself on the tape. I think too, he knew he was on because there was an audience there."

As Vivian's popularity exceeded even her own expectations, Phil's true feelings began to surface in a more dramatic fashion. During difficult periods, Vivian often confided in Irma. "She had to keep a record of every moment of her day—what she was going to do, who she was going to talk with—probably, he was keeping track for his own safety," Irma said. "If he were seeing someone else and he knew her every move, he knew what he could do."

Whenever the work days turned into work nights, Irma and Vivian would shuffle off to Vivian's dressing room and share a drink. "This would upset Phil greatly," Kusely said. She feels that the couple's problems had a great deal to do with his jealousy of her success. "He wasn't really nice to her. He was always around, but not because he was possessive. He just thought he was missing something which he might be interested in."

Growing restless, Phil spent most of his time playing cards with Burt Lancaster and tennis with some of the biggest names in Hollywood. One of his partners on the court, Katharine Hepburn, particularly enjoyed Ober's haughtiness. Meanwhile, Vivian never stopped trying to help her husband find work. On a few occasions, he did stints on the show but as Lucille Ball noted, "He wasn't fun to be around." In an early episode, "The Quiz Show," he appears as Lucy's "second first husband" and rewards her with a prize of $1,000 dollars. In another, "Don Juan Is Shelved," he played movie producer Dore Schary. When he was introduced to the studio audience as Vivian's real husband, Phil Ober, they sat there in disbelief.

When in public with his wife, Ober frequently overheard strangers say, "What right has she got to be out with that guy?" or "Who does he think he is being out with Ethel?" Vivian assured columnists that Phil got a kick out of it. Ober accepted the taunts humorously but at home, he would vent his frustrations on his wife.

Bill Asher, who took over as director of *I Love Lucy* the second season, recalls how they avoided using Phil. "There were other parts Phil could have done but we used actors from the stock group we had instead. Though Vivian may have been hurt, she never showed it."

In the early fifties, Vivian ran into Anne Denove Farleigh on the studio lot. Farleigh, whose husband produced commercials, now lived in Los Angeles. When Vivian told Anne about Phil's difficulty in finding employment, Anne offered to introduce him to her husband if he would consider doing commercials. Vivian replied that "though she wished he would do it, television was beneath him. Phil was accustomed to the style she had accustomed him to."

The third year of *I Love Lucy* meant a move to a bigger studio, a private bungalow for Vivian on the lot, some of the best shows of the series, and Emmy nominations for Ball, Frawley, and Vivian. The show received an Emmy for "Best Situation Comedy" that year for the second time in a row. Though Ball had won the previous year for "Best Actress in a Comedy," that year she lost to Eve Arden for her work on *Our Miss Brooks*. Frawley failed to receive a statuette when Art Carney clinched it for his portrayal of Ed Norton on *The Honeymooners*.

That ceremony, held at the Hollywood Palladium on February 11, 1954, featured the category of "Best Supporting Actress in a Series" for the first time. The cast of *I Love Lucy* was sitting together when they heard "Vivian Vance" announced as the winner of the Emmy. "I knew Desi and Lucille were screaming with excitement and everybody else was turning around to look and applaud, but I didn't hear a thing," Vance said. "The two of them hoisted me to my feet and pushed me out of my chair. I stumbled through a few words of gratitude, thanking Anna Ingleman and saying, 'I want to thank the greatest straight woman in show business.' Lucille liked that."

At that point, Frawley said, "It goes to prove that the whole vote is rigged."

When Vivian arrived home that night, she proudly displayed her Emmy on the mantelpiece. The next day she received a telegram from Kathryn Kennedy O'Connor who wrote, "Congratulations. I said you'd make it after forty." O'Connor had intuitively understood that Vivian would not reach stardom as a starlet but would have to wait until she reached maturity. She had told her so during the early days of the Albuquerque Little Theatre but Vivian had resented the prediction and had fought to prove her mentor wrong. After winning the Emmy, Vivian remembered this conversation with O'Connor which had taken place years before:

> "Your acting has improved greatly," she told me over a cup of coffee one day when I had one of my low spells.
>
> "Thanks to you," I said. "But, let's face it—I don't look like a glamorous leading lady and I never will."
>
> "I know," she replied.
>
> "Then why do you keep telling me I'll make the grade?" I asked.
>
> Kathryn said, "I didn't say as a leading lady. Your

chance lies in comedy and character parts. And I don't think you'll reach the top till you're over forty. And then as a comedienne."

Later, when Vivian returned home from a trip to Albuquerque, her Emmy had vanished from the mantelpiece. Phil had taken it. Vivian later identified this incident as the turning point in her marriage. "I went searching around the house, and there it was, tucked away in a glass-fronted case upstairs," she said. "Leaving it in full view to be seen by one and all was something only a peasant would do. But envy had to be justified."

Frustrated with Phil's jealousy and the growing pressures of the show, Vivian began fearing a second breakdown. On her drive to the studio, she'd often find herself a few blocks away, confused and hesitant. "I'd have to pull over to talk myself into making the rest of the ride in."

Later, the Monday morning blues also descended on director William Asher. "We all dreaded coming in. Viv and I laughed about how I'd start looking for gentle accidents to get into on those terrible Mondays. That's when I knew it was time to go to [directing] movies."

On the surface, it looked as if Vivian didn't need therapy. William Asher and many others described Vivian as steady, well-adjusted, and happy-go-lucky. Instead of showing her true feelings, it still seemed easier for her to project these qualities. Even while in therapy she fought against facing her problems, choosing to ignore them or pretending they did not exist. She had her marriage and career as concrete proof against those who judged her that she had developed into a responsible person living a balanced life.

Vivian may not have wanted to face the fact that many of the misfortunes in her life had been self-created. Ironically, after she achieved what she had sought most of her life, it did not produce the expected outcome. Rather it reinforced her pattern of being a struggling victim.

In the midst of success, traumatic childhood events continued to color Vivian's views on life. She remembered this incident in particular:

> I couldn't have been more than five or six years old. Brother Bobby wasn't born yet, Dorothy was a toddler, and Mickey was a baby, being nursed every four hours. Venus could have been in school—she wasn't around. Mama went off into one of her ranting and raving scenes. "I'm sick to death of the lot of you," she screamed. "I've had enough of it. I'm going. I'm leaving you, and shan't come back." She got in the car and drove away.
>
> A child believes what a parent says because it has no means of detecting truth from falsehood. Mama had left forever as far as I was concerned. I was traumatized by the sudden overwhelming responsibility, far beyond my capacity to handle it. The neurotic seed of feeling responsible took root and flourished. Even when I was in my middle years, the feeling was as much part of me as my arms and legs. I was responsible to my work, my home, and my husband but sometimes the load would be almost too much to bear, especially where my sisters were concerned.

According to Lou Ann, Vivian diligently carried out the role of family caretaker throughout her life. "Vivian set herself up as surrogate mother/adviser to all of us. She always had the feeling of being responsible for us, probably because she didn't think Mom was capable of it. As a result, all of us looked up to her. She was always very generous to us."

Growing up, Vivian truly believed everything her mother told her, including the time she confided to her second oldest daughter that Mae and Bob would have preferred a boy instead of a girl. "According to Mama, I was the wrong sex ever to win Dad's approval. One more fragment fell into place. All my life up to the present, as I remembered it, I'd been afraid of my own femininity."

In trying to prove her mother wrong, Vivian attempted to win her father's attention. "I never really felt that my father loved me. How could he, when Mama said he wanted a boy in my place? So I put on boots and learned to shoot, to go hunting with him, striving to be a son. When I was old enough to be boy crazy in the normal way of adolescence, which Mama thought was a sin, he reacted by being so strict that I rebelled. That shotgun routine was too much to take. It led up to the biggest fight the two of us ever got into. 'I know why you're so tough on me,' I said. 'I know why you try to keep me home all the time. You're afraid I'll turn out like you.' From the way he swatted me, I should have known I'd hit on the truth. He was harsh because he cared. I had to wait nearly twenty-five years to realize that."

Vivian's time on the couch often overwhelmed her but she found comfort when her analyst told her, "If this all works out, you're going to find a woman you never expected, complete and calm."

I Love Lucy writer Bob Schiller recalls a favorite story Vivian liked telling of a particular therapy session. She had spent close to an hour crying hysterically at the memories she had of her mother. Her analyst, knowing that the one thing Vivian had on her side was humor, told her, "Your mother spent so much time warning you about showing your legs and being a sinner, that you've spent half your life hiding—under men."

In spite of her therapy, Vivian justified her father's actions while stubbornly refusing to understand anything concerning her mother's behavior. "I remember one bout of sobbing that brought a question from my analyst, 'What does a whore look like?' I'd always believed that I had to be terribly careful because I looked like a whore. That fit in with what Mama had told me. It was one reason I'd played the 'other woman' so often on the stage. A showgirl, a girl who knew the insides of speakeasies and nightclubs, a mistress, a sinner, [I felt] the role was ready-made.

"I learned that if you missed having an understanding parent, you must fill the gap for yourself. In a strange but real sense, I turned myself into my own mother. It was essential to recognize what had produced the crackup. It was no time to keep saying, 'Oh, poor woman.' Of course, Mama had great problems with six children, live-in relatives, poverty, and Dad, but it was wrong to sympathize too soon. That was how I'd covered up hostility. Covering up for Mama was a means of suppressing natural anger. Covering up for my husband and pretending we were having the time of our lives together was more of the same. I wanted to keep that anger down because I thought it might destroy me if it ever came out."

Analysis finally gave Vivian the green light to unleash that anger, especially toward Phil. During this period, many noticed a marked change in Vivian. She developed quite a sharp tongue, she wasn't afraid to voice her true feelings, and often used this newly acquired strength when confronting problems on the set.

Lucille Ball had by now recognized the importance of a strong supporting cast and understood that the success of the show lay with the core of the ensemble. As a fledgling actor, Robert Osborne joined the Desilu Players, an apprentice program begun by Ball in the late 1950s to train young actors. He later became a published author and columnist for the *Hollywood Reporter*. During his time at Desilu, he observed the behind-the-scenes happenings while studying the actors and their techniques. He feels that "it was Vivian and Bill Frawley that were the catalysts that made the whole thing work so well. Lucy was always first to admit it wasn't just Lucy and Ricky. Lucy was wonderfully talented but I'm not sure it would have been that great of a show [without Vivian and Bill]. It would perhaps not be a show we still talk about today or still watch if it hadn't been for Vivian and Bill."

Television and stage director Paul Blake feels that "the cast was bringing in years of experience and each one had a lot to offer. Unlike today when you do stand-up for six months and get a show and there's no technique or experience to carry them through the moments of mediocrity. But the Lucy cast could do mediocre material and Vivian was brilliant at making things better. Not just about making herself better but about making others better."

Vivian had become an asset to the show and formed an alliance with Ball and frequently offered suggestions. But Bill Frawley adamantly refused to incorporate any business suggested by Vivian or anyone else. In his opinion, he was a professional film actor and above taking suggestions from this New York stage actress. Bernie Weitzman, who later developed a close relationship with Frawley, suggests that "Bill and Vivian came from two different worlds. Viv considered herself literate and Frawley illiterate. She was a stage actress, which she felt immediately put her on a higher level. Sometimes Broadway stage actors see the stage as being heaven. But Frawley didn't give a shit about Broadway—he couldn't have cared less."

Desi Arnaz often had to act as mediator to keep peace between the two co-stars. "Bill couldn't stand Vivian,"

Desi remembered. " 'Where the hell did you find this bitch?' he would ask. 'She can't sing worth a damn. You're going to have her sing again?' "

Arnaz would come to Vivian's defense. "Bill, she's a hell of a good actress and Ethel Mertz, the part she's playing, is not supposed to sing good."

"Well, she bugs me," Frawley said. "You know that dance routine she and I are supposed to do next week? Well, this silly broad tells the choreographer she doesn't think we'll be able to do it because I'll never be able to learn it. Like it was some kind of Fred Astaire and Ginger Rogers number or something. All we are supposed to do in this thing is an old-fashioned soft-shoe routine. Well, for Chrissakes, I was in vaudeville since I was five years old and I guarantee you, I'll wind up teaching fat-ass how to do the fucking thing!"

The now-legendary feud between these second bananas began early in the series. Her sister Dorothy said that Vivian cringed at Frawley's barroom jokes, his drinking, and his unprofessional conduct. Though this is partly true, there were other factors in the feud. During the first season of the show, Frawley overheard Vivian voicing displeasure about Frawley being cast in the role of her husband. "How can anyone believe that I'm married to that old coot," he'd heard her say. In retaliation, Frawley referred to Vivian as "a dried up old cunt." Vivian did not find this amusing.

Today's gossip columnists would have had a field day with the ongoing feud between Frawley and Vivian but in the fifties, studios avoided any negative publicity by issuing carefully worded press releases. It also helped that Lucille Ball and Hedda Hopper, one of the most influential gossip columnists in Hollywood, shared a close friendship. Hopper used her influence in Hollywood to insure that any negative publicity about *I Love Lucy* and its players never saw print. Clearly, viewers of *I Love Lucy* enjoyed reading that "Vivian, Bill, and the Arnazes have a four-way admiration society." When asked about Vivian, Bill responded, "She's one of the cleverest actresses I've ever known, and one of the funniest dolls in the world, both on and off stage." And Vivian reported that "Bill is a darling."

When another writer reported that Vivian and Bill behaved as candidly off the set as their television counterparts did on the show, it was obviously in reference to their bickering. Charles Pomerantz, the head of public relations for Desilu, decided from that point on to have the two co-stars interviewed separately. Vivian explained that "press interviews featuring Fred and Ethel side by side tapered off when at too many of them, the reporter would need a hole in his head to believe everything was peachy between the Mertzes and that old Bill and I were two real lovebirds."

Frawley often presented his co-stars with problems. He frequently fell asleep during rehearsals and constantly complained about the amount of time spent preparing for shows. He often bad-mouthed Arnaz, referring to him as a "Cuban heel" while calling Lucy and Vivian "brass-bound bitches." He once told an interviewer that "I just say what I have to say when I want to say it." Frustrated, Lucy, Desi, and Vivian tried to think of ways to have his character written out but unanimously decided that the public loved Fred Mertz too much and would never accept Ethel without Fred. Interestingly enough, soon after this Vivian's and Bill's contracts included a clause which stated that if either one decided to quit, for whatever reason, the other would also be dropped.

Ball appreciated Vivian's frequent suggestions and her reworking of bits to make scenes funnier and this frustrated Frawley even more. This type of give-and-take afforded everyone the opportunity to pitch their ideas. The writers outlined the scenes but the actors physically shaped them to their best advantage. Lucille Ball always choreographed physical moments, especially when using props. "We never discussed anything with the writers," she said. "After two readings, we'd get on our feet and throw the scripts away."

When these scenes included Vivian, both women worked tirelessly until they achieved perfection because they wanted to feel completely confident before stepping out in front of an audience. "Vivian, like me, was a perfectionist who took her profession very seriously," Lucy said. " 'Now what's my motivation here?' she'd ask me or Desi or Jess [Oppenheimer], and this would launch a half-hour discussion.

"During one early rehearsal, Vivian was championing a particular way in which a line should be spoken," Lucy went on. "Nobody agreed with her but she kept explaining until finally we did see the logic of her position. By this time, it was two a.m. and she was so wound up, she couldn't stop talking. Bill Frawley couldn't care less. If he got his big laugh, he didn't care how or why, and actually, Bill can be funny doing nothing. He has that kind of face and in any kind of costume, he's hilarious. I could sense a flaw in a story line or dialogue but I couldn't always put my objections into words. Then Desi would burst into a flood of Spanish and I'd express my frustrations by getting mad. Vivian was a tower of strength in such circumstances. She would intuitively guess what bothered us and then analyze it."

The constant rehearsing infuriated Frawley whose real interest, baseball, took up most of his time and attention. He was a stockholder in the Hollywood Baseball Stars and had his agent negotiate in his contract that if his favorite team, the New York Yankees, won the American League Pennant, he would have time off to see them play in the

World Series. His apathy toward the rehearsal process exasperated his fellow actors. Frawley employed a different method of working. When he received a new script, he would tear off and keep only those pages that pertained to his character. Sometimes he'd forget what pages belonged to what script and turned to Vivian, his number one enemy, to put him back on track.

"Right from the start, we knew Bill was going to be a holy terror," Vivian said. "He refused to learn one single word of anybody else's lines but his own. He had no idea in the world what the rest of us were saying. He tore all those pages out of his copy. I was being made up one night when he wandered over and said, 'Viv, is this next week's script I just picked up?'

" 'What's the title on the cover?'

" 'It says, 'Lucy Has Her Eyes Examined.'

" 'We've been rehearsing that all week,' Vivian said. 'We start shooting in fifteen minutes.' "

When episodes of *I Love Lucy* included singing and dancing, as several of them did, there were additional problems. Vivian often told this story:

Bill fancied himself a singer. He barely tolerated our efforts in that department. In his Dublin barroom baritone, he'd hang on to each note forever, always a stave or two behind the rest. I still hadn't got enough confidence back to go it alone, but I could hold my own in a barbershop quartet [with something] like "Sweet Adeline." Bill insisted that he should handle the repeats, and it was my job to take him aside to convince him otherwise.

"Lucille has to do them, Bill," Vivian would tell her co-star. "She's the star. It'll be funnier that way."

He wouldn't budge. I think he somehow got me and

the original Mrs. Frawley confused, so very soon the
fur was flying. "Shut up!" I yelled. "We've got to work
this song as we've rehearsed it. Keep still about it!" At
last he gave in but it was no surrender. "You know
what she's going to sound like, don't you?" he
growled. "Like putting a shovel full of shit on a baked
Alaska."

It was not unusual for Frawley to transfer his feelings
about marriage and his wife to his fictitious television
union and partner. "He was mad at me most of the time
because I happened to be cast as his wife, and Bill plain
hated wives," Vivian remembered. "In a rare calm
moment, he told me he'd once had one of his own. Marriage suited him so sorely that he never bothered with the
divorce. [He said] 'I'll never do it again.' "

Frawley's rule of acting was to memorize lines, go on,
say them, and "take the money and run." He despised waiting. On one occasion, technicians delayed his entrance
while they adjusted some of the lighting. Fuming, Bill bel-
lowed, "What's taking so long out there? I could have lit
Rome by now!"

Madelyn Pugh Davis, one of the three original writers of
I Love Lucy, once analyzed the different styles of the
show's co-stars. "Vivian and Bill worked in different
ways. Bill was from film, where everything is shot out of
sequence—you work your three or four days, go home and
never really know what the film was about. While Viv was
asking, 'What's my motivation?' That drove Bill Frawley
crazy."

But no matter how much he drove his fellow actors
crazy, no one could argue that Frawley carried out his
scenes efficiently, and at times delivered comedic brilliance. There was a backstage bulletin board listing the
names of the cast and crew with a series of gold stars next

to each name. The stars represented ad-libs. Frawley's stars ran the length of the board so quickly that the project was abandoned because, as Ball remarked, there was a lack of competition.

Vivian, like Lucy, wanted to be completely familiar with every detail before going on. Even after their characters had been fully defined, Vivian would never just walk through a scene as Frawley did. William Asher noted, "It bothered Vivian on Monday morning readings when Bill showed up with his sides only. That really used to bug her, but the feud has been blown out of proportion. There were times when they were outspoken to one another, but it helped the scenes, because their characters were so much like that. I think it added to the flow, playing right into the theme of boys against girls. If anything, they were funny."

Bill would never let an opportunity pass to goad Vivian. Once a script called for Fred to tell Ethel that she looked like Frankenstein's wife. Vivian, who couldn't care less what she looked like during rehearsals, walked onto the set wearing faded jeans and a Mexican peasant blouse with her hair tied in a bandanna and her face free of makeup. After speaking his line, Bill suddenly glared at Vivian and said, "Goddamn, Vivian! You do look like Frankenstein's wife!"

Through the years, several of Vivian's friends appeared on the show. Like Ball, who employed friends in need of work, Vivian tried to help those she had known from her theater days by suggesting them for small roles. John Emery, who had worked with Vivian in *Skylark*, appeared as a tramp in "The Quiz Show" and the grumpy neighbor in "Little Ricky Gets a Dog." In "New Neighbors," K.T. Stevens, who had co-starred with Vivian in *Voice of the Turtle*, played an actress mistaken for an international spy. Edith Meiser, who sang alongside Vivian in *Let's Face It!*, played Mrs. Littlefield in "Lucy's Schedule" and "Ricky

Asks for a Raise." Longtime friend Adele Longmire is the admissions nurse in "Lucy Goes to the Hospital." Though his career had taken off and he may not have needed Vivian's help in securing a job, Sheldon Leonard, who had a small role with her in *Burlesque*, appeared as the Handy-Dandy product salesman in "Sales Resistance."

As the show progressed, the writers wrote more for Ethel to do. Vivian, who had little experience with physical comedy, at first shied away from attempting anything risky. Ball, however, made it a point to introduce new gags. Never one to be outdone, Vivian decided to try anything once as long as Ball did it first. Sometimes this led to problems because Vivian refused to acknowledge any discomfort. For example, while rehearsing for the episode "Men Are Messy," she had to stand perfectly still, waiting for her cue to speak while hanging on a clothesline completely zipped inside a dress. As she waited, the director called "cut" and started a discussion on the set. After several minutes, Vivian passed out inside the dress waiting for someone to release her.

I Love Lucy still has the impact today that it had in the fifties. Although we are now all familiar with it and have our favorite episodes, it still elicits spontaneous laughter. Many have written about Lucille Ball's contributions and talent but few have mentioned the impact that Vivian had on comedy, television, and *I Love Lucy*.

"You believed every word that came out of her mouth," Lucie Arnaz says. "She wasn't doing schtick. Her reactions were honest and she knew how to listen."

Jay Sandrich, who began his career on *I Love Lucy* as second assistant director and went on to direct such hit shows as *The Mary Tyler Moore Show, Soap, Golden Girls,* and *The Cosby Show,* believes that "Vivian was, if there is such a thing, a method comedian. Everything was thought through, read carefully, and studied. Nothing was left to chance in her performance. She took comedy very seriously."

Unlike Lucille Ball, whose mastery in comedy lay in her physicality, Vivian's artistry rested in her line delivery and the way she elicited a laugh with a mere gesture or expression. Director Herbert Kenwith asserts that "Vivian was a real artist. You could give her basic direction and she'd have the imagination to broaden it. She made any director look good. Lucy's comedy was broad, Vivian's comedy was subtle and pulled back, but she knew how to extract whatever humor, or physical comedy from it."

There are many priceless moments in *I Love Lucy* that underscore Vivian Vance's brilliance as a comedienne. In "Pioneer Women," after churning cream for two hours, Ethel produces a plate with just a pat of butter. She dryly notes, "Our grandmothers must have had arms like Gorgeous George. All this butter and it only cost twenty-three dollars and seventy-five cents."

In "The Seance," playing Medium Raya, Vivian calls on the spirit world as if paging someone on a loudspeaker: "Ethel to Tillie, Ethel to Tillie, come in Tillie."

And Ethel and Lucy have this great exchange when they have their first fight in "Break the Lease":

Lucy: You mean that one-sided binding contract that you forced us to sign before giving us the privilege to move into this broken-down hovel?
Ethel: Broken down is right! It'll take the next five months' rent to redecorate.
Lucy: Redecorate!?
Ethel: Yes! After we fumigate!

In "The Operetta," a Wednesday Afternoon Fine Arts League fund-raiser finds Ethel singing "Lily of the Valley."

*Lucy Ricardo and Ethel Mertz end up in tears
in the episode "Vacation from Marriage."*

Vivian hadn't sung for years after her breakdown, and until the actual shooting of the show, she didn't quite believe she could do it. But this episode was the last for Marc Daniels as director of *I Love Lucy* and she may have felt more confidence with her friend at the helm. Still, Vivian was very concerned and talked about it with Irma Kusely. "Vivian held back on her singing because she wanted to present her voice right. She didn't have the confidence to sing at this time," Irma said. Nevertheless, she delivered a hilarious rendition of "Lily of the Valley" complete with a bluesy, torchy ending reminiscent of her nightclub singing days.

In the episode "Changing the Boys' Wardrobe," Lucy, while on the phone with Ricky (who along with Fred have asked their wives out for dinner and dancing), turns and asks Ethel if she'd like to go out with the boys. Not knowing who's on the phone with Lucy, Ethel responds excitedly, "YES!! . . . What boys?" The director wanted Vivian to deliver the line sarcastically, as written: "What boys?" But her addition of the "Yes!" with a pause before the next line guaranteed she would bring the house down.

"Whenever Lucy was doing a comic stunt, we'd pan the camera to Vivian and she always had a look of horror or astonishment that made it twice as funny," writer Madelyn Pugh Davis said. The expression on Vivian's face as she attempts to keep Ricky from noticing Lucy dangling from Cornel Wilde's balcony in "The Star Upstairs" is a perfect example. "Vivian made it funnier with her reactions. When she [saw] Lucy go by on the balcony, her reactions were a marvel," Davis said.

When Fred accepts Lucy's offer to buy Ethel a birthday present on his behalf, the two women share this exchange in "Ethel's Birthday" after Ethel finds the gift in her closet:

Ethel: I wanted a toaster!
Lucy: Well, Fred told me, but I couldn't believe you
could be that dull!
Ethel: Well, I'd look better wearing a toaster than I
would those checkerboard britches!

The longest laugh ever recorded on an *I Love Lucy*
episode, sixty-five seconds, occurred during the taping of
"Lucy Does the Tango." Writer Bob Carroll credits the
success of the scene to Vivian's reaction. "Viv had all that
presence. When Lucy does the tango with three dozen eggs
in her blouse, Viv's face tells you that someone is doing
the tango with three dozen eggs in her blouse—'My God,
she's not really going to do that, is she? Uh-oh!' You
watch her face. She was magnificent."

These "Ethel moments" are as priceless as any of
Lucy's. However, the viewer registers a physical action
more quickly than spoken words. Jay Sandrich agrees,
adding that "There's never been a physical comedy like *I
Love Lucy*. Vivian could do physical comedy too, obviously. If she hadn't been standing next to Lucille Ball, she
would have been considered a great physical comic."

The focus of the show, as written, centers around the
character of Lucy, and at first all eyes are glued on her.
However, the benefit of re-runs gives the viewer a second
chance (or thousands of chances) to appreciate the contributions of the other players. The character of Lucy Ricardo
was obviously the force which propelled *I Love Lucy* but
Ethel Mertz was a more-than-competent copilot, serving as
Lucy's confidante, gofer, lookout, and adviser as well as
instigator.

The older and wiser Ethel shared the ways and rules of
marriage with the younger, more inexperienced Lucy
Ricardo. Often, this well-meaning advice planted a strange

seed in the overactive mind of Lucy Ricardo, causing a conflict with Ricky. Ethel Mertz, on the other hand, always responded to her own Fred's teasing with strength or humor, never allowing it to diminish her affection for him. She was settled into her married life, and accepted all aspects of it, whether good or bad. Though she went along with Lucy Ricardo's schemes to "teach the boys a lesson," or "prove women deserve equal rights," she would also attack Lucy for getting her into another mess when things didn't go as planned.

For the most part, Ethel was a poor church mouse, never turning down second-hand furniture, hand-me-down clothing, or outings paid for by the Ricardos. Ethel finds herself in this predicament because of her penny-pinching husband who hoards his money and refuses to spend it. So instead of feeling sorry for Ethel, the viewer empathizes with her while admiring her control and endurance. Vivian played the role with total conviction and without judgment, even though, as Sandrich notes, "She was the opposite of the scatterbrained Ethel."

Vivian fought to develop Mrs. Mertz as a multi-dimensional character despite the limitations placed on her. "At first it was quite a struggle to keep Ethel as I saw her and have her character grow as I wanted it to," Vivian said. "There were times on the set when I yelled loud enough to be a credit to Mama. Marc (Daniels) had a method for handling those blow-ups. 'Your Yo-Yo string is tangled,' he'd tell me."

No one could deny Vivian's perseverance. This persistence stemmed from her years of training and developing her craft in the theater. This training produced an actress whose goal was to give a convincing and truthful performance despite any physical or mental discomfort. For example, in shooting "Lucy Goes to Scotland," Vivian had a musical number to do in which she shared the costume of a dragon with Bill Frawley. She despised the idea of being wrapped arm in arm with a man she hated while they were enclosed in a rubber suit. She feared that Frawley, known for having flatulence, would at some point break wind. Yet Vivian went on with the scene as written, keeping those concerns to herself.

In "The Housewarming," one scene required Vivian to down a couple of Lucy's sandwiches. The director, Jim Kern, kept interrupting with cuts. By the third take, Vivian had eaten well over six samplings and was beginning to feel a bit queasy. On the final take, she picked up one of the remaining sandwiches and flung it directly at Kern.

It's also in this particular episode that Vivian delivers one of her most famous ad-libs. "Lucy has a new friend that she's paying lots of attention to," Bob Schiller explained. "Ethel's nose is out of joint. Vivian came up with a perfect line to show just how unhappy Ethel was. When Lucy offers her a sandwich she glares at Lucy and says, 'I have sufficient!' She said it in rehearsal and we kept it in. It became my favorite line."

The writers often borrowed situations from the actors' real life experiences and incorporated them into their scripts. For example, Desi Arnaz's first Broadway show was *Too Many Girls*. So was Ricky Ricardo's. And Lucille Ball and Lucy Ricardo shared the same hometown of Jamestown, New York, and attended the same high school in Celeron, New York. To help the cast remember the names of unseen characters, the actors sometimes used the names of family and friends. In the episodes "Lucy and Ethel Buy the Same Dress," "The Fashion Show," and "The Club Dance," Vivian refers to her friend from New York, Jane Sebastian. When asking about a mutual friend from vaudeville in "Mertz and Kurtz," Vivian uses her sister's name in the line, "Whatever happened to Venus

Jones?" In "The Girls Go into Business," Vivian's brother-in-law's name, Ralph Bowyer, is given to the man who buys the dress shop from the girls at the end of the episode. Vivian borrowed Jimmy O'Connor's name—he was from the Albuquerque Little Theatre—for an old vaudeville pal of Ethel and Fred's who gives them parts in a movie in "Lucy Gets into Pictures."

Perhaps this practice explains why Ethel Mertz had three middle names. When Bill Frawley calls Ethel by her full name in "Lucy and Ethel Buy the Same Dress," he

Vivian and Lucy dressed up for "Little Ricky's School Pageant."

calls her "Ethel Louise Mertz." This was a pointed reference to his estranged wife, Louise, whom Frawley loathed as much as her television counterpart. In "The Million Dollar Idea," Lucy uses Vivian's real middle name when she calls her "Ethel Roberta." And in "Ethel's Hometown," the famous banner proclaims "Ethel Mae Potter We Never Forgot Her" in an obvious nod to Vivian's mother, Mae. Also in this episode, her sister Venus's husband, Hank Speer, is referred to in Ethel's list of her old flames.

Like many other working and personal friendships, the relationship between Vivian Vance and Lucille Ball had its ups and downs. Clearly the star of the show cared little for Vivian when they first met. Ball had an impersonal way of dealing with people and often tested the capabilities of those who worked for her. However, once Lucy saw that Vivian's commitment to her craft and her work ethics ran parallel to her own, she slowly warmed up to her.

Director William Asher attests to Lucy's scrutiny. "I was called in when Marc Daniels left the show because of a conflict with Lucille Ball. Lucy was always directing from behind the scenes. She had a habit of pretending not to know what she was doing. This was [a test] to make sure the director knew what he was doing. Vivian was aware of this, and was wonderful about it. I never had any conflict with her. Since I was the youngest one there, at age twenty-four, Vivian would often say, 'Let's help the kid out.'"

Vivian's youngest sister, Lou Ann, says that Vivian had a soothing affect on Lucille who, despite her callousness, allowed her supporting player a familiarity impossible for others. "Vivian was in charge of almost all her relationships except with Lucy. But she did know how to placate and get along with her."

On the set, Lucy grew more dependent on Vivian as a friend and as a sidekick and always considered her opinions before making decisions. Vivian's sister Lou Ann believes that a dependent, complex, and sometimes one-sided relationship developed out of Lucy's need for friendship and support. "Unfortunately, Lucy loved Viv a lot more than Viv loved her. Viv didn't necessarily love her, she admired her. She felt that Lucy was too hard, but never crossed her about it. Rarely did Vivian look to Lucille for advice."

Vivian later explained the intricate relationship shared by the two women. "She and I were just like sisters. We fought like sisters and made up the same way. We shared a rare sense of balance, Lucille and I, much like the instinct of a diver who judges precisely the right moment to leave the springboard. I was sure that if she and I got up from sitting side by side on a sofa and went our different ways to walk around the block, we'd arrive back in the room at the same second. We could take off together, singing or dancing, matching the notes and the steps without having to think about it."

Lucille Ball was the controlling force in most areas of their relationship but Vivian was the glue that held things together. Maury Thompson believes that "Vivian was the balancing wheel. She'd have Lucille laughing just a few minutes after some explosion. But not in the area where Desi and his drinking problem was concerned." At those times Vivian would back right off, knowing that was one line even she could not cross.

Arnaz had taken to drinking daily to relieve the stress brought on by his rapidly growing empire. In later episodes, his bloated face clearly shows the signs of years of alcohol abuse. Vivian liked Arnaz tremendously and felt indebted to him for having stood by her and believing in her talent from the onset. Unlike others who never bypassed an opportunity to criticize Arnaz, Irma Kusely testifies that Vivian never passed any judgment on her

boss. "Vivian really loved Desi. She respected his talents
and input on everything. She often resented it when Lucy
gave him a hard time." Vivian once told actress Kaye Ballard as she was getting ready to work on *The Mothers-in-
Law,* a show produced by Arnaz, "You are going to work
for the most tasteful gentleman in show business."

Over the course of the show, Vivian began to realize
that the opportunity to achieve the kind of stardom she had
dreamed of throughout her career had passed. No matter
how much money she made or fame she achieved, she had
no choice but to accept that her position would always be
that of second banana to Lucille Ball. This created an ani-
mosity which Vivian rarely spoke about but one which she
harbored throughout the years of her alliance with Lucy.
As friend Dorothy Konrad remarked, "As a fellow actor
she couldn't help it. You always resent the lead."

To cover up her disappointment, Vivian had a stock
answer to the question "What does it feel like to be a second banana?" Her response was that she had never wanted
to be a star. Vivian's friend from her Broadway days, Marjorie Lord, never believed that answer. "Vivian really
desired to be a major star and I think she did become a star.
But I don't know whether she became the star she wanted
to be."

Even though Ethel Mertz was the second banana, the
audience expected her character to appear every week and
Maury Thompson, for one, believes that Vivian thor-
oughly enjoyed her performances. "Viv would come into
the studio the next day after the shows aired and say, 'Did
you see how funny I was?' Lucille would sit there, staring
at Vivian in disbelief, thinking, 'What in the hell is the
matter with her?' Yes, she was funny, but it was Lucille
bouncing off her and she bouncing off Lucille that made it
funny. But Vivian had to be admired because Lucille was

so hard. Working with her so closely, reacting on camera and never being allowed to make mistakes, not ever. We had very few retakes."

Though Vivian had the freedom to voice her opinion, she still could not cross certain boundaries set by Lucille. This power annoyed Vivian who yearned for control. Lucy agreed that both women shared incredible strengths and weaknesses and both were extremely stubborn. Lucy remembers:

> Occasionally our tempers grew short. One day Vivian and I had a disagreement on the set and stopped speaking. The silence went much longer than either of us anticipated. It got to be a nuisance, since we were so used to listening carefully to each other's lines and making suggestions. But this particular Thursday we spent in stony silence. Finally, it was only an hour before the actual performance. We usually spent this time buoying each other up to get into the proper relaxed and joyous mood for performing. We sat side by side, putting on our makeup. Although not a word had been spoken, I suddenly blurted out, "Vivian, you know that line"—I repeated it—"You're not reading it right. It should be. . . " and gave her my interpretation. "Well, why the hell didn't you tell me before?" "Well," I replied heatedly, "we weren't speaking, and I'd be damned if I'd tell you!" Our eyes met in the mirror and we collapsed in laughter. We could never stay cross with each other for very long.

It was clearly a challenge to maintain a balanced relationship with Lucille Ball but Vivian found a way to do it. By the end of the show's first season, Vivian had earned the trust and respect of its star while proving herself an asset to *I Love Lucy*. Still, it took years to learn how to maintain that delicate balance and to develop a tolerance for the eccentricities of the comic genius.

Vivian had a difficult time understanding the impact the show had on its audience. It annoyed her when people associated her so closely with the character of Ethel Mertz. Everyone got caught up in the make-believe, including her father, who once asked her "Why don't you use your own name on the show? Fred Mertz does!" For Vivian, Mrs. Mertz was just another mask which she put on and took off at will. But the public's fusing of Ethel and Vivian made her ongoing personal search to find the true identity of Vivian Roberta Jones even more difficult. It isn't surprising, therefore, that Vivian detested people calling her Ethel.

Maury Thompson remembers, however, that the perks of her success elevated Vivian's spirits, especially when making public appearances. "Viv would say, 'See, we really are as famous as movie stars.' " Lucille Ball, who had lived in Hollywood most of her life, felt that the likes of Carole Lombard or Ginger Rogers deserved the title of star. She considered herself a working woman and seemed uncomfortable with self-praise.

Ball taught Vivian the etiquette to follow when making public appearances. "Lucille taught me to dress when we went places," Vivian said. "I'd been kind of casual up to these times. She insisted on how important it was to make an entrance and look like a star at a press conference, even if you didn't feel like one. The furs and the eyelashes always helped. I couldn't fool everybody, though. One woman along the way said to me, 'Why, you aren't bad looking. You look so homely on television.' Great, that word homely. People like that make you feel you're working for a worthy cause."

Irma Kusely still marvels at the memories of hundreds of people welcoming their favorite foursome. "We trav-

At the Arnaz home Vivian takes the time to read a story to Lucie and Desi Jr.

eled on the same train as the President had. The reception [for the cast] was the same [as his] wherever we went."

Something inevitably happened to make each trip by the cast of *I Love Lucy* even more memorable than the last. On a particular junket, Irma recounts that as the train pulled into a small town, Vivian noticed a quilt hanging from a clothesline. "I must have it," she told Irma. When the train pulled into the station, Vivian took a cab and drove to the house. Through a screen door, Vivian noticed a woman ironing and watching an episode of *I Love Lucy*. When Vivian knocked, the woman opened the screen, did a double-take of Vivian and the television set, and nearly fainted.

Vivian's niece, Vivian Wilkison, thinks it ironic that some members of Vivian's family living in the small towns of New Mexico hardly knew of the show's popularity. "The interesting thing was that for nearly the entire 1950s, when *I Love Lucy* was number one, we had no idea," Wilkison said. "We didn't have a television because there was no television reception in Carlsbad. The only time we ever saw it was when Vivian would send us some films in cans and my uncle would bring the projector, and we'd look at them on our living room wall."

In Albuquerque, everyone basked in the success of their favorite daughter, including Mae, even though she seldom voiced her pride to Vivian. "Mama still couldn't bring herself to admit that maybe it hadn't been such a bad idea for me to become an actress," Vivian said. "Not a word of approval came from her direct. It was left to my sisters to say, 'Oh, she brags about how she gave you all those lessons.' The Ragans on the whole preferred to believe that what I was up to was the devil's work. One aunt told me so in a letter which stirred a memory of the days when cousins weren't allowed to play with me."

Vivian's success led to a truce between her and Mae but it did not resolve any of their differences. Vivian eventually accepted this compromise with one of the important people in her life. But her relationship with her husband Phil was another story.

Phil saw his wife's achievements as his own demise in the business. Though their union had had some problems in the past, it now took a turn for the worse. But Vivian would not give up. In order to try and reconcile their differences, Vivian suggested to Phil that she give up her career and dedicate her time to their marriage. Phil did not think it was a good idea.

Members of Vivian's family remember Phil's outgoing and pleasant personality. Dorothy saw Phil as a big brother who loved her sister very much and liked spending his time with her. Vivian Wilkison agrees with her mother, adding that "Phil was a lot of fun. He was always so sweet to me and my sister. There is nothing derogatory I could say about him."

On the other hand, those who worked with Vivian saw Phil as pompous and controlling, including makeup coordinator Hal King who adamantly states that "No one really cared for Phil. But Vivian never liked to discuss her problems. She'd say, 'Why should I bore my friends when they have problems of their own.'"

In public, Vivian and Phil never spoke disparagingly of each other but everyone felt something brewing. Helene and Edward Lobherr, who for years lived next door to the Obers, agree that "all through the years of the *I Love Lucy* show, when Vivian came home from work, Phil would have a candlelit dinner waiting for her. However, he [began] to resent the fact that he had become a househusband. Somehow the roles had reversed."

Vivian's career reached its peak while she was contending with these personal problems. Estimates show that well over ten million sets across the country tuned in to *I Love Lucy* weekly with approximately three viewers per set relishing the antics of the Ricardos and the Mertzes. As *I Love Lucy* solidified its place as the number one show of the decade, invitations poured in for its stars to make special appearances. Along with other entertainers, the Ricardos and Mertzes performed for President Eisenhower at the fortieth anniversary celebration of the Anti-Defamation League. Frawley and Vivian reprised their number from the episode "Ricky Loses His Voice" where they sing "Nothing Could Be Finer Than to Be in Carolina in the Morning." While backstage, Vivian stood alongside Ethel Merman as the star of *Annie Get Your Gun* waited to go on. Vivian recalled the days when she had understudied Merman in *Anything Goes!* and *Red, Hot and Blue!* At one point, Vivian leaned over and whispered in Merman's ear, "This is the first time I've ever stood with you in the wings and didn't pray you'd drop dead." Merman roared with laughter.

Vivian rode the crest of her success by appearing on *Shower of Stars, The Milton Berle Show,* and *The Ed Sullivan Show,* as well as planning shows at the Albuquerque Little Theatre. In 1957, the Pacific Palisades Chamber of Commerce bestowed on Vivian the title of Honorary Mayor. For a time, rumors circulated that Vivian would play opposite Rosalind Russell in the movie version of *Auntie Mame.* Much to Vivian's disappointment, the deal fell through because of scheduling problems. Several commercials also came her way, including one for Schaeffer pens where she reenacted her Ethel character.

In 1958, the *Los Angeles Times* named Lucille Ball Woman of the Year. As Maury Thompson remembers it, Lucy invited Vivian to attend the ceremony. "Lucy begged Viv to go with her. Vivian said, 'No! I hate those kind of things.' Lucy told her, 'So do I. But come and sit with me. I can't sit there and talk to all those people I don't know.' So Viv went along. It got to a question and answer period and a lady asked, 'Miss Ball, do you and Vivian get along?'

"Lucy said, 'Oh yes.'

" 'Do you quarrel?'

" 'Oh, once in awhile.'

" 'Well, do you fight?'

" 'No, we never fight.' At this point Lucy asked Viv, 'Viv, what is it that we do?'

"Vivian said, 'Fight!'

"It just brought the house down. Lucy said, 'See—she always just tops me.' "

In order to maintain the show's momentum, the writers used different locales to involve the Ricardos and the Mertzes in new situations. Using the success of Ricky's career as the basis, the writers cleverly transplanted the foursome from the confines of their New York apartments to California, Europe, and Florida before moving them to the suburbs of Connecticut.

Vivian, Lucy, and Desi in "The Ricardos Go to Japan" from one of the episodes of The Lucy-Desi Comedy Hour

In May 1957, the last of the half-hour *I Love Lucy* episodes was filmed. After their seven-year contracts with CBS expired, Lucy and Desi contemplated retirement to try and rekindle their marriage. But they were at the height of their success and had numerous projects in development so both soon realized that retirement was not an option. However, Arnaz did not want to continue doing the half-hour shows, so in 1957 an hour-long format was put together. Thirteen episodes of *The Lucy-Desi Comedy Hour* were filmed from 1957–1960.

Vivian struggled over her decision to remain with the show. She finally signed on but only after her agent successfully negotiated with Desilu that she'd be able to wear better costumes. Still, one can easily spot her wearing the same bathrobe she had worn on the first episode of *I Love Lucy*.

Years later, Vivian fondly recalled particular moments she shared with the many celebrities who appeared on the half-hour and hour episodes. "I behaved like a schoolgirl movie fan, pinching myself to make sure I really was on a set with all these men whose names meant a special kind of magic. When Harpo Marx was a guest, I immediately added him to my list of silent loves. He had his harp standing by. We'd go off together during breaks, and he'd play for me the song he'd written. I'd sing along after I'd choked down the tears that came as his fingers started to weave over the strings."

Tallulah Bankhead guest-starred on one of the hour-long episodes. "I wanted her to be extra special because I knew her as the ex-wife of my great friend John Emery. I didn't know how I had the guts to do it, but I went to her dressing room for a heart-to-heart. 'Please, when you play you're the star next door, play the Tallulah Bankhead I saw on the stage years ago—not the lady who has become a caricature of herself. Go back and do it the way you did *Camille*.' She did just that and we saw a marvelous performance."

Others, however, tell a different story about Vivian and Tallulah. According to some, they despised the sight of each other. According to Desi and Lucy, the Broadway diva terrorized the set for a week, frequently using her way with the saltier parts of the English language to refer to Vivian. Nevertheless, once the taping ended, Tallulah gave Vivian a lovely Louis XIV chaise longue as a gift. This particular episode rated the highest of any of the hour-long episodes.

Desi considered it a coup when he booked his hero Maurice Chevalier on the show. But everyone's excitement, including Vivian's, dissipated once they met the French crooner. "Lucille and I fixed a meal that we hoped would be worthy of a Frenchman, and Maurice was pleased to join us," Vivian said. "We basked briefly in one Chevalier smile as we all sat down, and that was it. He had nothing to say. We started off on the small talk—he had none to offer. We dropped in a question or two—a polite, solemn 'Oh, yes' was the only response. He was as joyful as Napoleon's Tomb. It was only when the lights flooded the set and the cameras began to roll that he turned on his switch. Then out on the stage walked a personality that wiped you out."

When Vivian told Maury Thompson that *I Love Lucy* could catapult her career into the stratosphere, she had predicted correctly. But after almost nine years, everyone involved with the show itched for other adventures. Vivian had finally grown weary of donning that same tired terry cloth bathrobe. Many things had changed since that first rehearsal. Perhaps the most important for Vivian was the loss of her father on December 3, 1958. Vivian returned to Albuquerque to share in the loss with her fam-

Robert Jones and his daughters circa 1955.
From left to right: Dorothy, Vivian, Venus, Robert, Lou Ann,
and Mickey

ily. Because she had always thought burying bodies a barbaric ritual, she steered away from the funeral but spent time after the service with sisters and other family members recounting the joys of their father's life. The man who set the standards by which Vivian compared all the other men in her life had left her and nothing ever filled that void.

The death of Bob Jones gave Vivian an opportunity to resolve her differences with Mae, but instead Vivian drew further away. From that point on, she gave her mother everything she needed to live a comfortable life but felt neither love nor hate toward Mae, just indifference.

The building of the Desilu empire had not come without its share of difficulties for the Arnazes as well. The show which they started so that they could keep their marriage together ultimately caused the break-up of two couples. Though Lucy and Desi continued to try to salvage their marriage until 1960, the Obers had come to the end of their road. Lucille Ball later voiced her anger toward Phil. "God! That man! He was terrible. He used to beat her up. Loved to embarrass her. One day Viv came to work with a shiner. That did it. I think I said to her, 'If you don't divorce him, I will.' "

Knowing that he could control his wife at home, Phil would berate her with taunts. He'd tell Vivian that "People are talking about you and Lucy, you ought to be careful about the hugging and kissing you do on the show. You behave like a couple of dykes in heat." He'd often tell friends that Vivian had lost her mind and that he stayed with her out of pity. Everything she did irritated him. While Vivian cooked dinner one night, Phil walked into the kitchen and found her using a silver spoon given to them by his parents. "It made no difference to a peasant like me," Vivian said. "The moment he saw what I was doing, the spoon was gone from my hand. 'Don't use my mother's silver like that! You'll wear it out!' I had never been so angry in my life. 'You and your goddamned precious silverware! If that spoon hasn't worn out in a hundred years, I'm not going to wear it out stirring chicken-à-la-king!' The battle was on." Their fights escalated. One night Phil chased Vivian through the house wielding a knife. She found safety by running into the guest house and locking herself inside.

Friend Dorothy Konrad is convinced there was another major problem in the Obers' marriage—Vivian's relationship with Emily, Phil's daughter. "Vivian would not allow her to visit them. When Emily was going through a divorce and needed money, Vivian absolutely refused to give her any. 'That bastard,' she'd say. 'I'm not giving him my money for his daughter. She's not my child and I'm not giving her anything!' "

Phil could accept the restrictions of the "allowance" he

got from Vivian but he could not tolerate how it made him look before his daughter. "Phil loved Viv and was subservient to her," Konrad said. "But Viv wouldn't tolerate Emily. They had some of their biggest fights because of her."

Her sister Dorothy O'Neal feels that Phil and Viv could have worked it all out except for one incident—the day Vivian arrived home to find Phil in a compromising position with one of her closest friends. He packed his bags and left their home on Frontera Drive.

Instead of waiting for Vivian to make a move, Phil sued his wife for divorce on the grounds of extreme cruelty to protect his financial interests. This outraged Vivian, who could not believe that a man would ask for alimony from his wife. Hedda Hopper knew about the Obers' problems firsthand and rallied to Vivian's defense. Every morning she'd call Vivian on the telephone, asking, "What's the son of a bitch doing to you today?" Hopper advised her to get rid of her present attorney, who hadn't acted on his client's behalf, and engage one who would countersue Phil in order to protect her interest.

After Phil left, Vivian found it difficult to concentrate on her work. She knew firsthand the problems she'd face once the public found out about her divorce. Director and producer Herbert Kenwith, a close friend of Lucy's who had also worked with Vivian years earlier, was spending a great deal of time on the set then. "I suspected she had mental problems after Phil left because there were strange moments. I remember she was sitting in one of those director's chairs, I was talking to her and she really didn't see me. It's like her mind totally shifted away from me. She had a lot of distractions after Phil. Her lines were never always there and she was brilliant about lines, but she started to falter."

Irma Kusely agrees, adding, "On the set she was very

depressed and unhappy, but you get her in front of the camera and ka-boom!"

Vivian later wrote of that period, "The second banana on those comedy hours cried a lot at the end of the day. Looking back at the shows made during that period, it's astonishing to see what grief and heartbreak can do to one's face. I looked twenty years older at that time, with telltale marks of sorrow around the eyes and mouth. Yet at the studio, the other side of life continued."

On April 24, 1959, Vivian entered a courtroom to get her divorce looking tired and worn but, at her friends' urging, dressed to the nines complete with white gloves. Phil did not show up for the proceedings. Testifying before Judge Burnett Wolfson, Vivian explained that she had wanted to give up her career in order to save her marriage. Her husband, however, did not want her to stop working out of fear of being unable to live the high life. Vivian covered her face with her hands and wept as the judge approved the divorce, citing cruelty on Phil's part and adding, "Damon Runyon used to say that they never had to hold a benefit for a man who saved his money. Mr. Ober might well hark those words." The judge went on to say, "If there ever was an illustration of a man who killed the goose who laid the golden egg, this is one. I ask myself, 'How stupid can a man be?' " Judge Wolfson then asked Vivian if the settlement giving Ober half of their $160,000 in community property pleased her. Vivian replied, "No sir, I think the terms are pretty liberal. After all, I made and saved all this money."

Vivian and Phil had truly loved each other and had it not been for her success on *I Love Lucy*, their relationship might have endured. He stood by her through her nervous breakdown, years of analysis, and the trauma of a failed pregnancy early in their marriage. Yet money, success, and professional jealousy caused mutual disdain. From this point on, whenever Vivian heard Phil's name mentioned, she spewed venom. "Vivian used to call Phil Medusa," recalls Konrad. "She'd say, 'He could charm the birds right out of the trees, but he was a son-of-a-bitch underneath.' "

Lucy, meanwhile, tried in vain to keep her own marriage from breaking up. The two women looked to each other for guidance during this difficult period. Viewers of the hour-long episodes can see that the women's faces show evidence of emotional distress. Vivian had problems having her eyes made up to conceal the fact that she'd spent hours crying. William Asher noted that when "Lucy and Desi were having problems of their own, Vivian and Lucy grew very, very close—like two schoolgirls who grew up together—both professionally and personally. When Lucy had her problems, Viv was consoling her so much that I don't know when Lucy had the chance to console Viv on her divorce."

The last episode of the *Lucy-Desi Comedy Hour* was called "The Redhead Meets the Mustache" and guest-starred Ernie Kovacs. It was truly the end of an era and it brought simultaneous feelings of relief and sadness. Along with her own divorce, Vivian recalled the break-up of America's favorite couple and the end of their successful show. "Those were emotional days for everyone on the show. After their [Lucy's and Desi's] last show together, a lot of us just stood there and cried. The reason we were so involved with the split was because we all shared a bond— the cast and the crew were right out of *Our Town*. We had a tight little circle and knew all about the fortunes and misfortunes of everyone's lives. It was like living in a small town and sharing every emotion."

Everyone who worked on *I Love Lucy* knew that the experience could never be repeated. They had had a once-in-a-lifetime opportunity to introduce and develop the blueprint for future situation comedies.

I Love Lucy gave Vivian fame, riches, and recognition. Once it came to an end, she realized that at fifty-one, she had reached another crossroads in life. "*I Love Lucy* provided me with a backbone. Working with Lucille, living side-by-side with her, seeing all the strength she had, all this was good and healthy. I could take another look at the remark I'd listened to so often at home, 'It's neurotic to stick up for oneself.' That made no sense any longer. It was one thing to choose not to fight until the time arrived when fighting was the only reasonable response to a situation. It was another when you couldn't strike back because you were afraid to give vent to your temper. The truth was directly opposite to what had been hammered into me. It was neurotic not to stand up for yourself. The new woman that the analyst had forecast might emerge was coming into her own, and the difference was scarcely to be believed."

Vivian and John Dodds on their wedding day

Chapter Eight

"I'm Not Ethel Mertz! My Name Is Vivian Vance!"

❧

When the Ricardos of *I Love Lucy* moved to Connecticut, Desi Arnaz saw an opportunity to develop a spin-off series based on the Mertzes. Nowadays spin-offs are common practice but before 1959, they were rare. Given Desilu's success developing new shows, Arnaz was convinced he would have no problem selling his idea to the network. He figured the writers could easily introduce other characters in *I Love Lucy* while constructing a new premise for Fred and Ethel who would continue living in their New York apartment building.

Arnaz took it for granted that Vivian would also be sold on the project but when he approached her with his good news, she flatly refused. "I could be pushed into a lot of things, but the point could be reached when I dug in my heels like a mule," she said.

Convinced that the Mertz series would skyrocket to number one, Desi, who had built an empire on instinct, tried a different approach. When the time came for Vivian to negotiate her new contract, Arnaz asked her to come up with a figure as an incentive to sign. She told him that she wanted $50,000. When Desi wondered how she came up with that amount she responded, "It kind of makes up for the four-fifty I was paid the first couple of years." Arnaz agreed, but told her that he would only approve the figure if she filmed the Mertz pilot with Bill. Again she refused. "No money in the world could persuade me to do a series with Mr. Frawley," she said.

Just the idea of working side by side with Frawley day in and day out made Vivian fear she would have another breakdown from which she would never recover. And she also believed that the Mertzes didn't have a chance going at it solo. They needed the Ricardos to bounce off of. She reminded Desi that most, if not all, of her truly funny moments involved scenes with Lucy, not Bill. Arnaz finally abandoned the idea. When Bill found out that Vivian refused to work with him, he never spoke to her again except to exchange lines on the set. He never forgave her. Had the show been a success, it would have made him a very rich man.

For some time, Vivian had had her eye on another project that she hoped Desi would develop for her. *Guestward Ho!* was a successful novel written by Patrick Dennis and Barbara Hooton. The book is an account of the adventures of Barbara Hooton and her husband Bill after moving from New York to run a dude ranch in rural New Mexico. Desi agreed to do a pilot if they could secure the rights. Vivian went to Santa Fe to speak with Barbara about acquiring them only to discover that CBS had already bought the rights in the fall of 1957 for a *Playhouse Ninety* presentation. The time Vivian spent with the Hootons was not a waste, however. They remained close friends of hers for nearly twenty years.

CBS did not develop the show and when the rights expired, Desilu bought them for Vivian. This was before her divorce from Phil Ober and he thought himself a perfect candidate for the part of the husband. Told by friends that "she [Vivian] is famous enough and big enough, that if she'd ask for you, they'd take you," Phil demanded that Vivian persuade Desi to cast him as Bill Hooton.

The role of the transplanted New Yorker would have suited Ober but Arnaz would not consider him and no amount of pleading from Vivian could convince him otherwise. Robert Osborne, who played the role of the hotel clerk in the pilot, also doubled as reader during screen tests for the role of the husband. "I did a lot of tests where they were trying to find a husband for Vivian. Maybe eight or ten scenes. I remember Leif Erickson and Hugh Marlowe. They were trying to match her up to see who she looked good with and who she had rapport with." The part went to Leif Erickson.

Since the public had known Vivian only as Ethel Mertz, no one involved in the making of the pilot thought that the viewers would believe her in a completely different role. And writers, who had become accustomed to her status as second banana to Lucy for nearly a decade, had doubts that Vivian could carry a show on her own.

Bob Weiskopf and Bob Schiller, commissioned to write the pilot, agreed. "We weren't sure whether we could sell her as a star." When they voiced their opinion to Martin Leeds, he replied, "not to worry about it and to leave it to me."

Ralph Levy, who directed the pilot, found Vivian's behavior peculiar on the first day of filming. "During the first take of the pilot I said 'action' and she did absolutely nothing. All of a sudden she collapsed laughing. I didn't

Still photographs take of Vivian and cast in the pilot episode of
Guestward Ho!

Guestward Ho!

Guestward Ho!

know what was wrong, so I asked if she wanted a doctor. Her reply was, 'This is the first time that I ever felt my light.' " Others have interpreted this remark as Vivian's inability to go it alone, that she felt lost without Lucy. Levy, however, interprets it differently. "She laughed and kidded that it was the first time in years that she was receiving any attention since Lucille Ball had always been the center of it."

Lucille Ball's biographer Tom Watson says that "Everyone who saw the pilot said, 'I kept waiting for Lucy to walk in.' It was too unusual to see Vivian in a sitcom without Lucy."

The pilot did not sell. Leeds explains that "Desi wanted to do something special for Vivian with *Guestward Ho!* There were several things wrong with it. He wanted Ralph Levy to direct it. Ralph was a very fine 'specials' director but this was not his kettle of fish. It was a bad show. To my knowledge, after *Guestward Ho!* Vivian knew it wasn't going to work. She may have known where she was in the hierarchy of good to great actresses, which in my opinion is what she was. Vivian's reactions and timing were excellent, right on the line, but she was a reactor. She was the best goddamned reactor I've ever seen since I've been in this business."

CBS dropped their option for the show in early June and on June 16, Leeds sold a remake of the series to ABC starring a younger actress, Joanne Dru. The revamped show premiered in 1960 but lasted only one season. Weiskopf and Schiller recall that Martin Leeds conceded their point—he couldn't sell Vivian as a star.

Unable to shed the character she'd played for nine years, Vivian became the first major casualty of a television sitcom. Many other actors have since faced the same problem. Some have faded away while others, fearing permanent unemployment, have accepted playing varia-

tions of their characters on different shows. Vivian, however, refused to give in and accept another version of Ethel
even while offers kept pouring in, many for parts resem-
bling that very character.

"She turned down a lot of parts after Lucy because she
didn't want to be thought of as a frump. She really wanted
to be glamorous—not Ethel," says her friend Pat Colby. If
everyone involved had believed in Vivian's capabilities
and had given her more time to develop a "persona sans
Lucy," Vivian could have carried a show on her own. The
network's refusal to allow her to continue with *Guestward
Ho!* did little for her self-esteem.

Between 1959–1961 she did a few stints on variety,
game, and talk shows. She appeared on *The Arthur Murray
Party, I've Got a Secret, The Jack Paar Show, The Red
Skelton Show* and made the first of several appearances on
Candid Camera. In a two-season western called *The
Deputy,* she guest-starred opposite Henry Fonda. There
was one offer for a series which Vivian did consider, but it
didn't pan out. In it, she would have starred opposite
another great comedian, Jackie Gleason.

Vivian's psychiatrist now felt his client could begin facing her problems without his help and he gave her a final
piece of advice. He recommended that she go back to the
theater to shed her Ethel Mertz identity and prove that she
could carry a show on her own. This presented Vivian with
a new set of problems. Dorothy Konrad explains Vivian's
reluctance. "She was very nervous, very insecure because
she hadn't been on stage for a long time."

Actually, Vivian had wet her feet in the theater a few
months earlier in *The Marriage-Go-Round,* a production
directed by John Emery and staged at the Royal Poinciana
Playhouse in Palm Beach, Florida. This short-lived experience, however, did not give her the confidence she needed
to star in a nationally advertised tour.

Before going back to work she decided to redo herself completely. The only cosmetic improvement she had allowed herself up to this point had been removable caps to camouflage her crooked front teeth. Whenever in public or on stage, she would pop them into her mouth. But now she underwent plastic surgery to adjust the crook of her nose and give her a face lift. She also went in for a new hairdo and began a strict diet that shaved years off of her appearance.

Her neighbor, Helene Lobherr, could not believe the transformation. "Vivian came to my door and when I opened it she was standing there with a bouquet of flowers. She had just had her surgery done and she looked fabulous. She looked much more relaxed."

Next, Vivian chose to tour in the part of Mary Hilliard in *Here Today* written by George Oppenheimer. She asked longtime friend John Emery to take on the role of Stanley Dale and he quickly accepted. They played authors whose work together extends beyond the literary field as they collaborate on drinking and cavorting with uninhibited joy. Billed as "a comedy of bad manners," the cast included Philip Terry, Dorothy Konrad, and Pat Colby.

On a personal level, Vivian had to contend with the loneliness of divorce. She missed having someone special in her life yet she rarely accepted invitations for dates. On those occasions when she had a function to attend, she'd ask close male friends to accompany her. For a brief time she dated writer Bob Schiller. Though still searching for a man on a white horse, Vivian feared making another mistake.

"I was looking for a husband through a fog of grief as thick as the smoke that once filled the theater for *Anna Christie*," she said, "and I was liable to pick another guy who was wrong for me."

While on tour, Vivian shared her concern over her lack of companionship with Dorothy Konrad. "Oh my God, this is terrible—here are two gals alone together. I haven't been without a man since I was sixteen."

Before going on the road, Vivian had approached Philip Terry, a charming, good-looking man who had been married to the actress Joan Crawford, with a proposition. "I'm taking you on as my leading man," she said, "but there is a prerequisite. I will expect some recompense. I'll have to have a man on the road, and I thought we could have a thing if you don't mind."

Terry told Vivian that he wouldn't sleep with her and would willingly give up the role in the play. Though wild with anger that Terry turned her down, she still allowed him to continue with the tour. After Terry's rejection, Vivian made it a point, while on the road, to meet with many of her old flames. However, they often left her disappointed because they had all grown older.

A young character actor in the company, Tom Toner, says that Vivian refused to let her television persona be used as publicity for the show. "Vivian stipulated to the producer-director, Mike Farrell, that any publicity should make no mention whatsoever of the name Ethel Mertz or *I Love Lucy*. Advance sales were nil, so Mike pleaded with her to allow him to cash in on her TV identity. She finally relented and we sold out." So Vivian's already bruised ego took another jab. This vehicle, meant to disassociate her from the dowdy character of Ethel Mertz, could only succeed by exploiting that very character's notoriety.

One reviewer wrote that "Miss Vance Labors but Lucy Lingers." Another wrote, "Miss Vance, struggling to overcome her close identification with the character of Ethel Mertz, is attractive and glib as the free-and-easy Mary. Her timing is superb, her clowning excellent. But, the character is too much like Ethel for her to really escape." Nevertheless, most critics agreed that "Vivian Vance knows the art of comedy," and "Miss Vance is a bouncy performer with a sure touch and an exuberance of style which makes her role as the hard-living, hard-drinking playwright credible."

Pat Colby and fellow cast members were frequently delighted to meet the many celebrities who dropped by backstage after the show to see Vivian. "She knew everybody, tons of celebrities and everybody loved her," Colby said. "We met Edward Everett Horton, June Havoc, Joan Fontaine, Joe E. Brown. I remember seeing her at the theater with Phil, before they divorced, and with them were Clark and Kay Gable. She was always so low-key about it."

In an attempt to make people see her as a new, improved, and elegant Vivian Vance, she'd raze anyone who mentioned Ethel Mertz. While playing the east coast, Vivian and some of the others in the cast entered an ice cream parlor. The owners approached Vivian and said, "Ethel, Ethel, you play such a beautiful part! Oh! we love you so much, you're so good, and your husband too."

Vivian's extreme reaction left Pat Colby and Dorothy Konrad speechless. "That finished it! She got furious when they mentioned Frawley," Konrad said. "She walked out and screamed, 'I'm leaving, I'm never coming back! Don't you dare ever call me that! I'm not Ethel Mertz! My name is Vivian Vance!' Those two people nearly cried."

Pat Colby and Dorothy Konrad left the parlor but then decided to return to the couple to say that Miss Vance didn't feel well and they would like to apologize on her behalf. The stunned fans sheepishly accepted the excuse. When they left, Colby and Konrad caught up with Vivian who was still rambling on. " 'That old son-of-a-bitch! That dirty old man!' she was saying. 'He was too old to play my husband, they should have cast someone younger to play opposite me!' "

Vivian began to drink heavily during the run of *Here Today*. Every night she would invite John Emery, Philip Terry, and Pat Colby to her suite for vodka martinis and "every night we would carry her to bed, passed out," recalls Colby. The amount of liquor the four consumed amazed Konrad, who did not participate in the binges. "They went through a case of vodka in a week and every night she'd end up in some dive, drunk."

Hoping to relive the good old days of singing in night clubs, Vivian often asked Konrad and the other cast members to accompany her to piano bars for singalongs. In one establishment in the Adirondacks "Vivian sang 'Love Is Wonderful the Second Time Around' while all the patrons were looking," Konrad said. "She had this kind of operatic quiver and we would just die sitting at the table wanting to hang our heads because she'd sing loud enough to be on a stage."

Every morning, Vivian would nurse her hangover and by showtime she'd give a polished performance. Konrad believes the drinking, however, affected her behavior toward her public. "In Detroit we shared a trailer together. Two middle-aged women came up after the show, knocked and asked for autographs. Vivian went to the door and without opening it yelled, 'Go away! Go away! Don't disturb me. Let me alone.' "

Two minutes later, the two women began throwing rocks at the trailer. It didn't faze Vivian but Konrad hid in a corner away from the window afraid that a rock would come through it. "Vivian never budged, she was very cruel in these situations," Konrad said. "She was living out all the venom she had in her."

Pat Colby didn't witness that particular episode but agrees that Vivian's irascible behavior resulted from her intense frustrations. "She was holding all that hatred all this time and just didn't know how to get rid of it. I think Vivian had a lot of soul. She had a lot of innate loving nature—but over the years [she] built up so many layers of defense. Sometimes she'd be that mean and shitty and other times she'd be absolutely wonderful—a mother and a best friend."

When the company took a break from the tour and returned to Los Angeles, Vivian received an invitation from Barbara and Bill Hooton to attend a gala event in Santa Fe. That weekend she flew to New Mexico, glad to have a break from the show. The Hootons paired her up for the evening with a man twelve years her junior named John Dodds. Vivian hoped that her date would have no connection with show business. After her experience with Phil, she came to believe that "no one should ever marry an actor. They look at themselves in the mirror before they say good morning."

Relieved to hear that John Dodds worked in publishing in San Francisco, Vivian took an immediate liking to the tall, dark-haired man. In Paige Matthews Peterson's opinion, "John was glamorous, handsome, sexy, gregarious, and brilliant. He was incredible. There was no one who lit up a room like him. I could completely understand why she fell in love with him."

That weekend, John swept Vivian off her feet. He made her feel young, vibrant, and beautiful. He also did what few others were able to do—he could make her laugh. Peterson believes that Vivian and John thrived on each other's humor and immediately bonded because of it. Peterson tells this story about their early courtship:

"The two had gone for a long drive. While riding in the car, John and Vivian had been kidding and laughing about something they had seen. John in mid-laughter passed gas and suddenly both were silent. To get him off the hook, Viv burst out in song 'Getting to know you . . . getting to know all about you.' "

According to Dorothy Konrad, the only obstacle in the way of their complete happiness was John's relationship with another man with whom he had shared a life and a home for close to twenty years. "He was very happy with his life and was not about to change," Konrad said. But this fact did not seem to bother Vivian who was determined to hook the handsome bachelor. Viv fell completely in love with him and he eventually fell for her. Still, Vivian had her doubts as to whether he could be faithful.

Born in Gray Eagle in northern California to cattle rancher G. Fullerton Dodds and his wife Theresa, John Dodds grew up in Feather River Canyon, a tiny farming community described by friend Corinne Wiley as "real redneck country." He had an artistic nature which confounded his family who had no tolerance for anyone different. While John attended Portola High School, an English professor and his wife took John under their wing and introduced him to literature and the arts. It infuriated John's father that his son preferred reading *The New Yorker* to learning about cattle ranching. Along with his older son, G. Fullerton Dodds taunted John and physically abused him in an attempt to change his behavior.

Once he graduated from high school, John had no intention of remaining on the farm. He escaped by running away from home and the torment of his father and brother. It took years before John mended his relationship with his family.

He put himself through the University of California at Berkeley and after graduating with a masters degree, he set his sights on writing. But a year in Paris did not produce the next great novel and he returned to the States disillusioned by his attempt. After working in a New York bookstore, he abandoned the idea of writing and went into publishing. He used his charms and good looks to slide into the upper echelon of society. John had not inherited his worldly savoir faire but acquired his sophistication by surrounding himself with people of power. As Corinne Wiley notes, "John was a star . . . well . . . let's just say he liked people that were important and gravitated to them."

When she got back on the road with *Here Today*, Vivian never stopped talking to Dorothy Konrad about John. "She chased John all over. She latched onto him and didn't let him alone. She hounded the blue blazes out of him. She loved him very much and wanted to marry him and nothing [else] mattered. One day she missed him so badly that she paid his airfare to meet her in the city where we were appearing."

The night before John's arrival, Vivian asked a bewildered Pat Colby "whether it was possible for a man to live with another man and then marry a woman and change." Colby responded with an emphatic "Never!" But Vivian set her sights on changing John's lifestyle, determined to put John in therapy and change him from a gay man to a heterosexual man.

After the tour ended, Vivian's obsession to rid herself of Ethel Mertz took a back seat. She decided, instead, to focus her energy on her new beau. The reception she received while on the road made her come to terms with the reality that the public could not separate Ethel from Vivian. She also accepted, albeit unwillingly, the fact that unless she embraced this notoriety, she might not have a career. Friend and colleague Walter Williamson notes that "Ethel Mertz seemed to be a sort of trap. It was so lucrative and so popular and such a defining role for her that she could not get away from it. It was not something she really wanted to do but she steeled herself and became very practical about it. It became a blessing and a curse because she could have done so much more in her career."

Pat Colby and Dorothy Konrad accepted Vivian's invitation to return with her and John Emery to her Pacific Palisades home. "I offered to drive her car cross-country from Boston to Los Angeles while Vivian flew home," Colby said. "Dorothy agreed to ride with me. Vivian gave me $100 to pay both of our expenses and told me to keep a list of everything I spent it on. She was so cheap with me but now I understand why. She was so pissed about Phil Ober. I never heard of Phil as the 'heavy' from anyone except Vivian and she was pissed off because of the money. I'm not surprised if Phil hit her. I would have hit her too. She had such a mouth. She had a way about her that she could just cut you, she could just dismiss you with words."

Although Vivian continued drinking, her personality changed dramatically once John entered her life. According to Konrad, she began to entice the man of her dreams to her side with presents, buying him "a real snazzy little sports car. They were living high on the hog. Vivian was spending money like mad. She bought him clothes and did a lot for him. My early experience with Vivian, I found her to be a bit cheap. I think she was just frightened to death of being poor again and that's why she hoarded her money so."

Every morning a huge stack of checks arrived in the mail. Vivian would say "Look—there's $5,000 on my desk and I didn't have to get out of bed this morning," Konrad continued. "Once when she made dinner for us she brought this big flat iron pan—a dish with beans and cheese, etc. Well, half of it was gone. She said, 'You kids finish it, I got hungry earlier and had to eat.' That was dinner, half a pan of garbage and nothing to drink. Later when John came into the picture everything changed. Suddenly the fridge was filled with steaks 'cause John had taste and class and she was not about to schlock him out with casseroles and the junk she threw at us."

One night during one of John's frequent visits to Frontera Drive, he told Konrad, Colby, and Emery that he wanted to take a shower. "He emptied his pockets on the table, wallet, bank book and everything. He left them on the davenport and went into the shower," Konrad said. John Emery, known for his pranks, decided to go through

John's personal items to find out how much money he had. John had twenty-three dollars and change in his savings prompting Emery to remark, "Now I know why he loves Vivian so much."

"John wanted the money and the fame," Konrad said. "He was a charmer and good looking, I didn't blame Viv. She wanted a man in her bed and he cooperated, he satisfied her and he took what he needed and she was happy. I remember the night they went to get married. Vivian was so happy she was just singing away. They realized they didn't have a best man yet and asked John Emery to do it. He replied, 'Great! Let's go,' so they opened a bottle of champagne to toast. I drove them to the airport singing and drinking all the way."

On January 15, 1961, Vivian, John, and his best man boarded a plane to Santa Fe "drunker than hell." The following day, the couple married in the home of Barbara and Bill Hooton. A few family members and close friends, including John's male companion, attended the small ceremony. Vivian later described for Konrad her disappointment at seeing this man at her wedding. "She was furious. Vivian had specifically told John that she didn't want this man at the wedding, to which John responded, 'He's been my friend for years, he said he wanted to come and I said why not.' "

Corinne Wiley had the impression that John "dropped his companion and all his gay friends like a hot potato and went into a new life." Others are convinced that John never really gave up his lifestyle but rather went underground with it. To outsiders, the marriage had fiasco written all over it but the newlyweds were determined to make it work despite the fact that their interests and lifestyles were opposites. Though Vivian constantly worried about her young husband straying, this union began the happiest time in her life. The Doddses headed to San Francisco for their honeymoon. Oddly, Vivian asked Max Showalter, whom she had known since her Broadway days, to accompany them. "We rented a house on Lombard Street for a week," Max said. "I knew that the only reason she took me along was to cook."

Now that she was married to a younger man, age became an obsession with Vivian. Whenever Colby and others brought up the subject, she shaved more and more years off her real age. "She was clinging to forty-five when we went out on tour. We all knew she was older than she claimed to be. She dressed like a young girl. Shorts rolled up with a midriff shirt tied up. She didn't have a bad body but she was a lady not a young girl."

In 1961, Vivian and William Inge received commendations for their accomplishments in the arts at the Kansas Centennial festivities. While in Independence, Vivian visited city hall. When she emerged from the building, she held a piece of crumpled paper. She told Dorothy Konrad, "I've done something terrible. I've stolen my birth certificate. Nobody is ever going to know how old I am." She then proceeded to burn it.

Vivian began her marriage to John by erasing her past. Pat Colby stood witness one day as she threw all her *I Love Lucy* things away in large trash bins. "All her life's memorabilia was gone. She said, 'I don't want any part of it.' She took all the film, every segment of it, took it apart and trashed it," Colby said. Included in the bonfire was a scrapbook that Lucy had given her as a Christmas gift entitled *This Is Your Life: Vivian Roberta Jones,* which contained the famous mock contract. Vivian wanted to get rid of all the things associated with the show and her marriage to Phil Ober in an attempt to rid herself of the memories.

"Vivian didn't deal with anything calmly," Colby said. "I met her after analysis and I don't think she was very straightened out. She seemed as messed up as I was."

Her friends describe Vivian as unyielding, especially in regards to Mae. "She hated her mother violently," Konrad said. " 'My mother never gave me a word of encouragement or praise,' she'd say. One day Vivian opened one of her mother's letters. Everything in it said, 'You're a child of the devil, you're going to hell.' Her mother was relentless. Vivian threw all the letters in the fireplace. She said to me, 'I sent her big checks when I first started making money. I knew they needed money and I could help. My mother sent the checks back saying, 'I don't want this money, it is the money of the devil.' "

Interestingly, Mae's religious zeal did not have the same impact on her other children. Dorothy O'Neal, Lou Ann, and Bob agree that Mae lived by certain beliefs and that her views of how others should behave were somewhat restrictive. But as Lou Ann notes, Mae did not demand that anyone else embrace those beliefs. "Mama was a completely different mother for me than the one Vivian grew up with. We were all spread out over twenty-one years. My mother was a very strong and willful woman too, the reason why we turned out such strong women. She was what you might call a religious fundamentalist. First she was Methodist, disapproving of smoking, drinking, and showing your flesh. By the time it got to me she was a Jehovah's Witness. None of us were very religious like her because she just turned us off. However, she liked to have a good time herself. She loved to dance and play cards. I think she was just frustrated because she too didn't have her dreams realized."

To celebrate her new marriage, Vivian threw a huge party. Eve Arden, Mary Wickes, and Hedda Hopper attended along with many of the Hollywood community. In all the excitement, John's mother Theresa drank a little too much. Dorothy Konrad helped to diffuse a potentially embarrassing situation. "We had to push her up the stairs to get her in bed, she was so tanked," Konrad said.

After that party, John's father, G. Fullerton Dodds, frequently appeared at their door, drunk and in need of money. "John's father was a humdinger," Konrad said. "He'd ask John to get him money from Vivian, saying, 'I'm broke. You're married to a rich lady now.' John would get so mad at him because he'd always come at inopportune times."

Vivian decided it was best for everyone concerned to get John to the east coast, away from his family and from his "friend" in San Francisco. They purchased a house in Stamford, Connecticut, and John began working for the publishing house of G. P. Putnam & Company. In a postcard sent to Pat Colby, Vivian described her new life. "Yes, Pat, he's a real true-blue, 100 percent guy. What a happy life we have together. We just bought our dream house in Connecticut, pool, red barn and all."

Vivian became the quintessential wife in her new home, decorating, cooking, working in the garden, and taking care of her pets. Max Showalter humorously notes that "Vivian always loved to be out in that garden. And she was probably the worst gardener I ever saw." Showalter may have found Vivian's horticultural techniques lacking but according to her sister Lou Ann, the end result was usually breathtaking. "Vivian had wonderful gardens. She always had a magnificent variety of colors mixed with great landscaping of the hills and rocks. They all thrived under her care on old Longridge and the Pacific Palisades. All her homes were simply wonderful."

Through the years Vivian had always cherished her dogs and often took them on the road. To an extent, her pets had taken the place of the children she never had. Vivian believed that actors should make a choice between career and family. She chose career. In her opinion, children born into famous Hollywood homes often took a back seat to their famous parents.

Vivian took great care of her pets and now that she had time, she began showing them in tournaments. And she often rescued pets abandoned by others. Dorothy recounts one such occasion when things didn't exactly work out. "Edie Van Cleve and I were riding around with Vivian. There was this dog, all mangy, dirty and terrible looking laying on the side of the road. Vivian slammed on the brakes. She and Edie got out, picked this dog up, and put him on the back seat with me and went home. She advertised in all the papers, she called the Humane Society, she did everything to find out who this dog belonged to. She had him cleaned up at the vet and taken care of. One day she called me—I was back in Albuquerque by this time—and said, 'Well, we found the owner of the dog.' He had been lying in front of his own home when we 'rescued' him."

Vivian also involved herself in community affairs. She had paid psychiatrists thousands of dollars for their services and now she wanted to find a way to help the mentally ill who did not have the means to pay high fees for their therapy. In her opinion, no one ever thought of depression as a real disease and she had realized early on that there were many others who, like her, lived in depressed states. Vivian had written in an article years earlier, "I have been informed by authorities whose opinions I not only respect but revere that there are millions like me—or millions, more properly, in the gray-night world from which I have been led. And if this is so, and it must be so, I know them and they are my friends. Not because we have met, but because of the sympathetic bond between us. I know that their hands perspire in strange unidentified fears, that their stomachs contract in nausea if the boss fails to smile at them, that they walk alone in queer, numbing depression wherever they may be and that always, they are afraid."

Helping the mentally ill became an important part of Vivian's life. Columnist Hollie Hochstein tells this story:

As a guest star on *Candid Camera,* Vivian was posted behind a Los Angeles department store lingerie counter while the camera registered her customers' reactions to their famous sales lady. A young man came to buy a nightgown and Viv asked who it was for. "Tears came into his eyes," Viv recalled, "and I yelled for them to cut off the camera. He was buying the gown for his wife who was in a mental hospital. I asked if his wife would like to talk to somebody who had been sick too but who was well now." Arrangements were made for Viv to visit the hospital. "I found I was good at it," she said. "Nobody knows what talent they have until somebody asks them to use it."

For four years, she volunteered as chairperson for the outreach program Operation Friendship. Her contributions to the National Mental Health Association garnered her several awards including having a street named after her by the Connecticut Mental Health Association. She also received their 1966 Outstanding Service Award. In the years Vivian worked for the association, she lobbied for increased state aid for the mentally ill. She not only lent her name to raise money but went into the psychiatric wards and helped in the process of rehabilitation by speaking one on one with patients.

Whenever she toured in a show she would visit hospitals, with the understanding that no one would publicize the event. Actor and friend Jay Bell once escorted Vivian on one of her trips to the wards. "The visits were strictly for the patients. I cried for hours. They would hear her voice and people who were just sitting there in a stupor would come out of it. The doctors told her that the one day she was there did more for those patients than months and months of therapy."

"She was one of the first celebrities to speak openly

Vivian cuts the ribbon at a ceremony naming a street after her in appreciation for her work with the Connecticut Mental Health Association.

about mental illness," says Paige Matthews Peterson. "The most important thing she felt she ever did in her life was bust open depression. Vivian would walk into those mental wards, take people in her arms and say, 'You know what, darling, you're just fine. I just went through this and you're going to be just fine.' She healed more people in this country than anybody has any idea of."

Vivian was particularly successful at raising the morale of the teenagers she met at treatment centers. She was effective with middle-aged women too because, ironically, they identified with Ethel Mertz. There are stories of almost miraculous responses to her friendliness, truthfulness, and sincerity with the patients. One patient who hadn't spoken for years opened up to Vivian and was subsequently discharged. Another who had been too hostile to take treatment became cooperative after talking with her. A Norwich, Connecticut, hospital doctor once remarked, "Because Miss Vance talks freely about her own illness and recovery, she gets across the idea that the patients can also be helped. She gives them the feeling that people on the outside are concerned about them, something they have great doubts about."

Vivian often used her humor to get her points across. At every question and answer session, some patient would inevitably ask Vivian, "My mother [father, relative, or friend] says I wouldn't be here if only I helped myself. What should I say to them?" Vivian's reply, "Tell them to go fuck themselves."

Vivian also became interested in education, her own education. Since she barely graduated from high school, she wasn't on an equal footing intellectually with John or his friends. One day Dorothy Konrad went for a drive with Vivian, still one of her favorite pastimes. "In the back seat she had a lot of books, all the classics. She said, 'John is educating me, he got me all these books; I don't understand all of them, but it doesn't matter. I'm reading them.' "

Every day she read all the newspapers and news magazines she could and became politically and socially aware of current issues. "She was real hard-core, cared about what happened in Portugal or the Soviet Union, and truly became a current events and literary person," Paige Peterson said.

Meanwhile, Lucille Ball, who had divorced Desi in 1960 and recently married comedian Gary Morton, moved back to the West Coast after finishing a stint on Broadway in the musical *Wildcat* and planned to do another weekly television series. Desi Arnaz had the book *Life Without George* by Irene Kampen adapted to suit his ex-wife's talents. The premise of the new show was that Lucy was a widowed mother of two who makes ends meet by renting a room to her recently divorced best friend and her son. Only one person, in Lucy's opinion, could play her best friend. When asked to do the series, Vivian responded with an emphatic "NOT ON YOUR LIFE!"

Accustomed to having her way, a determined Lucille Ball traveled east with script in hand to convince Vivian to accept the role. Vivian told her, "Don't take it out! I won't read it!" But Lucille Ball didn't budge. "I refused to even consider being in a continuing series without Vivian. Since we had gone off the air, she had married a handsome and successful New York editor. Vivian was ecstatic about her flower garden and lecturing on behalf of mental health. Her loyalty to me—and a hefty paycheck which was spread out over years and years to avoid a big tax bite—won her over to my side."

After discussing the pros and cons with John, Vivian accepted the offer. However, before finalizing the deal, she approached executive producer Desi Arnaz with a few demands: She wanted the character's name changed to Viv so that the audience would no longer associate her with tacky Ethel Mertz, she demanded co-star billing, and a wardrobe equal in glamour to Lucy's, along with a huge pay increase. This was a sore subject for Lucille Ball who, as Hal King says, never discussed money with Vivian. "Money was Lucille's god," he said, and though she felt Vivian deserved whatever she asked for, she did not want to know the exact figures. Vivian landed $8,000 a week besides additional bonuses spread out over a five-year contract. She had final say on every costume she wore and received co-star billing. The character's name was changed to Vivian Bagley. Once established in a new, swank suite on the Desilu lot, Vivian reflected, "This is quite a change from when we started *I Love Lucy*. Our first dressing rooms were so bad that Lucille and I brought some cleanser and scrubbed the toilets."

Desi Arnaz and Lucille Ball, known for their allegiance to loyal friends, hired most of the crew from *I Love Lucy* for the new venture. New faces joined the cast, including Dick Martin (the male interest for Lucy Carmichael), Candy Moore and Jimmy Garrett who played Lucy's children, and Ralph Hart as Vivian's son. A pool of actors, among them Kathleen Freeman, Mary Jane Croft, Mary Wickes, Dorothy Konrad, and Lucy's protégé Carole Cook, regularly appeared on the show.

Vivian began making weekly commutes between coasts. On either Sunday nights or Monday mornings she'd arrive in Los Angeles, and return home on Thursday nights after filming the show. Pat Colby remembers, "Vivian was afraid of flying. But she'd say, 'Oh I'm not worried, I just drink enough vodka, get on the plane and sleep soundly all the way.'"

The first day of rehearsals for *The Lucy Show* bore no resemblance to that first day eleven years before when Vivian walked into the General Service Studio only to be

Hans Conreid and Vivian on the set of The Lucy Show *in the episode entitled "Lucy Plays Cleopatra"*

scrutinized and tested by Lucille Ball. When Vivian entered stage 19, she found two director's chairs, one positioned at the head of the table with Lucy's name written on the back, and the other one directly to the right with her name on it. In Hollywood that meant you had made it.

Vivian's position had changed in the hierarchy. She was no longer an easily replaceable actor. Lucy now looked to Vivian for support and depended on her strength, especially since Lucy's own personal life had changed so dramatically. That first day was difficult for everyone. A teary-eyed Desi Arnaz stood high up on the catwalk watching as his ex-wife rehearsed one of her scenes. Vivian, noticing his sad face, approached him. As she embraced him she said, "Oh Desi, it isn't the same, is it?" She later commented, "Here we were, starting again, only

Lucy, Arthur Godfrey, and Vivian as Steamboat Bessie in The Lucy Show

this time he was on the outside looking in, and it wasn't fun anymore. So much had happened to so many people but most of all to Desi, leaving him alone and a little sad, although he tried to hide it."

Vivian's look had completely changed from her days on *I Love Lucy*. Those who had not met her before, including Helen Garrett, marveled at how different she appeared in person. "She was much more attractive than I expected her to be. She had quite a nice figure. I had always thought she was heavier but she was very well put together. I was surprised so many times at how tiny her waist actually was."

Regardless of the changes in the characters' names and descriptions, most saw *The Lucy Show* as an extension of *I Love Lucy*. Tom Watson says that "the second series together put the nail in the coffin for both ladies. Essentially Lucille was back as Lucy Ricardo and Vivian was Ethel in different clothes. That sealed it—they could not get out of it." Though both had tried and to some degree succeeded at other ventures, neither could separate herself from the other or from the characters who still resided, in the minds of the audience, at 623 East 68th Street.

Since the days of *I Love Lucy*, several television series have tried to duplicate the formula which made this duo so appealing. "*Laverne & Shirley* was a good take-off in a younger version. They were funny and a lot of them were Lucy and Ethel situations, whether copied knowingly or not," says Lucie Arnaz. Today we can still see traces of Ethel in television characters who serve as the bosom buddy of the star. Even though they are no longer a frumpy, dowdy next-door neighbor setting up the joke, TV sidekicks still serve as confidante, companion, and foil. Only now they are as attractive as the star and their quick-wittedness often supersedes that of the lead.

As the original second banana, Ethel Mertz is still used to define this particular television character and Vivian is finally being credited for her contributions in the development of this type. Actress Valerie Harper agrees that Vivian brought second bananas out of the shadows. "Vivian was always so full of truth and that's what was funny. She is less a clown than Lucy and that was the glue of their scenes. Ethel broke a hell of a lot of ground for people. Ethel was a powerful thing in the American psyche."

Actress and comedienne Kathleen Freeman explains that the two most important factors between star and sidekick are a cohesiveness and a natural chemistry. "No two people are funny in the same way. If you have synchronicity with somebody, it's priceless. And Vivian had that with Lucille Ball and Lucille Ball had that with her. Vivian was

Lucille Ball, Vivian, Mary Wickes, Mary Jane Croft, and Lucy's and Vivian's stand-ins form a line on The Lucy Show.

Vivian (right) takes a kitchen job in a wealthy household presided over by Norma Varden on The Lucy Show.

terrific with Lucille and a lot of it was damn near unconscious. That fabulous, inherent, innate timing—and they had it like gangbusters."

Like the comedy routines used repeatedly by Gleason and Carney, Abbott & Costello, and Lewis & Martin, the writers of *The Lucy Show* rewrote scenarios from *I Love Lucy* because they guaranteed laughter. The two comediennes publicly denied any similarity between the two shows. However, episodes like "Lucy's Barbershop Quartet," "Lucy and Viv Become Tycoons," and "Lucy Buys a Boat" bore a striking resemblance to plots from *I Love Lucy* such as "Lucy's Showbiz Swan Song," "The Million Dollar Idea," and "Desert Island." Many other episodes had familiar routines woven into different circumstances.

Vivian thought her work on this series was funnier than her work on *I Love Lucy*. She appeared more at ease with the new character of Vivian Bagley, who she felt differed a great deal from Ethel Mertz. The divorced Bagley had a confident, assertive quality lacking in Ethel. She also had fewer money problems than the ever-budgeting Mrs. Mertz. Critic Cecil Smith commented, "Although her Ethel Mertz of the old *I Love Lucy* was a very funny gal, I prefer her Vivian Bagley—a warmer person and more Vivian."

Vivian herself conceded that "The character I do now is much more to my liking because she is nearer my own personality. As Ethel I was always asked to make the down remark. I got bored with that. I like to smile."

While rehearsing, she no longer took a cautious approach when it came to voicing her opinions but rather gave suggestions without trepidation. Carole Cook and others began to refer to Lucy and Vivian as "Leopold and Loeb" because on several occasions, the actors didn't know who to take their direction from—Lucy, Vivian, or the director, Jack Donohue.

Kathleen Freeman appeared in several episodes. "It's

funny and frustrating when you have two people on the same show, one telling you to do one thing, the other something else. It drove most people absolutely crazy. I'd go to the director and say, 'Who do I listen to—you, Lucille, or Vivian? Give me a clue 'cause I'll go with any one of the three of you.' The director just broke up laughing. They weren't diametrically opposed but it would make a difference to the scene."

Pat Colby, who also appeared on *The Lucy Show*, describes the confused state of the hierarchy. "Vivian was being bossy. It was Vivian, Lucy, and the director, you couldn't tell who was who. They were all alike." Helen Garrett, Jimmy Garrett's mom, agrees. "My son Jimmy came to me and said, 'I never know who to listen to.' Lucy would tell him one thing, Jack another, and Vivian another. I told him to ask Lucy. Tell her you feel confused." Ultimately, Lucille Ball gave six-year-old Jimmy the definitive response to everyone's dilemma. "To put it in Lucille's exact words, she laughed and said, 'Stick with the money, honey!' "

Whatever their differences, Vivian and Lucy did agree on how to play comedy. They believed that young actors did not have the tools nor an understanding of the subject. When the two women once arranged to teach a course, Vivian commented, "We were astounded at the lack of interest young actors have in comedy. Comedy embarrasses them. It's beneath them. Like one fellow said, 'You want me to overplay everything like you do on television?' They want to toss the lines away! You can't toss a line away until you can overplay it! So we put them on their feet. They were all sitting there taking a lot of notes. I told them, 'You can't get through a producer's door by taking notes!' "

When actors responded to her approach by spouting cerebral justifications for their characters' behavior,

Vivian would go berserk. "Oh God! I hate to hear actors talk about themselves! It really bores me to death. 'This character doesn't make me feel . . . 'Who cares!? Actors can go on and on and on. If you want the truth, it's all I can do to get my foot out of the mud and go out there and play the part. Get up and do it! I don't have any time to think who I am or if I'm a tree."

In the same vein, as Maury Thompson points out, Lucy would annihilate any actor who did not use his full energy and speak loudly. "A guest star kept mumbling his lines during rehearsals. Lucy said, 'I can't hear him.' They'd redo it again and again he mumbled. Lucy attacked him and told him to speak up. He said, 'I'll speak up when the cameras rolls.' 'Oh no,' said Lucy. 'You'll read it loud right now!' 'Perhaps you'd like to read it for me?' he said. 'Out!' she said. 'I want him out of here right now! I won't go on until he leaves.' " When Lucy returned from her dressing room the guest star had been replaced by a new actor.

By the second season of the show, Desi Arnaz had given up his position as producer. An observer recalls that during that first year's rehearsals "Arnaz would frequently fall asleep sitting in his director's chair. Lucy would discreetly send someone over and instruct them to pretend bumping into his chair so he would awaken without embarrassment."

The overwhelming demands of running the studio, his drinking problem, and ill health caused Desi's instincts and judgments to waiver. Lucille Ball felt obligated to take the reins, not only to protect her interest but to safeguard Arnaz's image. At the end of the first season of *The Lucy Show,* Arnaz sold his shares of Desilu to Ball, making her the first woman in Hollywood history to own a major studio. This additional responsibility placed a huge amount of pressure on Ball, who, many felt, had now turned into a tyrant to

The cast of The Lucy Show. *From left to right: Jimmy Garrett, Candy Moore, Ralph Hart, Gale Gordon, Vivian, and Lucille*

work for. It didn't matter who walked on the set—if Lucille Ball thought someone couldn't cut the mustard, they received a tongue-lashing. No one appearing on the show was exempt from Lucy's wrath, and this included close friends. After a particularly exhausting and tense week of rehearsals in which Lucy had put comedy great Jack Benny through the wringer, he called Herbert Kenwith and pleaded with him, "Get her to a psychiatrist, she's going nuts!"

Helen Garrett remarks, "Lucy was very demanding as far as everyone being prepared. I saw her replace people if they couldn't or wouldn't do it the way she wanted." Carole Cook notes, "It was always Viv and Lucy with the guest stars. Lucy was always tougher and Viv was always jolly, trying to make the guest star feel welcome. She was more diplomatic than Lucy. Vivian was a great help to her—remember, she didn't have Desi—so Vivian assumed a more powerful position. Lucy depended on her a great deal; they were a powerful twosome. I always thought of the two of them against the world; they were Laurel & Hardy, Fricke & Fracke."

When stars walked on the set for their first day of rehearsals, Vivian went out of her way to make them feel at home while preparing them for what was in store. She'd usually quip, "Just don't count on any close-up in a two-shot. It's either a group shot or a close-up on Lucy."

"Lucy didn't touch Vivian," says Herbert Kenwith. "Vivian was such a strong lady, I think Lucy was intimidated by her." Still, Lucy knew what to do to get under Vivian's skin. Maury Thompson tells this story about a bit where Lucy tosses Vivian a baseball bat:

> Vivian had to grab it so that Lucille would win. Lucy was throwing it so that Viv couldn't catch it at the right spot. Viv said, "Lucille, if you throw it decently I can catch it," so they did it again. This was a weakness she saw in Viv so again, she threw it badly. Viv came running over to me crying, "Tell her! For God's sake I'm doing the best I can." Lucille just turned and ran to her dressing room. The property guy said he would put tape on the spot where Viv was supposed to catch the bat and I told Viv, "No matter how she throws it to you, just grab it where the tape is." We called Lucy out after a twenty-minute break. Lucy never said a word about the tape. They did it again and it worked. But I've never seen Viv like that, she just went to pieces.

It's obvious that Vivian knew Lucy's weak spots as well as Lucy knew hers. Lucy, who would try anything scripted for her, once refused to do a scene involving an elephant. "Lucy was afraid of the elephant," writer Madelyn Pugh Davis said. "It was the first time I'd ever heard her say no, she couldn't do a scene. We went upstairs to our office, not knowing what to do because it was the final scene of the episode. Vivian later called and said, 'Lucy will do the scene as written.' When we asked her how she coerced Lucy into doing it, Viv said, 'I just told her that if she didn't want to do the scene with the elephant, I would do it.' "

Most agree with Carole Cook that the relationship between Vivian and Lucy had taken a new turn from the days of the *I Love Lucy* series. "Vivian by this time was very sure of herself and wasn't in the position of trying to cement her place with Lucy. On the set she was basically on equal footing and Lucy would defer to her. Very few people, even directors on the show, would take that type of control."

But even in her new position of power, Vivian realized that Lucille Ball was still the captain of the ship. This awareness and Lucy's occasional tantrums caused Vivian to harbor resentments which surfaced at inappropriate times. Lucy would often give generously to Vivian on holidays and birthdays but Vivian accepted Lucy's gifts with the contempt of an employee receiving a token from a boss rather than a heartfelt gesture from a friend.

Dorothy Konrad, who had been a witness to Vivian's outbursts of anger, calmly watched this scenario one day as others were left speechless. "During a party on the set, Lucy gave Vivian a bedcover made of mink bellies. It was gorgeous. When she gave it to Vivian you should have heard her. 'Stinking old rotten fur pieces, and cheap too!' She said it out loud, everyone heard her but no one said a word. Another time, Lucy gave Vivian a $7,000 red station wagon. She had it delivered in front of her door for Christmas with a big bow. Vivian said, 'Oh, what a horrible thing! Who needs a station wagon? She's so cheap!' I thought—come on, lady. She really resented Lucy. I think she was really jealous of her in her heart, although she played the role of being fond of her."

After two seasons of *The Lucy Show,* Vivian, tired of the

weekly commutes between Los Angeles and New York, wanted out. "After so many years on a series you realize that as an actor the show isn't going to do you any more good. It'll take you to the bank every week but it's not helping your career if you want to do other things," reasons Marjorie Lord. Vivian told an interviewer in the beginning of the third season, "I'm quitting the show this year. I want to live at home with my husband. I'm tired of commuting."

In some ways, Lucy agreed with Vivian. She would have liked to spend more time with Gary and considered not coming back for a third season. Vivian believed that Lucy truly intended to end the run. One observer noted that "During this period Vivian made public statements that weren't very flattering and it was a very foolish thing to do. She thought Lucille was done with the show but she picked it up again."

The threat to end the show was still a favorite ploy used by Lucy to extract more money from the network and because of her contract, Vivian had to return. When asked about the rumors of her departure, Vivian responded, "We're in negotiations now, trying to work something out. At present, we've agreed that I will do twenty shows next season, and will be out of the fourth and fifth years altogether. I'm still hoping I can do fewer shows. I have a beautiful life waiting for me in New York and I'm ready to live it."

Immediately after filming the first four episodes of the season, Vivian left on a trip to London with John. "He is going over to see his clients and I'm going over to see the shows," she said. "I want to see Laurence Olivier in *Othello*."

Vivian's participation in the third season of *The Lucy Show* was not as prominent as in the two previous years.

"Lucille accepted her back but I remember Viv was real embarrassed about the things she had said. I think being written out was her own fault," Dorothy Konrad said.

Whatever the reason, it's apparent that the writers began to slowly wean the public off Vivian Bagley and allowed the audience to get comfortable with Lucy Carmichael minus her best friend. Vivian usually made an entrance at the beginning of the show, à la Ethel Mertz, and then retreated leaving Lucy free to solve whatever dilemma had been set up. Included among the episodes in which Vivian did not appear are three of the four shows guest-starring Ann Sothern as a countess. Along with Gale Gordon, whose character Mr. Mooney first appeared in the second season, other semiregulars, like Carol Burnett, Mary Jane Croft, Mary Wickes, functioned as Lucy's second in later episodes.

In "Lucy and Arthur Godfrey," Lucy and Viv convince Godfrey to appear in a musical with their community players. This episode marked one of the rare times in that third season when Vivian's character does more than just make a few entrances. Along with Bob Lees and Peter Walker, Max Showalter wrote the musical numbers for the show which included "Steamboat Bessie," a song specifically suited to Vivian. Bessie is a gold-digging saloon singer who tries to vamp the millionaire (Gale Gordon) and take him away from the sweet and virginal Lucy Bell. Bessie reels him in by strutting her stuff as she sings "Steamboat Bessie."

"It was one of the most expensive episodes of *The Lucy Show*," Showalter said. "I wrote a song just for Vivian. Lucy thought the song was so much better than any song she had. Viv could sell the pants off a song and Lucy told me, 'I think Viv is doing too much. Tell her to tone it down.' I went to Viv and said, 'Honey, just keep on doing what you are doing.' There was resentment of Lucy on

Vivian's part, too. Lucy would never speak badly of Vivian. I told her, 'She's made you an icon in television,' but Vivian was not pleased."

At the end of the third season, Lucy and Vivian had a private discussion regarding their future working together. Vivian was at odds over continuing with the series. She genuinely wanted to spend more time with her husband, to travel around the world, and to go back to the theater where she hoped to begin directing. Ball realized that if she wanted Vivian back she had to compromise on time and scheduling to allow her to do all she wanted. Believing that Vivian wanted to direct, write, and produce, Lucy proposed that if she stayed on with Desilu, a creative package could be put together where she could do all she wished in accordance with her time schedule. Lucy understood that Vivian must have had a certain amount of frustration building up because of her position as second banana and wanted to pay Vivian back for her past performance and dedication through the years. When the conversation came to an end, Lucy walked away convinced that she had reached an understanding with Vivian.

Lucy was not a great businesswoman but believed above all that an understanding between friends meant more than a written contract. Desilu executive, Bernard Weitzman, verifies that "Lucille was never really aware of deals; it wasn't her specialty. She was extremely generous in risking these things with Vivian. Lucille told me, 'We will pay her very handsomely, give her a small piece of the show, and keep it short and sweet.' Lucy thought it was a done deal.

"Lucy called me to her home," Weitzman went on, "and said, 'I love Vivian; she's like a Rock of Gibraltar to me. She's a marvelous director and writer and I want to use her in these capacities.' Gale Gordon and Vivian were the two stalwarts to her life as an actress as far as the series was concerned. Gale did not want to direct. He was happy being an actor. He would have made a great director but he had no inclination to do it.

"Lucille wanted to cut a deal that would make Vivian happy. In addition to acting, she wanted to give Vivian the creative opportunity to do more. They were going to be, in effect, almost partners although we never spoke of a partnership with Vivian. We thought it was going to be very, very simple until we turned to her agent, Phil Weltman. We sat down at my office at Gower Street to discuss how to make this happen. After a cordial fifteen to twenty minutes he gave me the numbers of what Vivian wanted. They were literally staggering. I said, 'Lucy is not going to be working for her.' Phil said, 'Bernie, it's really a take it or leave it deal. This is what Vivian wants.' I think her husband, John Dodds, had told her that she was entitled to this. I think it was bad advice from those around her. It was not just the formality Lucy expected it would be. I left it up to Lucy but I had to tell her in my opinion that the deal was outrageous. It would have put Vivian on the same level as Lucy and though Lucy was keeping her in a second level, the deal would have been an expansion."

As he reflected on Lucy's options after his round of negotiations with Phil Weltman, Weitzman said, "Lucille had to make the decision whether she was going to stand on her own two feet or continue to depend on Vivian Vance. She rejected the deal with Vivian's agent."

From a professional point of view, Vivian's decision had not been a wise one. Besides Ida Lupino and a handful of others, women did not produce or direct on television at that time. Whether she was aware of it or not, Lucille Ball had given Vivian the green light to explore territories rarely explored by women in the business. By rejecting Lucy's offer, Vivian closed the door on an opportunity which would have given her a whole new career. Eventually she would have been able to write her own ticket. Instead she had made it impossible for a compromise to be reached. She may have priced herself right out of the contract because she truly did not want to return to weekly television and setting up a no-compromise scenario may have been her way of saying "all this is no longer important to me."

Weitzman concedes that "Vivian at that moment didn't care, unless it was an incredibly rich deal." Clearly, her priorities had completely changed from the days of wanting to make it no matter what the cost. Because her past ambitions to become a star never materialized, Vivian had no desire to set herself up for failure and this may be the reason why she readily voiced her discontentment with stardom. "My ambition was never to be a big star," she said more than once. "I've seen very few happy stars, and I was determined that that wasn't going to happen to me . . . Ambition doesn't go too well with age or companionship."

At 58, Vivian may have simply wanted to look after her 46-year-old husband and enjoy a fulfilling life without the worries and responsibilities that come with directing, producing, and writing a major television show. Accepting Ball's offer would have cemented her association to Desilu, stripping her of any individuality. Vivian may have also been embittered by the fact that through the years of *I Love Lucy,* she had not reaped the pecuniary benefits that others had. Jess Oppenheimer, Madelyn Pugh Davis, and Bob Carroll owned a percentage of *I Love Lucy* because they had been part of its birth, but some of the executives who entered the picture when the program was at its peak also received profit sharing while Vivian and Bill Frawley did not. That knowledge, and the fact that Vivian and Bill were the only ones who didn't get rich from *I Love Lucy*, may have played a part in Vivian's decision to demand an astronomical amount of money for her work on *The Lucy Show*.

But it was a move which backfired. She stood her ground and lost the gamble. Vivian's friend Walter Williamson assessed the situation this way. "Vivian Vance was a triumphant victim. She got a lot in life and she knew that, but she didn't get all of what she wanted. This may have been a pattern in her life that she made happen. That win/lose combination may have come by mistake at the beginning, but over time it became something she enforced."

Gale Gordon recalled Lucy's disappointment when she heard of the outcome of the negotiations. "Lucy cried in private talking to me because she depended on Vivian. She told me she could never do a show without Vivian. Lucy told me that, just prior to the break, Vivian was asking for more money than Lucy was willing to accept. It broke Lucy's heart really. Vivian thought she was a great, great star. She was wonderful and worked beautifully with Lucy. But she wasn't that great on her own, or as great as she thought she was."

But Hal King sees it differently. "It would have meant nothing to Lucy to give Vivian more money. She was making so much goddamned money, she could have afforded a few more thousand dollars."

Personally, the two women were growing apart. For all intents and purposes, Vivian didn't see eye-to-eye with Lucy's new husband and producer, Gary Morton. "Vivian and Gary, I don't think liked each other and that was one of the wedges that got driven between Lucy and Viv," Tom Watson says. "Vivian really adored Desi and no one replaced him in her mind."

In the first episode of the fourth season of *The Lucy Show,* the only evidence that Vivian Bagley ever existed was a quick mention made in the opening scene. *I Love Lucy* aficionado Neil Wilburn asserts, "I've always hated the way they handled her departure, with a one-line reference to her marriage to 'Vern Bunson' in the fourth season opener. Then it was off to Marineland! Think of the un-mined plots—Viv dating, the wedding, and the tearful Lucy-Viv parting. No, these Lucy writers were not into character development. Instead, the last episode of the third season had Vivian and Lucy in one of those everything-mechanical-goes-wrong plots that has not aged well."

By the end of the second season, the show's original writers, Madelyn Pugh Davis and Bob Carroll, had departed because of a disagreement with Ball. Bob Schiller and Bob Weiskopf left after writing only four episodes of the third season to explore more contemporary comedy situations. The new writers, most of them working as free-lance artists, had a difficult time writing zany, funny, and believable situations and this is perhaps the reason why later episodes of *The Lucy Show* seemed stilted and forced. Most agree that the best of this series include episodes featuring Vivian alongside Lucy. When she left, the public had the same response to *The Lucy Show* as CBS executives had for the *Guestward Ho!* pilot. "People said that *The Lucy Show* didn't touch *I Love Lucy* because the guys were missing but as long as you had Vivian, there was something of the old show. There was something missing when Vivian left," Helen Garrett said. "You kept expecting that door to open and for her to walk through it. There was a dead space."

Lucille Ball later wrote, "Vivian's the greatest supporting player anyone could ask for. During one of the earlier shows, we were supposed to be trapped in a glass shower stall, with the water turned on full blast. The script called for me to dive down and pull out the plug at the bottom of the shower, but when I did this in front of a live audience I found I had no room to maneuver. I couldn't get back to the surface again and moreover I had swallowed a lot of water, and was actually drowning right there in front of three hundred people who were splitting their sides laughing. Vivian, realizing in cold terror what was happening, never changed expression. She reached down, pulled me safely to the surface by the roots of my hair, and then calmly spoke both sides of our dialogue, putting my lines in the form of questions. Whatta girl! And whatta night!"

In a later interview, the two recalled the incident in a different way. Vivian had been an expert swimmer and had originally wanted to do the dive. She said, "Remember the time the shower flooded and I put my foot on your back to push you to the bottom so you could pull the stopper?" "I do indeed remember. You almost drowned me," replied Lucy. "Well, it was your fault. That was the one thing I could have done—dived to the bottom. But nooo, you were the star—you had to do it!"

Vivian did not return for any of the fourth season. She did make an appearance in the fifth season in the episode "Viv Visits Lucy" in which the two dress as hippies and hit the Sunset Strip in Hollywood. In the sixth season, Vivian comes to the rescue after Lucy breaks her leg and decides to help nurse her friend back to health in a show which aired on New Year's day in 1968. Through flashbacks, the two recall some of the funniest moments from the first two seasons of *The Lucy Show*. The end of the episode finds Vivian also breaking her leg and remaining with her friend.

Vivian again returned in the last season for "Lucy and

the Lost Star/Lucy Meets Joan" in which Joan Crawford
guest-starred. Crawford had heard all about Lucy's tyran-
nical behavior on the set and voiced her terror of working
with the redhead to Herbert Kenwith. He tells this story
about that show:

> Joan had to do a time step, a little Charleston. Well,
> the bleachers were filled with everyone from the studio
> to see Joan Crawford, the movie star. While Joan is
> doing the step, Lucy comes over, hits her on the arm
> and says, "Stop! You can't dance!"
> Joan said, "I haven't really rehearsed and the pianist
> is playing at a tempo I'm not accustomed to."
> Lucy said, "Let me see you do a Charleston!"
> Joan was a lousy dancer but she could do the
> Charleston—but not when pressured in front of three
> hundred people. So Lucy yelled, "Stop! Stop the music.
> I'm going to give you another chance. If you don't get
> it right we are going to cut the number." Joan was so
> nervous she couldn't talk, she was visibly shaken. They
> started it again. I don't think more than four bars played
> when Lucy yelled, "Okay! Cut!! The number is out!"
> Joan Crawford ran to her dressing room crying.
> Kenwith followed the distraught star, finding her on
> the floor of her dressing room sobbing and muttering,
> "And they call me a bitch!" Vivian must have agreed
> with Lucy's assessment of Crawford's dancing skills
> because she later wrote, "In my opinion, I could out-
> Charleston Joan Crawford any day and without stirring
> a leg. I realized I could when she appeared on one of
> our shows."

During her time away from the show, Vivian turned her
energies toward the stage where she still enjoyed honing
her technical acting skills. This technical savvy had always

been her forte. She'd often turned to these skills when playing Ethel in order to mask her hostility of the character while simultaneously trying to make her believable. Lucille Ball archivist Tom Watson comments, "The real true actor on the show was Vivian Vance. The rest were sort of personalities playing characters, even Lucy, bless her heart. Vivian was always in character. You never saw anything but Ethel Mertz when she was on camera. She was constantly Ethel Mertz. Even when the scene was totally about Lucy or Ricky or Fred you'd look over at [Vivian] on the sidelines and she was always in the moment of the activity on stage and never broke character. As far as being a trained actor, I think she had more than the others, although they all contributed in their own way."

After six seasons *The Lucy Show* went off the air. At this point in her onstage career, Vivian could have simply glided on the crest of her success. But as Larry Maraviglia, who worked at the Drury Lane Theatre in Chicago, points out, "Vivian would never break character and be 'the star,' which is very tempting to do when you're a big name in a role. Vivian was very true to the text, extremely fastidious about working on her moments and the business she did on stage. And this carried over into her admiration and interest in seeing how other people worked.

"While Vivian was appearing at the Drury Lane in a revival of *Over Twenty-one*, Gloria Swanson was rehearsing *The Inkwell,* a comedy written for her. Vivian sat in the back of the empty theater most of the day watching Miss Swanson rehearse, which was unusual. Rarely did one star come in to watch another unless they were old friends or had worked together. Vivian was really interested in what was going on on that stage, breaking it down technically, never being critical or catty, rather she was respectful. She felt she had something to learn from Swanson. I saw a very keen woman dedicated to her work."

Vivian and Bernie Thomas in The Marriage-Go-Round

Vivian and the cast of Here Today

Although Swanson knew that Vivian had spent hours studying her, she never acknowledged her presence. While others went up to the screen legend and introduced themselves, Vivian did not. At this point in her life, she now felt confident enough that she no longer had to ingratiate herself to anyone.

The stage remained Vivian's primary focus. She wanted to direct and she frequently took advice on the subject from her Connecticut neighbor, theater great Josh Logan. Vivian returned to the Albuquerque Little Theatre to codirect and star in the premiere of *Everybody's Girl* by John Patrick, a play he wrote specifically with Vivian in mind. She toured summer stock and dinner theaters with *The Marriage-Go-Round, The Time of the Cuckoo,* and *Barefoot in the Park.* While touring in the latter with Jay Bell, Vivian was concerned "that when she came out for her final bow, she just got nice applause. She said, 'Something's wrong.' She decided one night to get all dolled up in this black lacy thing. The audience stood and cheered. 'That's it!' she said. 'We gotta use the old showgirl gimmick.' "

In 1966 David Merrick offered Vivian the part of Marion Hollander in Woody Allen's new play, *Don't Drink the Water,* with rehearsals slated for that summer and a Broadway opening scheduled in the fall. From the outset, Vivian did not jibe with the director or the star of the show, Lou Jacobi. Vivian told friend Dody Goodman that "every piece of business she invented, the director gave to Jacobi." Later Vivian confided to Jay Bell that " 'Lou Jacobi made life unbearable for her as far as she was concerned. She was very unhappy and left two days before the opening. Kay Medford, who replaced Vivian, told her, 'You gotta realize that he became a star late in life.' "

Before her departure, Vivian had the opportunity to open the show out-of-town at the Walnut Street Theatre in

Philadelphia. Reviews unanimously agreed that Allen's writing had little substance. However, Henry T. Murdock of the *Philadelphia Inquirer* wrote that "as his [Jacobi's] ever-loving wife, Vivian Vance has her way with off-beat lines."

On March 3, 1966, while attending a party at Sardi's, Vivian heard the news that William Frawley had collapsed on a Hollywood street, dying of a massive heart attack. After *I Love Lucy*, the character actor had not waited for Arnaz to cast him in another Desilu project so that the studio could profit on Fred Mertz's popularity. Instead, he quickly accepted a costarring role on another series, *My Three Sons*. Through the years, when asked about Vivian, he would reply in his usual uncensored manner, "She's one of the finest gals to come out of Kansas, but I often wish she'd go back there. I don't know where she is now and she doesn't know where I am and that's exactly the way I like it."

When a guest told Vivian the news of the departure of her old nemesis, she picked up her glass and announced, "Champagne for everyone!" After that, whenever a fan asked of Fred's whereabouts, she'd respond, "He's dead . . . Thank God!"

Producer Gary Tomlin recalls a similar incident. "We were doing a show up on Cape [Cod]. As we were leaving a restaurant one night, someone said, 'Oh, it's Ethel Mertz! Hey Ethel, how's Fred?' Vivian said, 'Dead! And it was the happiest day in my life when he died!' "

Through the 1960s, Vivian made several television and film appearances on shows such as *Candid Camera, The Dick Cavett Show, ABC Nightlife, Love American Style, The Mike Douglas Show* (as a cohost), and sat on the panels of several game shows. She had not done a film since the 1950s. When she landed a small role in *The Great*

Race directed by Blake Edwards and starring Tony Curtis, Jack Lemmon, Natalie Wood, and Peter Falk, Vivian hoped to rekindle a movie career that she had abandoned before it really began. But when Vivian saw the previews, she quipped, "I had more costumes than lines." This time, humor could not hide her disappointment. Robert Osborne says, "One great heartbreak for Vivian was that she thought *The Great Race* would open up a whole phase for her in film but nothing ever happened. It was a big disappointment."

When reporters asked why she didn't do another series, she said, "Why, honey, what series would I do? I did the best one they ever had in *I Love Lucy*. Why settle for second best? But I'll always do television because of something Claudette Colbert told me when we did a movie together years ago. She said, 'Get before the public every year—let them see you every year—then they don't realize you're getting any older because they're getting older right along with you.'"

Vivian also received several awards during the sixties: the TV & Radio Mirror Award for Best-Supporting Female on Television for two years in a row and in 1964, the Genii Award from The Radio and Television Women of Southern California. When she stood up to make her speech, she addressed an audience of mostly women. She talked of analysis and said when her psychiatrist led her through the steps of her life, she got along famously retracing her childhood while doing the *I Love Lucy* series but then she hit a snag. "How," she asked her doctor, "can you go through adolescence and menopause all at the same time?" Vivian didn't know that her speech had gone out live on the radio. When she found out, she laughed and said, "Well, I thought it was just among us girls."

In their eighteen years of marriage, Vivian and John

moved cross-country four times, living in Connecticut and
then Santa Fe where, for a brief time, they tried early
retirement and bought a travel agency. Then they moved
back east to their Beekman Place penthouse in Manhattan.
Between John's literary crowd and her theatrical cronies,
the Dodds received invitations to many of New York's
most sumptuous parties. Though Vivian enjoyed quiet
nights at home, John would often prompt her to attend
these gatherings. Vivian shared with Paige Matthews
Peterson the events of one particular soiree that took place
in the mid-sixties:

> While at some incredibly fancy party with lots of
> celebrities sitting around, everyone was getting up and
> performing something. Viv had gotten up and sang her
> song and then sat next to this young, homely girl. She
> told her, "Oh come on, honey, you're on Broadway,
> now get up and sing a little something."
> And the girl said, "No, I don't do that unless I'm
> paid."
> Vivian told her, "Now listen, girlie, you're in a room
> full of these great theater people, now get up and sing
> that little song you sing." She wouldn't get up and that
> made Vivian really mad. She said to me, "You know,
> that little Barbra Streisand was a real little shit!'" The
> "little song" Vivian wanted Streisand to sing was
> "People."

John's business dictated that he live primarily in New
York City and though Vivian willingly moved anywhere to
keep John happy, Dorothy, now living with her second husband Walter O'Neal in Carlsbad, New Mexico, says that
Vivian had grown to detest the confinement of Manhattan.
She wanted to leave their Beekman Place apartment for the
country, so she sold some property in Solvang and bought

a two-hundred-year-old schoolhouse in North Salem, Westchester County, which they completely remodeled. Gary Tomlin recalls that "the schoolhouse in the country was all white with flowers and light. Vivian said, 'My therapist told me to surround myself with light so when I wake up in the morning I am not waking up to dark colors.' She deliberately decorated that house so that even on gloomy days, there was light. The whole back of the house was glass so that light could come in no matter what."

Walter Williamson adds, "The schoolhouse was their love nest with one bedroom on purpose. It was just for them." Vivian was thrilled when *House & Garden* magazine featured this home in one of their issues.

While on the east coast, Vivian again visited a plastic surgeon. She had often suggested to Lucy that she should get a nip here and a tuck there but Lucy, who had difficulty healing as well as a fear of operations, preferred to have her wrinkles disappear by having her skin pulled back and taped under her wig, giving her an astonishingly—if only temporary—younger look. Adele Longmire Franz visited Vivian after one of her surgeries when John invited her to spend the weekend to console Vivian because the operation had gone awry. "She had a face-lift and something terrible had happened. Her eyes drooped, the red was showing and wouldn't close up. John was just frantic. God only knows what she paid that doctor. He said, 'She'll have to go through surgery again, we don't know how they'll repair it.' This condition had existed for about two weeks and they kept telling her it's going to go back in place, but it didn't. They finally had to operate again."

The Dodds moved once more, this time west to Belvedere, a suburb of San Francisco. Vivian sold the remaining property in Solvang, California, to finance a publishing company in San Francisco for John, who had held several important positions in the publishing world and now decided to go out on his own. He had worked as editor for William Morrow & Co., editor-in-chief of both Holt, Rinehart & Winston and the New American Library, and as general manager of G. P. Putnam's Sons and Simon & Schuster. While at Rinehart, he took on the monumental task of assembling the private papers of President Lyndon B. Johnson for publication in four volumes, though he never received full credit once they were published. The many other books he edited include *Ladybird's Journal*, *My Life with Martin Luther King* by Coretta Scott King, David Niven's *Send in the Empty Horses*, and Golda Meir's autobiography.

Those who knew the Dodds agree that they had a blissful life and marriage. Although few would bring up the subject, many had an inkling of John's sexual preference. A stage manager once asked Vivian in actor Larry Maraviglia's presence why she had married a gay man since she was not a lesbian. She laughingly joked, "It's wonderful to marry a gay man because when he has to please you sexually, he has to work so hard that it is a tremendous experience." Larry Maraviglia thought it was a flip way of answering an embarrassing question. Vivian did have concerns over John's fidelity and though she didn't share them with those she worked with, close friends witnessed her moments of frustration when John did not arrive home as scheduled. She'd call everyone in New York to see whether they knew of his whereabouts. Sometimes, asserts talent agent William Blake, when John returned, "They would stay up all night drinking and arguing and they would solve it that way."

Immediately after *The Lucy Show*, Lucy geared herself up to do a new series, *Here's Lucy*. Despite the tension from the failed negotiations only a few years before, Lucy labored diligently to get her sidekick to return. But Vivian made it clear she would not take part.

> When Lucille telephoned to talk about doing another show, I said, "I'm going to stay with John. It's that simple. I want to live with him seven days a week."
>
> Lucy said, "But how am I going to go on without you?"
>
> "Lucille, you mustn't worry. With your talent, you mustn't feel that way about anybody. You can go anyplace without anybody." Yet, I was sure I was deserting her. She had a tremendous fear of rejection, and unless she thought it through, it could seem that I was deserting her, giving her up after years of closeness and clowning for a husband and a home I wanted to share with him. She and I would go on chatting together, seeing each other, staying friends but the relationship inevitably changed.

Lucy chose her own children, Lucie and Desi Jr., to play her on-screen children for *Here's Lucy*. Desi Jr., who had inherited his father's ability for music, had become a teen idol with his band Dino, Desi, and Billy. Lucie, who had always had a love for acting, wanted to make her mark. Since the divorce of their parents, Lucie and Desi Jr. had grown distant from their mother. Lucy saw this as a way to further her children's careers and strengthen her relationship with them.

Vivian did make occasional appearances on *Here's Lucy*. Herbert Kenwith tells this story about her return for an episode guest-starring Lawrence Welk:

> Lucy said, "We're going to have Vivian back." I was delighted. Vivian was so spirited, so wonderful and I remember the first reading around the table. Lucy came

with a script that was blue-penciled in many areas of
lines she didn't want said. She thought it held things up
but Vivian said, "Just a minute." She threw her pencil
down on the table with a bit of noise and said, "I just
flew three thousand miles to do this script and this is the
script I am doing. If you want to cut your lines, you cut
them, but I'm still saying my lines." And I thought that
was wonderful because she really stood up to her. Lucy
said, "Well, the lines aren't good." Vivian said, "No,
they're not good because they're funny for me and not
funny for you. I am saying those lines." So Lucy said,
"Well, we'll talk about it later." Vivian said, "No, I
want to talk about it now. I think we have to discuss it
now so I'll know what I'm reading, what you're reading, and what the rest of the cast is reading." Meanwhile, every time anything like this happened, Gale
Gordon, who was the sweetest, most tolerant man in the
business, just excluded himself from everything. He
never said "boo" when Lucy argued on the set. He disappeared, you never saw him leave. It was like the floor
opened and swallowed him up. Well, we went on with
this thing and Vivian won out. Her lines were all kept in
and rehearsals were a ball.

Today, Lucie Arnaz gives much of the credit to Vivian
for her own devotion to the theater:

Vivian used to do cameos on the show, "Aunt Viv"
kind of thing. My greatest memory is her taking me
aside one afternoon and saying, "So, girl, what do you
do on your hiatus?" I started listing all the wonderful
vacation spots of the world that I had an opportunity to
visit in my four months off and she got this real stern
look on her face and said, "You forgetting about theater? You're a theater person. I've seen you in high
school plays, you know about theater and have loved it

since you were a little girl. You are a stage person, don't you forget about that talent. Don't get stuck on a sitcom for the rest of your life playing second banana to Big Red."

Coming from her that was an interesting comment, oddly enough. As if being on that sitcom was a terrible thing. People would kill for that. She always knew that it was hard for her to go back out and take those wonderful parts she'd had before and have people see her after she was Ethel Mertz. She didn't say get off the show and go do theater, she was saying don't let people think this is all you know how to do. Because this is easy compared with what theater people do. I really listened and literally within two nights I was on the phone with my manager, asking, "How do I get into summer stock?" Vivian loved the theater; she was a theater person. It takes a special kind of talent and it's very hard to explain why we give up so much other stuff and say no to so many other things and truck on and on eight times a week to do that foolish thing we do. She was one of those special people. I'm assuming that in me she saw a kindred spirit and wanted to encourage it. We were mentor and mentee.

On April 11, 1974, after a grueling opening night performance of the musical *Seesaw*, Lucie Arnaz stood on stage ready to take her bows. "The curtain fell and my heart just jumped out of my soul. The fact that I had actually done it and I looked offstage left and there's Vivian applauding. I want to cry even now when I think about it. Vivian Vance! I didn't even know she was there. She was there even before the cast was onstage to take their bows. I cried so hard and when I went offstage she said, 'See, girl! You did it!' "

In 1969, Phoebe and Henry Ephron wrote a play for

Vivian entitled *My Daughter, Your Son,* in which she played Maggie Gordon. The lighthearted comedy, directed by Larry Arrick, also starred Bill McCutcheon, Robert Alda, Don Scardino, and Dody Goodman. This play marked Vivian's return to Broadway after a twenty-year absence. Her comeback lasted only six weeks, however. Critics panned the show but spared Vivian. "You expect Vivian to be wonderful and she is." "Miss Vance and Miss Goodman are such skillful comediennes that they can make even bad lines so good." The play fared better in stock and regional theater where, Dody Goodman jokingly explains, it opened whenever she and Vivian needed money for new drapes. Producer Gary Tomlin, who toured with Vivian and Dody Goodman, played Vivian's son. He remembers "Vivian and Dody were a wonderful combination. I guess the time just wasn't right. But I never understood why someone didn't see that show and say, 'We have to do a series with those two.' They were hysterical together. It could've had the same kind of dynamics as she and Lucy had but in its own way. It allowed Vivian to be a little more on the aggressive side and Dody more passive. They knew how to use each other very well."

Vivian was finally living the life she had always desired. She worked when she wanted, took part in charities, and traveled around the world. On one occasion, Vivian took the money she earned from a special she had done with Lucy and treated all of her sisters to a trip to Hawaii. Despite being overwhelmed by her feelings of responsibility for her sisters, Vivian remained very close to them. They kept their relationships together by writing to each other once a week.

Barring the occasional doubt, her marriage seemed happy and fulfilling. In the early seventies, she continued her appearances on *Here's Lucy*, took part in a production of the play *The Front Page* as Mrs. Grant for NBC, played May Brodey on the ABC Television Movie *Getting Away from It All* starring Larry Hagman, and continued working in the theater.

But in 1973 her life took a dramatic turn. One day as she looked in the mirror, she noticed something strange about one of her breasts. It did not take long for her doctor to discover that she had a large tumor that was quickly spreading. She kept the news from everyone except for Dorothy, close family members, and friends. "She called me in Carlsbad when she found out she had breast cancer," Dorothy said. "She never had an examination because Viv had always been so healthy."

When the news of her hospital stay reached the public, the cause was undisclosed. The breast cancer had metastasized toward the underside of her arm. "The surgery was done at Columbia Presbyterian Hospital. The cancer was very severe and it took six hours to do it but they thought they got it all," Dorothy said. After the grueling operation the doctors, confident that Vivian would survive, gave her a clean bill of health.

Though relieved by the outcome, the operation left her emotionally as well as physically scarred. "Viv was really proud of her figure and the way she looked. It bothered her not to be all there," says Dorothy who joined Vivian on Cape Cod while she appeared in *Butterflies Are Free*. "She was so unhappy. I had never seen her so depressed." Gary Tomlin, who was appearing in the same play, recalls that "Vivian was in a lot of pain partially because it was humid and that seemed to intensify all the pain. But she was a trooper."

Vivian no longer saw herself as a complete woman and feared that John would no longer be attracted to her physically. But "Her worries were unfounded. Her relationship with John didn't seem to change after the mastectomy. He felt a lot for her and was very good to her," Dorothy said. Vivian later told a friend that John had diligently supported her while she recuperated.

Vivian made up her mind not to give in to the disease and began physical therapy to regain the use of her arm. Later that year she appeared in Florida in a production of *Arsenic and Old Lace.* When she arrived at the airport, actor Walter Williamson, who had arrived at the same time, walked up to her and introduced himself. "The first thing she said was, 'Oh God, there's a photographer. Let me put my teeth in.' "

During the run of the show, she shared intimate details of her recent ordeal with Williamson. "She talked about a network of women who had been through this. People she never expected started rallying around her showing their scars and showing her how to manage and wear all the appliances."

When Vivian saw that the costumes for the show would present problems for someone who had undergone breast surgery, she called on Williamson, who had previously done costumes, to help her find something suitable to wear. "We went through the stores to try and find something but later decided that I would build her some stuff," Williamson said. "We rented a sewing machine and set up shop in her suite. She explained that everything would have to be fitted because of her mastectomy. Up to this point, I didn't know about her breast surgery."

Making light of an uncomfortable situation had always been Vivian's way to ease the pain, but her feeble attempt to find humor in this case made it that much more poignant when she remarked to Williamson, "I can always get work as a model for Picasso."

That following year, while Vivian toured in *Everybody Loves Opal*, life again dealt her an emotional blow. On the evening of March 2, 1974, while riding in her limousine along with other cast members, she quietly announced that earlier in the day her mother had died. The stunned cast poured out their condolences but Vivian seemed void of any emotion.

In the two years before Mae's death, Vivian had not appeared as rigid in her relationship with her mother. She had candidly remarked in several articles that "Only recently have I made my peace with my Mother. Now she can sit in the living room and say, 'That's my girl there on TV.' " Lou Ann recalls their mother's allegiance to Vivian during these years. "Once when I visited Mother in the nursing home, I told her that I was in theater now and was acting. She looked up at me and said, 'Well, you won't take Viv's place.' "

Vivian's refusal to cancel her performance could be interpreted as a heartless gesture but given the problems in her relationship with Mae, it doesn't seem surprising. Choosing not to go on would have been a futile and hypocritical gesture of respect that Vivian deemed inappropriate.

Unfortunately, the problems of the past remained too deeply rooted and her struggle would continue despite her mother's passing. However, Vivian did find some emotion in her heart for her mother. She wrote the following when she visited her home state:

> Today Kansas looked so beautiful it put a gulp in my throat . . . I thought about Mama, who had lived out her days in the Carlsbad nursing home, with all the misery she suffered forgotten. She remembered only the time she was a girl who loved to sing and dance a jig, and nurses adored her. I was glad that what doctor Levy had

said turned out to be right and compassion did come once I worked through all the hostilities. I wished she'd known that one of her ambitions for her second-born daughter had been realized. A teacher was what she wanted me to be, and a teacher I had become in directing the young actors and actresses who worked with me on the fine points of winning laughter.

Because of the breast cancer, producers could not insure Vivian for long-term projects. Still, an offer to do a television series based on the play *Everybody Loves Opal* came her way when the show proved successful in regional theaters. The idea did not materialize because Vivian decided that she couldn't move to Los Angeles and leave John. However, she continued touring just to prove that she had completely recovered from her bout with cancer.

In the early seventies, Vivian campaigned to win roles in the movie versions of Neil Simon's *Plaza Suite* opposite Walter Matthau as well as in Jerry Herman's *Mame* opposite Lucille Ball. Producer Gary Tomlin recalls, "She desperately wanted to play the Maureen Stapleton role in *Plaza Suite*. She fought really hard for it. The role of Vera Charles in *Mame* eventually went to Bea Arthur. But Vivian saw it as a role in which she would've been great. She said, 'Ah honey, they wouldn't even consider it. It would have been too much like Lucy and Ethel again.' "

In 1975, she appeared on the *Dinah Shore Show*. She also accepted a role on the television show *Rhoda* starring Valerie Harper. The two actresses had met in Hawaii. When Valerie returned to Los Angeles, she mentioned the meeting to Charlotte Brown, writer and executive producer of the show, who, having admired Vivian for years, quickly had the idea to write a guest-starring role. "Charlotte thought it a great idea to approach Vivian with the role of the older friend who makes Nancy Walker's char-

Vivian onstage with her friend and neighbor Paige Matthews Peterson

acter jealous. It is an incident that had happened to Charlotte and her mother," Harper said.

Vivian played Maggie Cox, a television commercial
writer who along with her husband, played by David
White of *Bewitched* fame, move into Rhoda's building.
Vivian's commercial agent, William Blake, accompanied
her to the set on the first day of rehearsals. "Vivian waited
time-wise so that she arrived in the hallway at the same
time as Valerie Harper. The star always arrives on the set
last. It was one of those little show business 'one upman-
ship' things. It was kind of cute."

"It was a red letter week," Valerie Harper fondly
remembers. "Vivian was an idol of mine and it was wonderful to see her work. She had a trademark voice and
style. She was everywoman yet she was very unique. She
had that common touch with a wonderful singular personality. Her talent contributed to the atmosphere to write for
a character like Rhoda. We are the sum totals of our life
experiences, and if I hadn't had Ethel to watch, I don't
think Rhoda would have been as good. Vivian contributed

to my career in that respect. Without Lucy and Ethel they wouldn't have wanted Mary and Rhoda. It was a satisfying and profound experience. She graced our set with her humor."

Several articles stated that Vivian had accepted a contract to join the cast of *Rhoda* as a regular. The rumor has persisted through the years among fans of the show, but Harper insists that "Vivian was never intended to be a regular on the show."

Gary Tomlin, however, vividly recalls Vivian sharing the news of the offer. "I remember she was so thrilled. She said, 'Oh great! I'm gonna play her real elegant. She's gonna be this character that's nothing like Ethel Mertz.' In the end, she just wasn't funny. She wasn't as good at that as she was at the other things. Towards the end of her career I don't think she wanted to do what she was really good at, and really funny at. She'd made up her mind about the type of role she wanted to play but that wasn't necessarily the right direction to go in."

Following her appearance on *Rhoda*, Vivian landed the role of Minnie in an ABC Television Movie of the Week, *The Great Houdinis*. It starred Paul Michael Glaser, Sally Struthers, and Ruth Gordon.

Jean Radcliff, who had written the Frances Farmer biography, had made a deal with John Dodds to collaborate on Vivian's memoirs. Vivian agreed and received a $10,000 advance for the book. The two women spent several sessions together as Vivian recalled her past, carefully leaving out anything that might be considered scandalous. Radcliff knew that Vivian's version would not sell and prompted her to open up and talk about her love affairs and to discuss more openly her relationship with Lucille Ball and her days on *I Love Lucy*. Vivian refused. Radcliff called Max Showalter venting her frustrations.

"John wanted Jean to write the book," Max said. "But

Jean told me that she'd come to a conclusion. 'I can't write this book. Vivian does not want to be remembered as Ethel Mertz and continues to give me all these glamorous photographs. She is not cooperating with me.' "

Finally Radcliff gave up and Vivian ditched the idea, returning the money to the publishing company, and storing away what had been written in the back of her closet. Vivian later justified her position to her sister Dorothy this way. "She said that it was good for her to write it but that she did not want to give up her privacy. She also knew that she would have to go on the talk show circuit and she did not want to do that."

Though Lucy and Vivian had worked together for years, they had personally grown distant, barely speaking or seeing each other. During a trip to Los Angeles with friend Jay Bell, Vivian decided to pay Lucy a visit. "She got as far as Beverly Hills, turned around and said she couldn't do it. They were kind of on the outs around this period but she never said what it was."

Vivian did, however, visit Desi Arnaz. Vivian's fondness for Desi had not diminished through the years, and whenever anyone mentioned his name, she made sure to credit him for her success. Jay Bell "drove her down to see her doctor in the lower part of California and to visit Desi, who lived in the area. She rented the house next to his just for the night." Bell didn't go in with Vivian, thinking it best to leave them alone to catch up.

Vivian and John by now had moved into a small Victorian cottage in Belvedere, California. The house had a magnificent view of the San Francisco Bay. Vivian seemed to enjoy this home more than any other. Her niece, Vivian Wilkison, described how Vivian "was always so appreciative of beauty, and would be in rhapsody over a sky or a sunset."

The Dodds had a hot tub installed and a deck added

where Vivian would sit for hours quietly indulging herself. She became very close to her next-door neighbor Corinne Wiley and her daughter Paige. "Vivian was at peace and content when she moved here. She felt like she really fit in. She'd sit and talk about life and philosophy. She didn't talk much about show business; she was really finished with it by this time. I remember she never learned to ride a bicycle so she bought a big three-wheel tricycle and rode it around the town. You'd see her on it or out walking her dogs, just enjoying her anonymity." Her contentment during this time had a great deal to do with her health. For the past few years, she had tested clean of any cancer.

Though Vivian's appearances on the stage fetched her $2,500 a week, except when she worked for the Albuquerque Little Theatre where she would accept only $250, she now wanted to find a quicker way of making money and looked toward doing television commercials. She had one stipulation—she refused to wear a maid's uniform. Many actors had cashed in on their notoriety but Vivian had no idea how much money celebrities made for this type of work. William Blake offered his services as her representative. "I told her, I'll get you a three-year contract at $250,000 per year. She was very happy and signed with me. I did all the work alerting commercial people, the actual companies, General Mills and General Foods. The money was no problem—we were just looking for a product. They were thinking of giving her Oleo, which Eve Arden was doing but [it] wasn't selling. An agent at William Morris who had originally said he could get $50,000 for a contract took my idea back to General Foods, changed the price, switched products to get Maxwell House coffee and I was left out in the cold even though she had a commercial contract with me. We sued, went into arbitration, and William Morris won."

Vivian appeared on television and in magazine advertisements as Maxine, the restaurant hostess who only served coffee "good to the last drop." She said, "One gets to a certain place in life where you are much more content to take it easy. Now I have my blessed commercial. That's the goal of most people in this business. Isn't that a wonderful new goal?"

Actually, the goal in this case was to make as much money as she could for as little work as possible. She continued to act on the stage in *Myrna and Clark, The Marriage-Go-Round,* and *My Daughter, Your Son.* Vivian also appeared in a production of *Harvey* with Pat Paulsen. "One matinee, we were standing onstage about to go on," Paulsen said. "We looked out on a sea of blue-haired ladies. Vivian, keeping a straight face, whispered to me as the lights went up, 'I bet there's not a tampon in the house.' "

During the run of this show, Vivian began complaining of a searing pain in her hip and left leg. She went to a doctor who told her not to worry, she had pulled a muscle and the pain would soon subside.

During this period, Lucy and Vivian made amends and once again became "best friends." They frequently discussed possible projects they could do together. "Lucy was sad that life had separated them, personally and professionally," notes Tom Watson. "Professionally she would rather have worked with Vivian than anyone else alive simply because they were like two pros playing tennis. Matched equals who knew each other's timing and sparks would fly. Personally, they were close personal girlfriends who didn't socialize a lot when working but always kept contact with each other."

Vivian once told Jay Bell, "If I walk down Fifth Avenue alone, people would recognize me and watch me go. If Lucy walked down Fifth Avenue alone, people would recognize her but not come up to her, just let her go. But if the two of us walked down Fifth Avenue, we'd stop traffic." Both women felt that working together would prove a success so they agreed on a female version of *The Sunshine Boys*. But whenever one could work it into her schedule, the other one couldn't. After this went on for a while, they abandoned the idea and the project never got off the ground.

In 1977, the two reunited for a television special, *Lucy Calls the President*. A bittersweet feeling filled the air on the set during rehearsals. Many of the actors who had worked with Lucy through the years participated in this hour-long special: Mary Wickes, Mary Jane Croft, and Gale Gordon. Clearly, many things had changed and everyone had grown older. Lucille Ball still grieved over the recent loss of her mother, DeDe. This was the first time since *I Love Lucy* that DeDe would not sit among the studio audience. Vivian had recently suffered a mild stroke which left her with a slight droop to the right side of her face. Author Jim Brochu watched the taping that evening. "Lucy was so protective of Vivian and insisted that Vivian only be photographed from the side that didn't show her paralysis. She only wanted Vivian to be presented at her best."

During the week of rehearsals, Vivian again complained of a persistent pain in her leg and hip. Lucy finally convinced Vivian to go see her doctor and take some tests. The lab notified her that it would take them a few days before the results came in.

On the night of filming *Lucy Calls the President*, there were several delays. Vivian didn't feel up to par and when the cast did not break for dinner, she voiced her anger. Paige Matthews Peterson, along with John Dodds, attended the taping that night to help Vivian. "We were sitting in the audience and Viv's mouth started quivering. John said, 'God, she looks really tired, she looks like she's not doing well.' We couldn't figure out whether she had a twitch or what was going on. When they came to a break, Lucy screamed, 'Goddamn it Viv, stop doing that face!' And Viv walked over to us and we suddenly realized that she had Bell's palsy and that her face was falling apart. John said, 'Oh God, I'm taking you to a hospital.' Viv said, 'I'm going to finish the show.' And that woman finished the show and by the end of it her face was completely paralyzed. We quickly packed her things and left for Belvedere. Lucy never called her, never checked on her, never focused in on her. It was stunning."

Vivian failed to mention that the results from Lucy's doctor had returned indicating that they had found cancer. Panicking, Vivian called her sister Dorothy. "You ask your doctor about this! I don't believe it, he says I have bone cancer." Dorothy reassured her sister as she'd done through the years and told Vivian to go see another doctor, which she did. Meanwhile, after a few weeks at home, Vivian's face returned to normal and she felt well enough to fly to New Mexico to meet Dorothy and to open the College of Santa Fe theater season with *The Matchmaker*.

"We were staying at La Prasada when her doctor called," Dorothy said. "She was very unhappy and crying when she repeated what the doctor said. 'I have bone cancer and must come home immediately. What am I to tell that director?' I said, 'You've got to go home!' We flew to San Francisco. She had extensive bone cancer and immediately went into the hospital for chemotherapy and radiation."

While appearing on stage in San Francisco, Dorothy Konrad stopped in Belvedere to see Vivian. The Dodds' determination to pursue every means to find a cure left her deeply touched. They tried every "guaranteed" remedy including "herbs, healers, and gurus from India." Hope always seemed just around the corner. The doctors did not promise Vivian a cure but they hoped that with aggressive treatment, the cancer would go into remission. Vivian's condition fluctuated as she went through the intense and painful therapy. Some days were better than others but Vivian treated each one as a beginning instead of the end. At one point she returned to work.

Director Paul Blake conceived an idea for a television show for the San Francisco Public Broadcasting System and offered Vivian a role. "When I met her she was a sage. She'd been through everything, a gypsy in the chorus, a Broadway star, come to Hollywood as a second banana and even then she was a huge star. It was very strange writing for Vivian because you heard her all the time. It was easy 'cause I didn't realize how that voice was so ingrained in my head." Blake cast Vivian as Audrey Christie's best friend in *Over Easy*. The show catered to an older viewing audience. "Hugh Downs narrated the show. *Over Easy* showed that growing older doesn't mean growing old. It was a major issue, when Vivian accepted the role, that she have a private dressing room. It wasn't important how much money she made but it was essential that she have privacy because of her cancer. We filmed three short episodes in one day. Once, we couldn't finish because she was too tired. She was able to do only one out of the three. We wanted her to come back and do more but by then she turned us down."

Lou Ann Graham and her husband, Ross, both artists in the theater, had staged *The Wizard of Oz* for the Attic Theatre, a local playhouse in San Francisco. They invited Vivian to one of the rehearsals. While there she shared a story about her experience with the show's creator, Yip Harburg:

After he'd finished the score and lyrics, he asked Vivian to listen to a particular song, which MGM executives thought too sad and refused to include in the film. After hearing the tune, she told Yip to stick to his guns and to keep the number in at all costs. He decided at that moment not to cut the song titled "Over the Rainbow" and to take his chances with the movie moguls.

During Vivian's fight with cancer, neighbor Corinne Wiley would often go next door and keep her neighbor

A very ill Vivian giving actors notes as they rehearse The Wizard of Oz *staged by Vivian's youngest sister, Lou Ann Graham.*

company. Though Vivian considered her show-business life now a thing of the past, she would reminisce with Wiley about her early days, the mistakes made, and people she'd hurt but "she'd left Hollywood. She prided herself that she didn't live in the past. Life was exciting enough not to have to talk about Hollywood stories."

John Dodds's support of his wife during her illness was unwavering. When the frustration of the disease became too great, making him doubt his own strength to go on, he would voice disgust at his weakness to Paige Matthews Peterson. Then he'd turn right around and go lie down next to Vivian to give her hope. "That was a true love affair to the last moment," Paige said. After chemotherapy sessions, John would be by her side to comfort her and was constantly trying to lift her spirits.

The chemotherapy injections caused Vivian's hair to fall out. She called on Irma Kusely, the best hairstylist she knew, to make a wig for her. Irma had done her hair innumerable times on *I Love Lucy.* "She mailed these pictures to me to have as a sample for the wig maker. They were horrible because of the chemo but I told her I'd do everything I could."

When they heard of her sickness, many of Vivian's friends tried to visit but rarely succeeded in their attempt because she was too weak and in too much pain to see anyone. One day her close friend Helene Lobherr told her husband, "We didn't receive a Christmas card from Vivian and I haven't heard from her in several months, which was very unusual. Vivian was always a prolific letter-writer. I got on the phone and called. John answered and said, 'Well, Helene, Viv is a very sick lady. I just brought her home from the hospital.' He left and came back to the phone and said, 'Viv says to tell you that she loves you and she'll call you when she feels better.' But I never heard from her."

One day after a chemotherapy session, as Vivian rested on the couch reading the newspaper, Paige Matthews Peterson noticed she was crying.

"Oh, this is so painful I can't stand it," Vivian said.

Paige asked, "Viv, what's wrong?"

"Lucie is opening tonight on Broadway and I would do anything in the world to be there but I can't."

"Viv was too sick to go and it killed her," Paige remembers. "The pain that she felt not being able to be supportive of little Lucie was incredible. She loved Lucie and felt she had protected her through the years."

Vivian had refused to apply for Medicare or Social Security benefits to pay for medical expenses, insisting to her sister Dorothy that she had more than enough money. But when the expenses got too great her insurance company required her to apply for benefits. "We went to the Social Security office. When the girl asked Viv for her age, Viv told her, 'Honey, I have no idea! I've lied about my age for so many years that I have no idea how old I really am!' "

Lucille Ball, who frequently called for updates on Vivian's condition, decided, along with Mary Wickes, that the time had come to visit their friend. Vivian initially told John that she'd rather not see anyone but he insisted that it would do her good. Once Lucy walked through the door, Vivian's face lit up and the two began their final visit together. As Paige Matthews Peterson explains, a very important chapter came to a close that day. "In the end those two women probably loved each other more than anyone in the world. Did they have problems? Absolutely. You can dislike someone and still love them. They worshiped each other and Viv was truly Lucy's best friend in the whole goddamned world up till the last moment. Vivian was thrilled that Lucy was there."

Vivian fought an admirable battle against her disease, never letting go of the hope and humor that had carried her this far. One day one of her nurses asked, "Is there anything I can get you, Viv?" She replied, "Yeah, a new body."

Toward the end, those closest to Vivian remained near. Her sister Mickey and her husband, Ralph Bowyer, visited. While there, Vivian asked Ralph what he knew about God and religion. They gave her some of their favorite scriptures, hoping they would bring some comfort. But Vivian could not find hope in them because her perception of religion was still so closely tied to her mother's fanatical views. She told her sister Dorothy, "I tried very hard to find a belief in God and to pray, but I just couldn't do it."

"She had no sincere feeling about it," Dorothy said. "Around this time is when she got her face all made up, put on her prettiest nightie, called John in and said, 'This is it. Don't do any more for me. No more radiation, no more chemotherapy, I don't want anything. Just keep me out of pain, I want to go.' "

Lou Ann Graham remembers Vivian's final days:

> I had been driving her to Marin County Hospital for two years for her radiation treatments. For the last year, I'd spent two days a week preparing meals so that John could be spared cooking. I tried to fix things that she really liked because her appetite was so bad.
>
> John called me and said Viv had decided it was time for her to go and that she "wants to talk to you." It was just her way. She wanted to tell me in person about her decision and she wanted me to be there when the doctor came in.
>
> When I got there Viv asked whether John had told me of her decision. I told her that he did. And then Viv said, "I want you to have my mink coat." And I laughed because it was so much like her. It was laughter mixed

with love and deep sadness that her long, difficult fight was coming to an end.

Once when I was giving her a shot, she woke up from a deep sleep and told me that she was going down a white tunnel. But then she saw Mama waiting for her at the end so she came back. She became very breathless telling me this.

I was there when she asked the doctor, "Could I please not be in any more pain?" I took the four-to-twelve shift and there were two other nurses to take care of her. From that time, she never ate a thing and drank very little water. She had been in pain so long, all she wanted was for it to end. I admired that she had the strength and the courage to just . . . not commit suicide . . . in a way that is what she was doing. But it was her choice, just dying little by little, and I thought the fact that she'd told John, "You've got to let me go" and then talked to us and talked to the doctor and made the decision and did it, was a very admirable thing.

We all sat around, and though most people wouldn't understand, Connie, Paige, my sister Dot, and I would sit around and have sessions, praying, "Please take her. Let her go. Please let her have her wish." Here we are praying for her to die. A lot of people might think that was weird but it was her wish and we wanted her to have her wish. When she did, it was a mixture of jubilation and great sadness.

On August 17, 1979, after two years of battling bone cancer, Vivian Vance died as she had wished—in grace. Lou Ann says, "I was at home when she died. Dot called and I went immediately to Belvedere. Peggy, the other nurse, and I cleaned up the bedroom . . . and I swear, my husband saw it too, that Vivian was sitting there on the windowsill watching us and smiling. Later we all went out because that's what John wanted."

Corinne Wiley recalls that night. "We went out to a restaurant and started telling Viv jokes. We had this fabulous evening celebrating her. We got in hysterics, laughing and reliving the joy of her life."

Years earlier, Jay Bell had asked Vivian how she would like to have her remains disposed of when she died. In true Vivian Vance fashion, she smiled and said, "Honey, surprise me!" But she surprised everyone when, before dying, she requested that instead of returning to her beloved New Mexico, her body be cremated and her ashes scattered by the Neptune Society in the San Francisco Bay.

Vivian Vance, July 26, 1909–August 17, 1979

Epilogue

❖

Vivian's sisters Venus and Mickey are deceased. Her niece Vivian Wilkison has passed on since work on this book began. Vivian's youngest sister, Lou Ann Graham, lives in San Francisco and sister Dorothy O'Neal resides in Albuquerque. Their brother, Robert Jones, lives in Arizona.

Vivian's first and second husbands, Joe Danneck and George Koch, never crossed paths with Vivian after their divorces. No one is certain what happened to Joe Danneck. Vivian's sister Dorothy did meet George Koch in the late forties in Chicago. He had remarried and had a young daughter. Phil Ober married Jane Westmore, a former press agent at NBC Television. He retired from acting and moved to Puerto Vallarta, Mexico, to act as emergency U.S. representative for the American consul. He died of heart failure on September 13, 1982. He was eighty years old. John Dodds died of cancer on October 9, 1986.

Of the incredible team from *I Love Lucy*, William Frawley was the first to die on March 3, 1966. Vivian died on August 17, 1979; Desi Arnaz on December 2, 1986, at the age of sixty-nine; and Lucille Ball succumbed to a fatal heart attack on April 26, 1989.

On June 14, 1990, a television news program featured a story about Vivian Vance. The report noted that she was the only member of the *I Love Lucy* team who did not have a star on the Hollywood Walk of Fame. The following morning, the Hollywood Chamber of Commerce received over 3,000 calls from outraged viewers who wondered how an oversight such as this could occur. The following year, on February 14, 1991, Vivian Vance finally received her star. Lucie Arnaz graciously paid the $5,000 fee required by the Hollywood Chamber of Commerce.

Today, Lucie Arnaz is a stage and film actress living with her husband, actor Laurence Luckinbill, and their children in New York State. Desi Arnaz Jr. lives with his family in Nevada.

Authors' Note

The authors gratefully acknowledge the following sources for their permission to reprint material in their control:

A Book by Desi Arnaz (William Morrow & Company, Inc., 1976) by special permission of Desilu too

As I Am: An Autobiography by Patricia Neal (Simon & Schuster Inc., 1988)

Desilu: The Story of Lucille Ball and Desi Arnaz by Coyne Steven Sanders and Tom Gilbert (William Morrow & Company, Inc., 1993)

Lucille: The Life of Lucille Ball by Kathleen Brady (Hyperion, 1994)

Lucy in the Afternoon: An Intimate Memoir of Lucille Ball by Jim Brochu (William Morrow & Company, Inc., 1990)

Portrait Gallery by Agnes de Mille (Houghton Mifflin Company, 1990)

With a Quiet Heart by Eva Le Gallienne (Viking Press, 1953)

Quotations from the unpublished manuscript of the memoirs of Vivian Vance is by permission of Serge Matt, c/o Collier Associates Literary Agency, Box 21361, West Palm Beach, FL 33416.

Photo Credits

Frontispiece: authors' collection

Page xxii: authors' collection

Pages 4 & 5: original note written by Vivian to Lucille Ball from the personal papers of Lucille Ball, used with permission from Lucie Arnaz

Page 12: courtesy of Lou Ann Graham

Page 13: courtesy of Imogene Littell

Page 17: courtesy of Lou Ann Graham

Page 30: courtesy of Lou Ann Graham

Page 46: courtesy of Albuquerque Little Theatre archives

Page 60: courtesy of Albuquerque Little Theatre archives

Page 76: courtesy of Billy Rose Collection, New York Public Library for the Performing Arts

Page 80: courtesy of Billy Rose Collection, New York Public Library for the Performing Arts

Page 81: courtesy of Albuquerque Little Theatre archives

Pages 86 & 87: courtesy of Albuquerque Little Theatre archives

Page 97: courtesy of Marjorie Lord

Page 99: courtesy of Albuquerque Little Theatre archives

Page 108: Pat Colby

Page 118: courtesy of Albuquerque Little Theatre archives

Page 122: courtesy of Billy Rose Collection, New York Public Library for the Performing Arts

Page 128 (top): courtesy of Pat Colby

Page 128 (bottom): courtesy of Pat Colby

Page 146: courtesy of the Academy of Motion Picture Arts and Sciences

Page 153: authors' collection

Page 155: authors' collection

Page 157: authors' collection

Page 158: authors' collection

Page 161: authors' collection

Page 163: authors' collection

Page 164: authors' collection

Page 165: courtesy of Photofest and Desilu too

Page 192: authors' collection

Page 197: authors' collection

Page 203: courtesy of Desilu too

Page 207 (top and bottom): authors' collection

Page 210: courtesy of Lou Ann Graham

Page 216: courtesy of Lou Ann Graham

Pages 220, 221 & 222: authors' collection

Page 239: courtesy of the Connecticut Mental Health Association

Page 243: authors' collection
Page 244: courtesy of Photofest and Desilu too
Page 246 (top): courtesy of Irma Kusely and Desilu too
Page 246 (bottom): authors' collection
Page 250: authors' collection
Page 263 (top): courtesy of Albuquerque Little Theatre archives
Page 263: courtesy of Pat Colby
Page 278: courtesy of Paige Matthews Peterson
Page 286: courtesy of Lou Ann Graham
Page 292: courtesy of Lou Ann Graham

Play List

Even though Vivian Vance was best known for her roles as Ethel Mertz and Vivian Bagley with Lucille Ball, she was most proud of her accomplishments on stage. This is a compilation of Vivian's theatrical accomplishments before and after *I Love Lucy*.

Broadway

This was Vivian's first experience as an actress in a commercial theatrical production. She joined a touring company of *Broadway* when it came through Tulsa, Oklahoma with the help of the man who became her first husband, Joe Danneck. She started in the chorus but eventually moved up to play the part of Pearl, the "gal who gets revenge on the guy what got her man." Vivian also appeared in this play during the second season of the Albuquerque Little Theatre.

Peggy Ann

Vivian and her then-husband Joe Danneck joined the touring company of this play in 1929, she to sing in the chorus while Joe did advance publicity work for the company.

Cushman's Revue

Strictly speaking, this was not a play but a traveling vaudeville show. It toured the South and Midwest as an extra-added attraction in movie theaters. Vivian sang torch songs such as "After You've Gone" and "My Man." Her appearances in *Cushman's Revue* made her popular in Albuquerque and gave her name a boost when she began to appear at the Little Theatre.

This Thing Called Love

Vivian played the part of a "fiery vamp" in the first play of the first season of the Albuquerque Little Theatre. Even though she was not born in Albuquerque, the townspeople of this small city in New Mexico supported her financially when she left for Broadway.

The Cradle Song

Vivian played the part of a Dominican nun in this comedy produced by the Albuquerque Little Theatre. During the run of this play, Vivian fell off a horse and had to appear on stage with heavy makeup to cover a black eye.

Rain

This is the story of a love triangle set in the tropics and Vivian played the part of Mrs. Davidson, a missionary's wife and the "wronged woman." Many doubted that Vivian, known for comedy even then, could play the part but were amazed at the changes in her appearance wrought by makeup and costume.

See Naples and Die

This comedy, written by Elmer Rice, showed off all of Vivian's comedy skills to perfection. One reviewer wrote, "It was Vivian Vance's show. *See Naples and Die* was one big laugh from the moment the Little Theatre star stepped on stage."

Within the Law
The founder of the Albuquerque Little Theatre, Kathryn Kennedy O'Connor, gave Vivian just a small role in this comedy about a woman who is wrongfully accused of theft by her employer and sent to jail. Her revenge once she is released is to marry her former employer's son.

Redemption
This play, written by the Russian great Leo Tolstoy, was produced by the Little Theatre in an attempt to personally involve great numbers of the community in a play. It was, in Kathryn Kennedy O'Connor's estimation, a disaster.

The Trial of Mary Dugan
This melodrama was very important to Vivian's career. Little Theatre founder Kathryn Kennedy O'Connor was convinced that Vivian could make it on the Broadway stage if she could just get to New York and used the proceeds of this production to finance Vivian's trip. The entire play takes place in a courtroom with Mary Dugan—Vivian—on stage the whole time. Albuquerqueans packed the Little Theatre in support of Vivian when the play opened on August 16, 1932.

Music in the Air
Vivian won a place in the chorus of her first Broadway musical after an audition in which she belted out "After You've Gone" in what her sister Dorothy called "in the smokiest Sophie Tucker manner."

Vivian's audition selection was in sharp contrast to the operatic arias sung by others as they tried out in front of Jerome Kern and Oscar Hammerstein II.

Anything Goes!
During its run, Vivian graduated from the chorus to a speaking role and became Merman's understudy in the role of Reno Sweeney. Merman, however, was renowned for her stamina and dedication so Vivian only had a couple of chances to head the cast. However, Vivian did get to star in the play when it went on tour in 1935.

One Viennese Night
Vivian appeared in this Little Theatre production while on a break from the *Anything Goes!* tour. The people of her adopted hometown were visibly proud of her accomplishments.

Red, Hot and Blue!
Vivian had expected a speaking role in this play but had to accept another chorus job—and understudy for Ethel Merman. Many years later, Vivian—now famous for her work in *I Love Lucy*—stood backstage next to Merman and whispered, "This is the first time I've ever stood next to you and not wished you were dead." Merman roared with laughter.

Hooray for What!
Though the circumstances were not the best, this musical starring Ed Wynn became Vivian's break out of the chorus and into the spot-

light. The production of the play was chaotic at best and Vivian inherited the role of Stefania Stevanovich when the producers fired the play's original star, Kay Thompson.

Kiss the Boys Good-bye

Vivian starred in a touring company of this popular Broadway play under the direction of the renowned Antoinette Perry. In addition to mentoring Vivian, Perry also introduced her to Philip Ober, a patrician New Englander who became Vivian's third husband.

Springtime for Henry

Vivian made lifelong friends everywhere she went and two of them were principals in the cast of this play when it was produced in Saratoga, New York—Edward Everett Horton and Marjorie Lord. Horton was the original Mr. Dewlip in this play and appeared in the role more than 3,000 times.

Burlesque

Vivian played opposite Gypsy Rose Lee in this play written about the stripper when it was produced in Saratoga. Despite Lee's hard work and notoriety, the play earned less-than-rave reviews.

Skylark

Vivian appeared in this play with the English *grande dame* of the theater, Gertrude Lawrence. In addition to learning her lines, Vivian learned what it was like to be upstaged by one of the best

practitioners in the business. Among other things, Lawrence had bells attached to her shoes and would wiggle her feet when Vivian had funny lines to speak.

Out from Under

Vivian gave her notice to the producers of *Skylark* when asked to join the cast of this play directed by Antoinette Perry and starring Phil Ober. It was one of Perry's few flops, however, and closed after nine performances.

Anna Christie

Vivian, now doing well in the theater, offered her services to this Albuquerque Little Theatre production free of charge. The play was not well received by the critics who, along with the rest of the audience, were driven out of the theater by gas that foamed out of cones that were supposed to be making fog on stage.

Let's Face It!

In addition to Vivian Vance, this wartime play starred Eve Arden—of *Our Miss Brooks* and *The Mothers-in-Law* fame—Nanette Fabray, and Danny Kaye. During the run of this play, Vivian and Phil bought a small ranch in Cubero, New Mexico.

Over Twenty-one

Vivian and Phil were both part of the cast that took this play to Europe with the USO to entertain U.S. troops who were pushing back the German army in Northern Africa and Italy.

Voice of the Turtle

Vivian took over the part of Olive Lashbrook and joined the touring company of this play while it was in Chicago. Of all the productions in her long career as a thespian, no play had quite the same impact on her as *Voice of the Turtle*. During her first run, Vivian was forced to leave the production because she suffered a nervous breakdown. During her second run as Olive in a touring company in La Jolla, California, Vivian's performance was seen by Desi Arnaz. Before the evening was over, Arnaz asked Vivian to take the part of Ethel Mertz in *I Love Lucy*.

It Takes Two

Director George Abbott played a key role in bolstering Vivian's shattered self-confidence when she returned to the stage in this comedy in 1947 after her breakdown. From this point on, Vivian never accepted a role in a musical because she did not trust her voice.

Counselor-at-Law

Vivian appeared in this play with Paul Muni for a month in Marblehead, Massachusetts. The play's director, Marc Daniels, was the man who persuaded Desi Arnaz to check out Vivian's performance in *Voice of the Turtle*. Daniels became the first director of *I Love Lucy*.

The Cradle Will Rock

Even though the critics praised this play, it closed after five weeks on Broadway. Soon after it closed,

Vivian took on a second stint as Olive Lashbrook in *Voice of the Turtle*. Before accepting the role of Ethel Mertz, Vivian appeared in another production of *Over Twenty-one* with her husband Phil. From there, she traveled to Hollywood to be part of television history and *I Love Lucy*.

Marriage-Go-Round

John Emery urged Vivian to get her feet wet in this play after her long absence from the theater. It was directed by Emery and staged at the Royal Poinciana Playhouse in Palm Beach, Florida.

Here Today

Vivian used this play as a vehicle to rid herself of her Ethel Mertz persona. Unfortunately critics and the public refused to cooperate with her plan.

Barefoot in the Park

After another long absence, Vivian returned to the stage in a short run of *Over Twenty-one* at the Drury Lane Theatre in Chicago. Then she appeared in *Barefoot* in the role of the mother played in the film version by Mildred Natwick.

Don't Drink the Water

Woody Allen's play was not well received before its Broadway debut. Vivian did appear in the role of Marion Hollander in its Philadelphia run but quit before the show's New York opening when she decided that she could never get along with her male lead, Lou Jacobi.

Time of the Cuckoo
In 1966 Vivian toured extensively
with this play which included in its
cast the then unknown Olympia
Dukakis who went on to win an
Oscar for her role in *Moonstruck.*

Everybody's Girl
Vivian returned to the Albuquerque Little Theatre to co-direct
and star in this vehicle written
specifically with her in mind by
friend and playwright John
Patrick. Vivian often toured with
this play.

My Daughter, Your Son
Vivian made her Broadway comeback in this play but it did not last
in New York. Critics loved her but
hated the play. However, Vivian
made a lifelong friend of her co-
star Dody Goodman and the two
of them would take the show on
the road whenever either of them
"needed money for new drapes."

Clark and Myrna
Vivian toured in this play in1972
in summer theaters in Stockbridge
and Dennis, Massachusetts and at
the Ogunquit Playhouse, Maine.
She played the role of Myrna.

Butterflies Are Free
Vivian appeared in this play

shortly after her mastectomy. She
went on night after night despite
her physical pain.

Arsenic and Old Lace
Walter Williamson helped Vivian
design special costumes to wear in
Arsenic which would minimize
any discomfort brought on by certain physical scenes required in
this play.

Everybody Loves Opal
Vivian's mother, Mae, died while
Vivian was on tour with this
play. Vivian waited until after that
night's performance to announce
the news to cast members who
were stunned when they found out
that she'd gone on despite her
mother's death.

Index